CARS

CARS

by Laura Hobbs

Illustrated by Barry Gurbutt

x629.2
H65c

AN EASY-READ FACT BOOK

FRANKLIN WATTS | NEW YORK | LONDON | 1977

EVANSTON PUBLIC LIBRARY
CHILDREN'S DEPARTMENT
1703 ORRINGTON AVENUE
EVANSTON, ILLINOIS 60201

Cover by Ginger Giles

Diagrams on pages 14 and 15 by Vantage Art, Inc.

Photographs courtesy of:
Ford Motor Company: pg. 6, top
General Motors: pg. 6, bottom, pg. 7, top, pg. 7, bottom

Library of Congress Cataloging in Publication Data
Hobbs, Laura.
  Cars.

  (An Easy-read fact book)
  Includes index.
  SUMMARY: An introduction to various types of cars and their parts.
    1. Automobiles—Juvenile literature. [1. Automobiles] I. Gurbutt, Barry. II. Title.
TL147.H57   629.22'22   76-47681
ISBN 0-531-00375-2

All rights reserved
Printed in the United States of America
7 8 9 10

Cars are very important to our way of life. Every day many, many cars travel the streets and highways of the world.

In many ways, cars make life easier. But they can also be harmful. They use up the country's supply of oil. They injure and kill many people each year. They dirty our air. Slowly, however, cars are being made safer and cleaner.

There are several kinds of cars and many different models. The **sedan** is the most common car. It has two or four doors. It has seats in the front and back. In the back of the car is a **trunk.** The spare tire and other things are carried there.

Two-door sedan

Four-door sedan

A **convertible** is a sedan with a top that comes down. It gives passengers a windy ride.

Station wagon

Convertible

The **station wagon** is usually longer than the sedan. It has a large space behind the back seat. This space can carry more than the sedan trunk. Even people fit in the back of a station wagon.

(7)

Sports car

Sports cars are small and do not weigh too much. They can usually perform better than other cars.

They are good for racing as well as driving. Many sports car drivers belong to clubs that race against each other.

One kind of sports car race is called a **rally.** The driver wins points by passing certain places at certain times. Other sports car races last up to 24 hours.

Maserati

Jaguar E Type

Other kinds of cars race, too. **Stock cars** have the bodies of sedans. But they have special racing engines. The cars race each other around a track.

Drag racers race along a straight, short **drag strip.** The driver sits behind the wide rear wheels. Drag racers can reach a speed of 250 miles (400 kilometers) an hour in just a few seconds.

They go so fast, they must stop themselves with parachutes. They use their brakes at the same time.

The most famous race in the United States is the Indianapolis 500. Special "Indy" or "Championship" cars circle the track 200 times. They reach speeds of more than 185 miles (300 kilometers) an hour.

Grand prix (GRAND PREE) racing cars look much like the Indy cars. They compete in grand prix races, held mostly in Europe (YOUR-up). These cars are made just for racing. They are low machines that can seat only the driver.

Grand prix drivers receive points in each race. There are at least 12 races each year. The final winner must win the most points for all the races.

Grand prix racer

(11)

All cars, from the slowest to the fastest, are powered by an **engine.**

In most cars, the engine is in the front and usually turns the rear **axle** (AKS-ell). This connects the two rear wheels. The two front wheels are also connected by an axle.

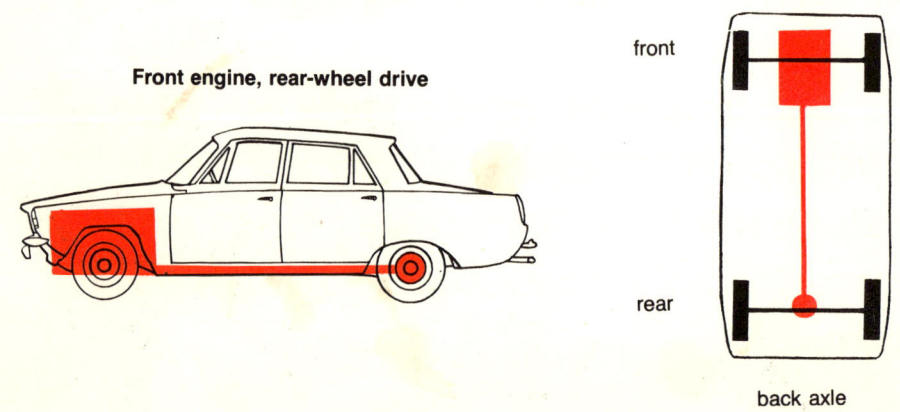

Some small cars, such as the Volkswagen, have the engine in the rear. The trunk is in the front.

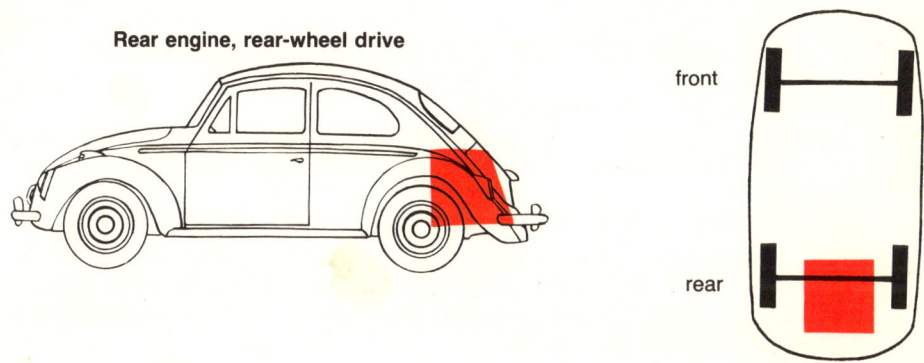

Some cars and trucks are very good for driving on bad roads. They are pulled by their front wheels or by all four wheels.

This **front-wheel drive** or **four-wheel drive** gives them better power to grip the road. This is called **traction.** They do not slide off icy or muddy roads. The cars and trucks can climb steep hills more easily.

This car is a **left-hand drive** car. The driver sits on the left. He or she drives on the right side of the road.

In some countries, cars are built the other way around. The driver sits on the right. He or she drives on the left side of the road.

Look at all the parts of this car. Each one makes driving safer or more comfortable.

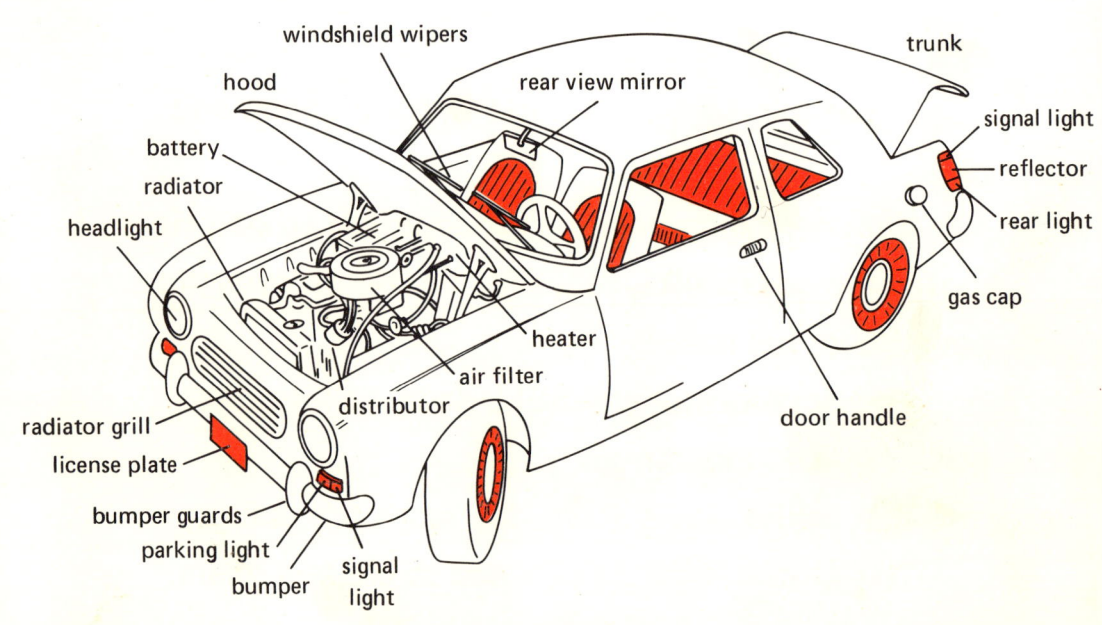

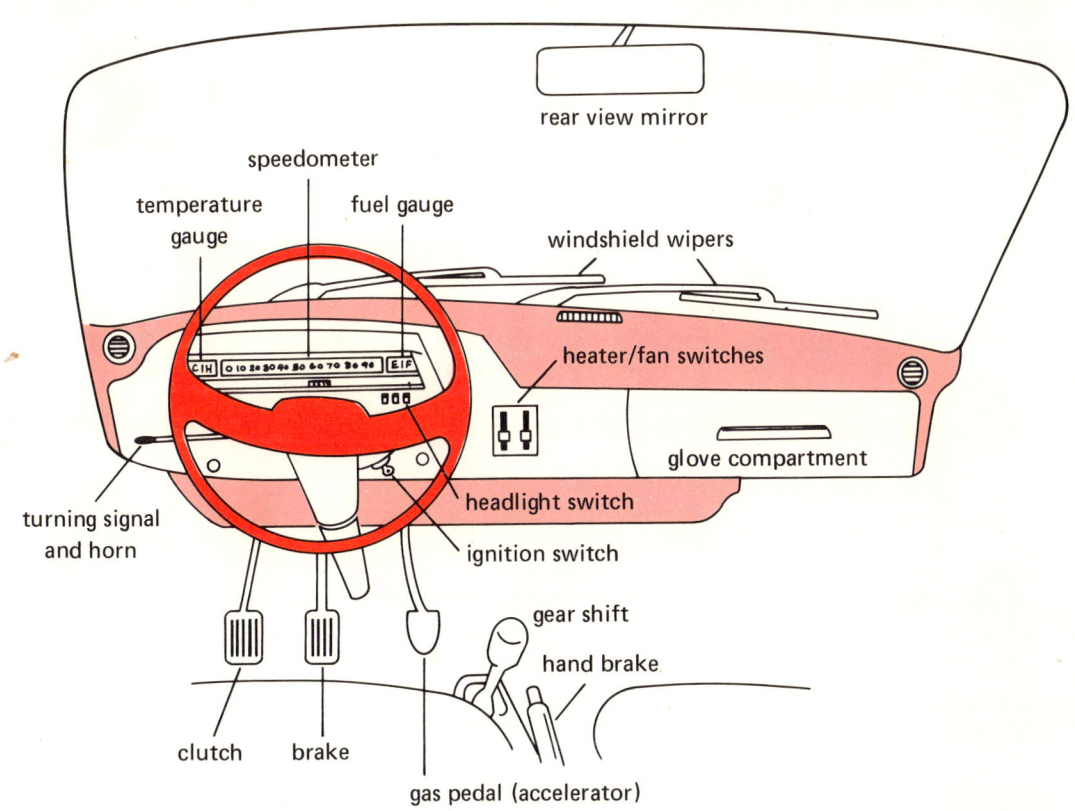

The driver controls the car with his hands and feet.

With his hands he turns the **steering wheel.** He moves the **gearshift** with his hands. He presses the pedals with his feet.

The **accelerator** (ak-SELL-er-ay-tur), or **gas pedal,** makes the car go.

The **brake** slows down and stops the car.

The **clutch** must be pressed to change gears.

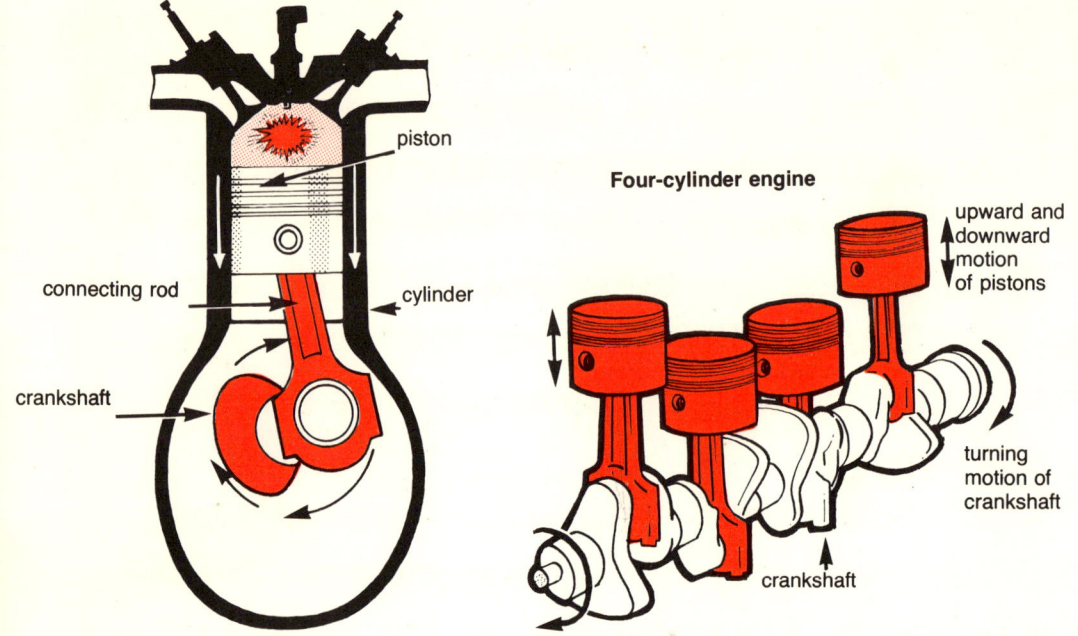

Engines have four, six, or eight chambers, called **cylinders** (SILL-in-durs). Inside each cylinder is something that looks like a can. This is called a **piston.** The pistons move up and down inside their cylinders.

Under the cylinders and connected to the pistons is the **crankshaft.** As the pistons move up and down, they turn the crankshaft.

The crankshaft, which is inside the engine, turns the **drive shaft** (see picture on page 30). The drive shaft runs from near the engine to the rear axle. The drive shaft turns the rear axle. This turns the rear wheels and makes the car move.

What makes the piston move?

First, it needs fuel, which is gasoline (GAS-uh-leen), or gas. Gas enters the **combustion chamber** through the **intake manifold.** There a **valve** acts as a door for the gas. This controls how much gas enters the cylinder.

Then the piston moves up. This forces the gas into the space near the **spark plug.** (We call this **compression**.)

Spark plugs are atop each cylinder. They spark over and over again while the engine is on. These sparks ignite (burn) the gasoline. This causes small explosions inside the combustion chamber. This forces the piston down.

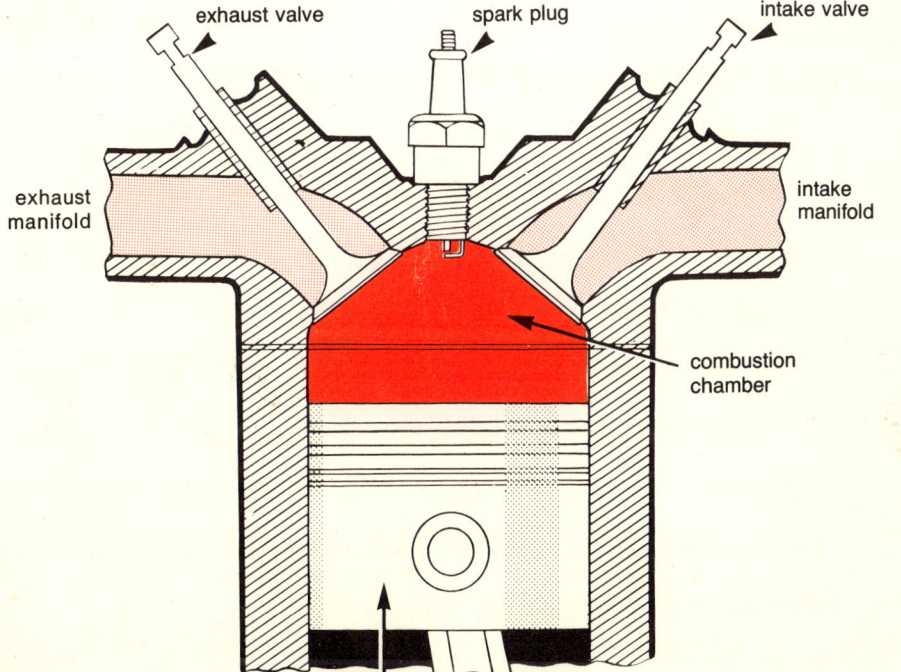

The piston comes back up. It forces out burned gas vapor, called **exhaust** (eggs-AWST), through the **exhaust manifold.** A valve opens and lets the exhaust out.

Here, again, is what happens to make power.

1. The intake valve opens to let gas in (induction).
2. The piston compresses the gas in the cylinder (compression).
3. The spark plug sparks and burns the gas. The hot gas pushes the piston down (power).
4. The piston goes back up and forces the burned gas from the cylinder (exhaust).

These steps make up the **four-stroke cycle** of the **internal-combustion engine.**

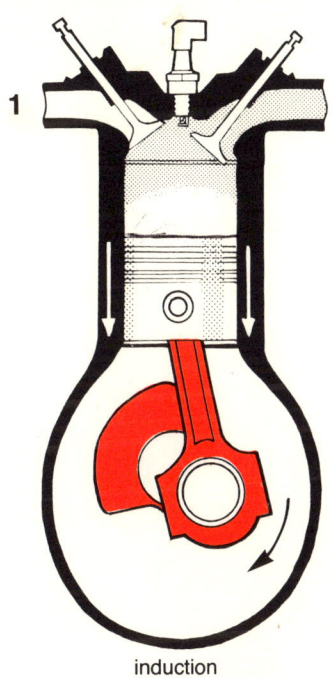
induction

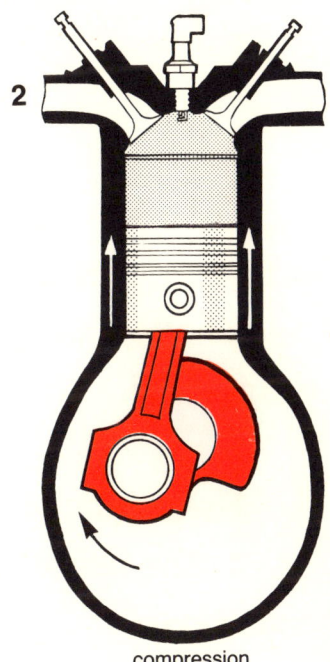
compression

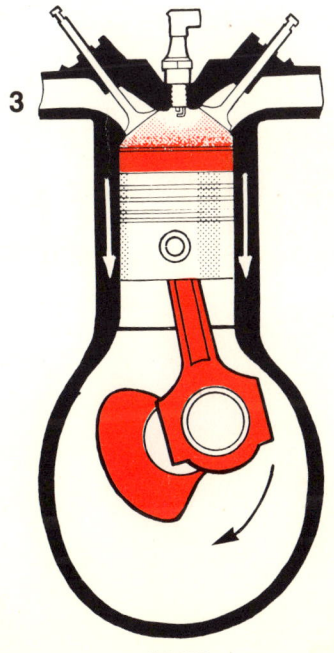
power

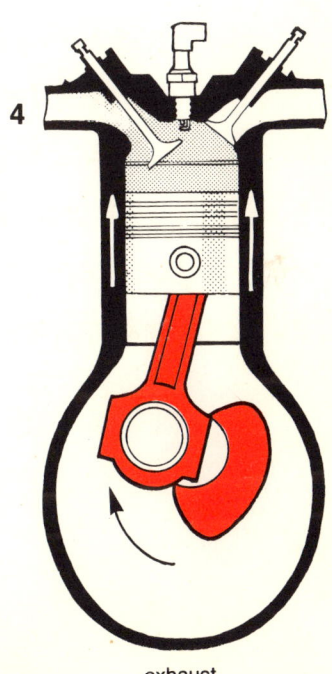
exhaust

This picture shows a four-cylinder engine. See the parts that make the moving pistons turn the crankshaft.

A heavy **flywheel** helps the crankshaft move smoothly. Without it a car would jerk when it runs.

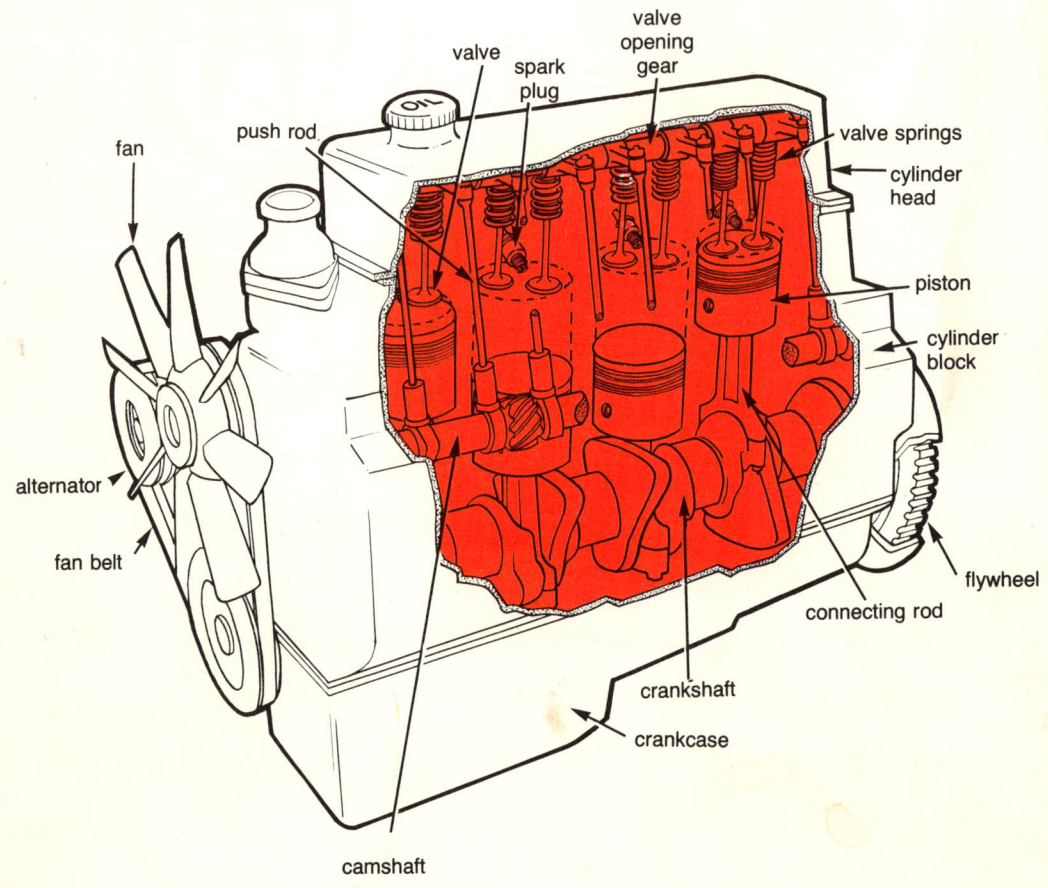

You may have heard of a **"V-8 engine."** It gets its name from the "V" shape the pistons form.

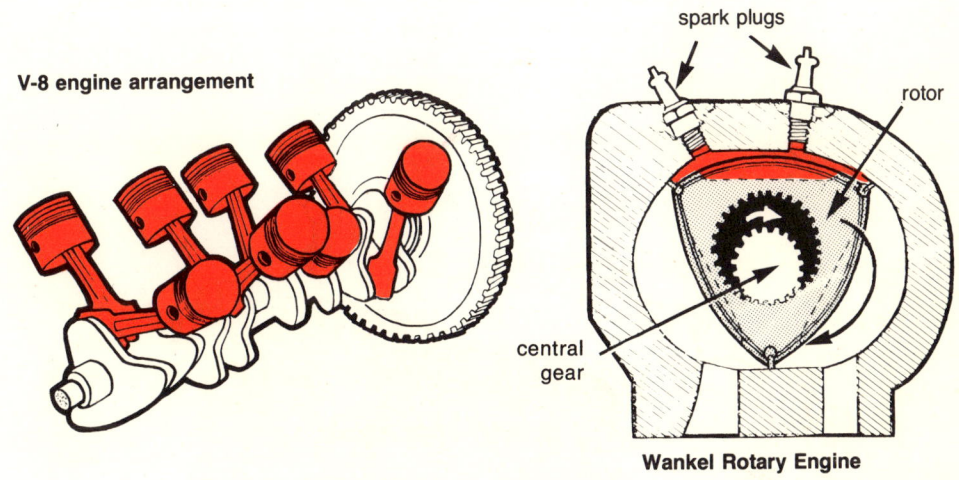

A few cars do not have cylinders or pistons. They have **rotary engines** and run more quietly.

The rotary engine works like an internal-combustion engine. But it doesn't have pistons that move up and down. Instead, it has a **rotor** that turns around.

(21)

THE FUEL SYSTEM

Look at an engine. First you will probably see the **air filter.** This large, round air filter sits atop the **carburetor** (KAR-byuh-ray-tur).

Air enters part of the filter. The air swirls through the tiny cells inside. And it is cleaned of its dirt. The air must be clean before it goes to the carburetor. This is where it is mixed with the gasoline.

The gas is pushed to the carburetor by the **fuel pump.** The gas moves to the engine through a pipeline. The pipeline is connected to the **gas tank.** Gasoline is stored in the gas tank.

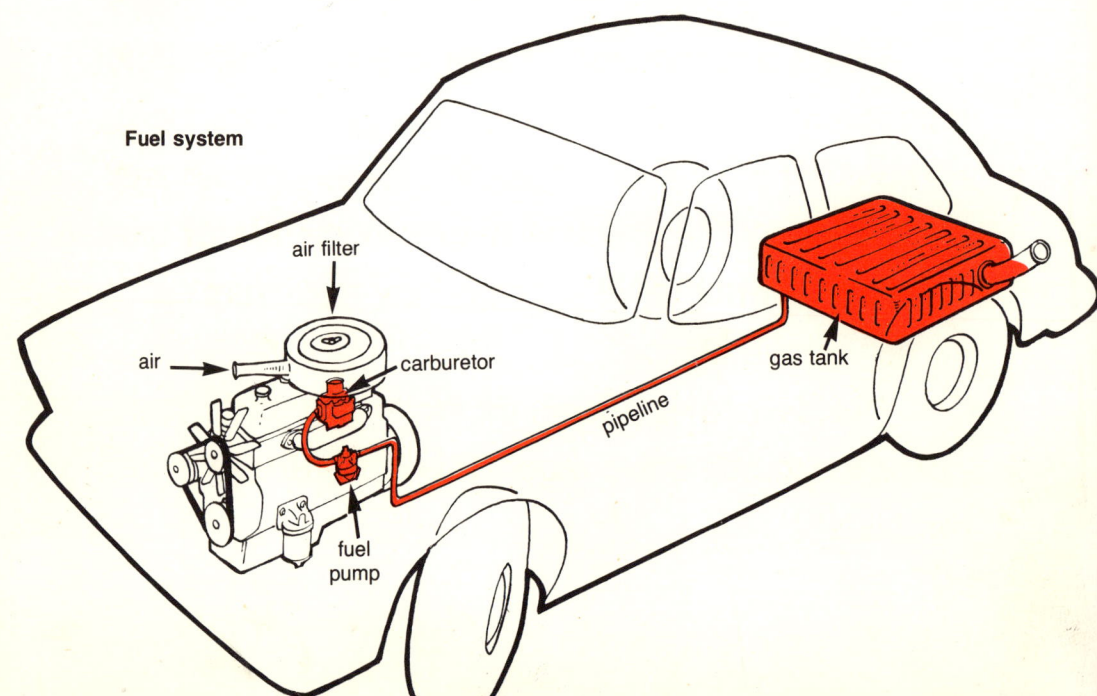

Fuel system

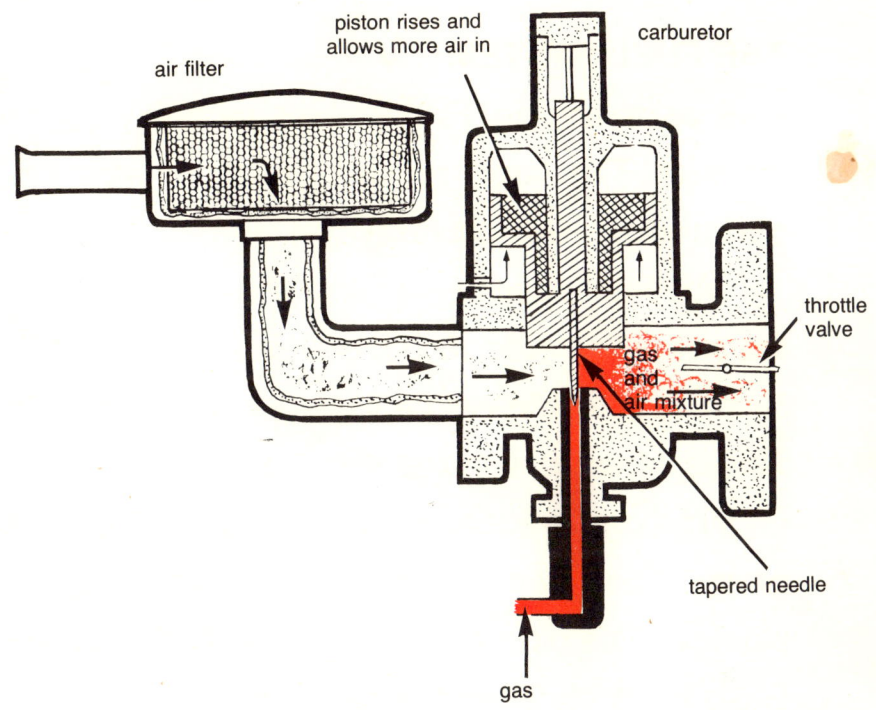

This is a carburetor. The air enters the carburetor from the air filter. At the same time, gas enters the carburetor from below. A needle between the air and the gas rises. The gasoline is sucked into the air stream.

The **throttle valve** controls how much gas and air go into the engine.

The driver steps down on the accelerator. This opens the throttle valve wider. This makes the engine run faster.

(23)

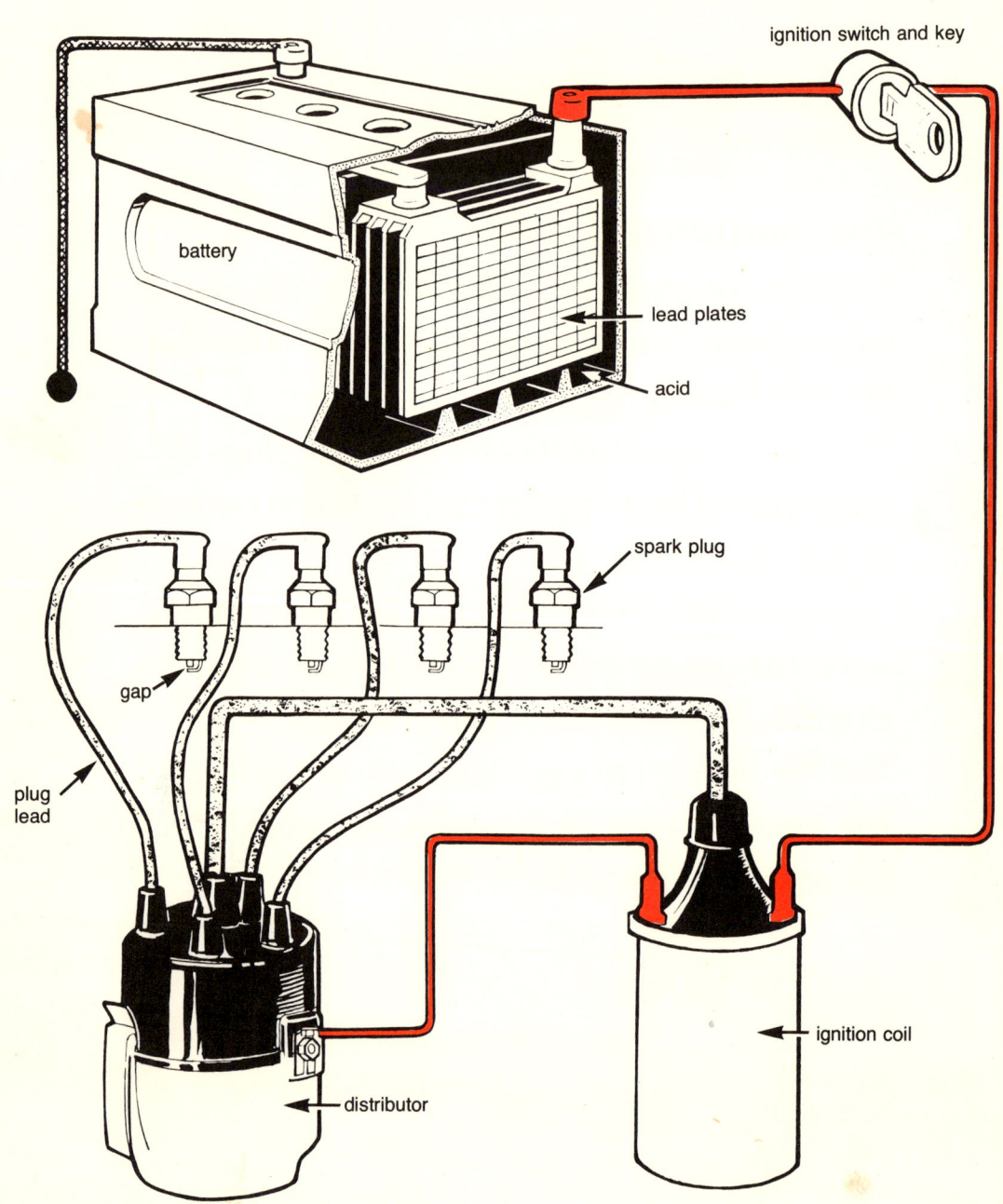

THE IGNITION SYSTEM

The spark plugs are the next stop for the gasoline. To make sparks, the plugs need electricity. They get it from the **battery.**

Between the battery and the spark plugs is the **distributor.** The distributor passes around electricity to each spark plug.

Flashlight or radio batteries run down after a while. But the car battery can last a long time. The **alternator** keeps it from running down.

The battery produces electricity at a low power. The **ignition** (ig-NI-shun) **coil** makes it very powerful.

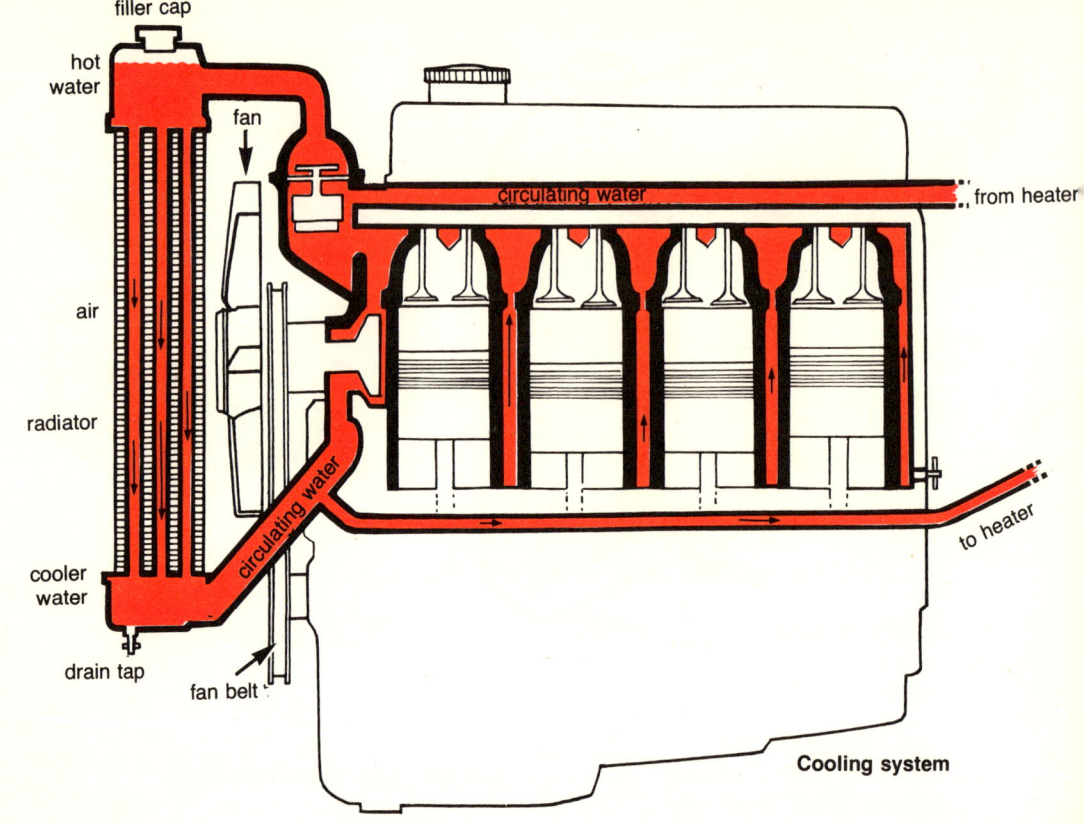

Cooling system

THE COOLING SYSTEM

With so much gasoline being burned, the engine gets very hot. The heat must be carried away. This is a job of the **cooling system.**

Most engines have a water cooling system. Water is pushed through passages around the cylinders. The water carries away much of the heat.

The water, of course, becomes hot. So it is led to the water storage tank called the **radiator.**

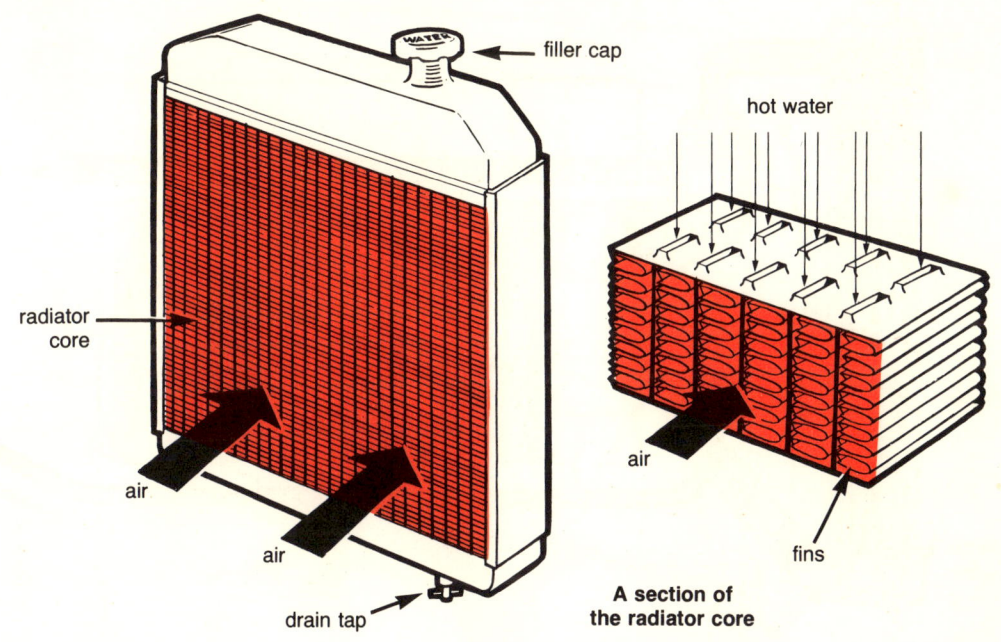

In the radiator the hot water passes through narrow tubes. On the tubes are thin fins.

A **fan** blows air over the tubes and fins. This cools the water passing through. A **fan belt**, which the crankshaft turns, powers the fan.

The cool water is then pumped back through the engine. It will remove more heat from the cylinders.

Some engines are air-cooled instead of water-cooled. A fan blows cool air over the cylinders. The cylinders have fins to help take the heat away. A Volkswagen is air-cooled.

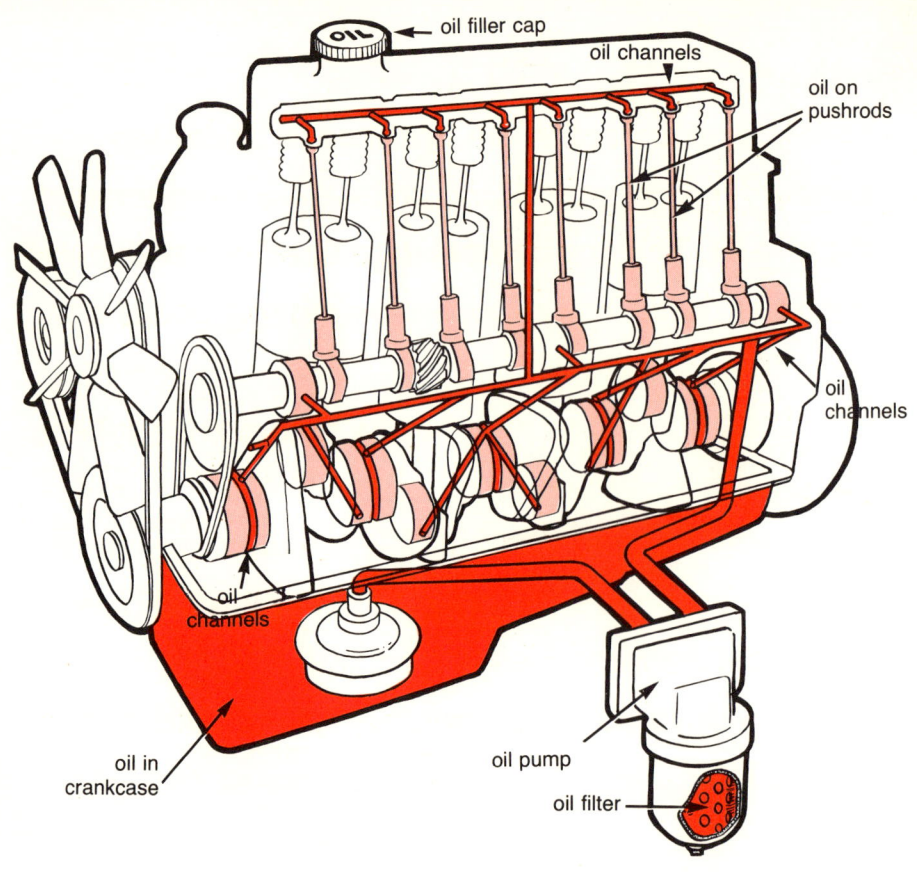

THE LUBRICATION SYSTEM

The car's engine has many moving parts. They need oil to continue to move smoothly. The job of the **lubrication** (loo-bri-KAY-shun) **system** is to oil the engine.

The oil is kept in the **crankcase** under the engine. The **oil pump** brings the oil up and through the engine. The engine **bearings** need more oil than the other parts. They support the moving shafts and allow them to turn.

The bearings turn and throw oil to other parts of the engine.

Remember how the air filter cleaned the air before reaching the carburetor? The **oil filter** cleans the oil before it reaches the engine.

The driver checks how much oil there is with a **dipstick.**

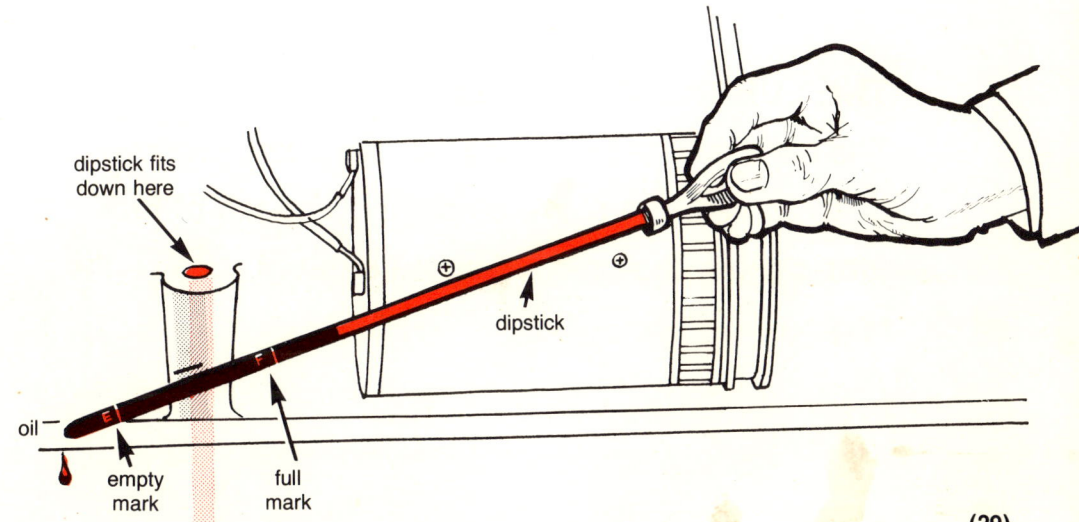

(29)

THE TRANSMISSION SYSTEM

Other systems are needed to make the car run. The **transmission** is just behind the engine. It makes the rear wheels turn slower or faster than the crankshaft.

A driver must shift gears as he goes faster. He must shift when slowing down. He must shift driving up or down a steep hill.

To shift gears, he pushes the clutch with his foot. While the clutch is down, gears can be shifted. Then they are not being turned by the engine's crankshaft.

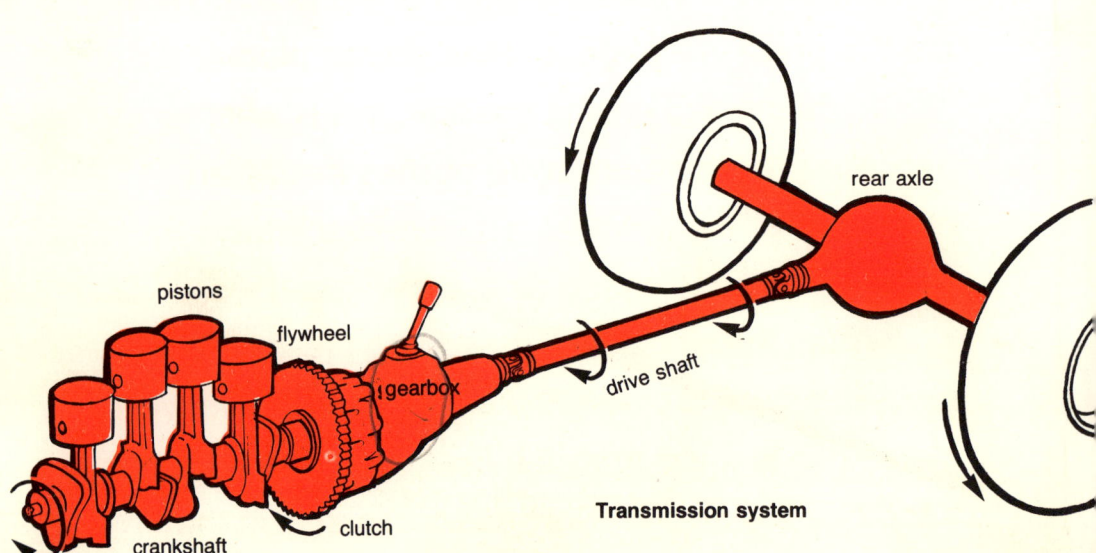

Transmission system

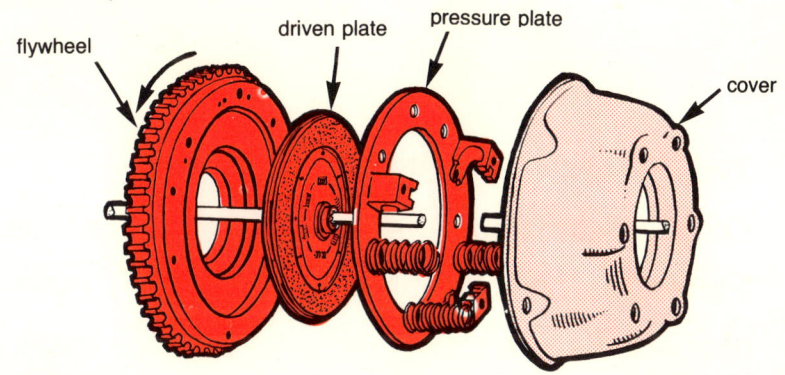

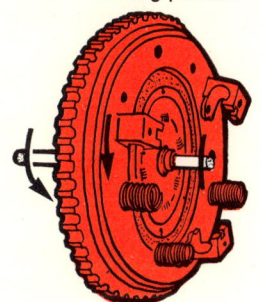
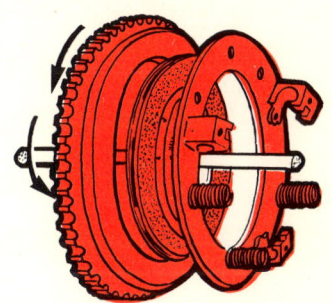

Here you can see the parts of the clutch. They are the **pressure plate** and the **driven plate.**

In the normal driving position, this is what happens. The pressure plate pushes the driven plate against the flywheel. The flywheel always turns at the same speed as the crankshaft.

When the clutch is pressed, the pressure plate moves. It stops pressing the driven plate. The driven plate springs away from the flywheel. It is no longer turned by the engine. Now gears can shift in the **gearbox.**

A gearbox is different size gears on shafts. Gears look like wheels with teeth. One gear can turn another gear when their teeth fit together.

The size of the wheel and the number of teeth it has is important. A large wheel with many teeth will turn slowly. A small wheel with few teeth will turn quickly.

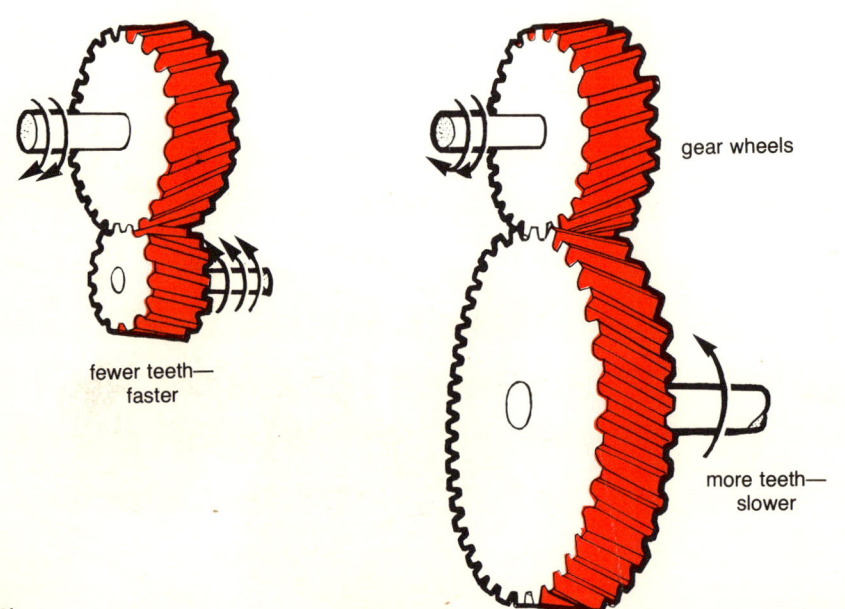

fewer teeth—
faster

gear wheels

more teeth—
slower

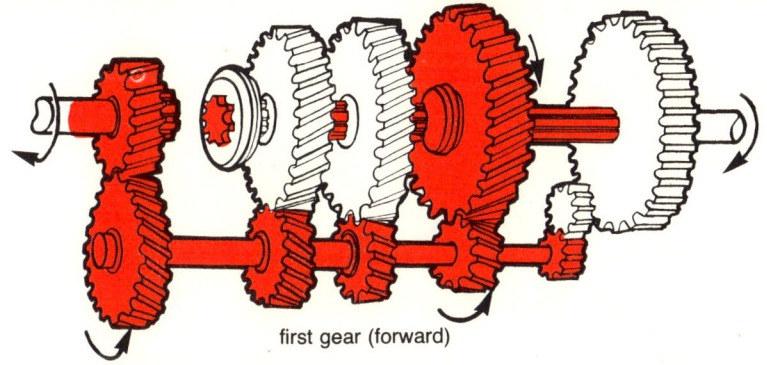

first gear (forward)

The different size gears are linked together in different ways. This lets the engine go faster than the wheels. This happens when the car is just beginning to move.

To shift gears, the driver moves a gearshift lever. It is beside the driver's right leg or on the steering wheel.

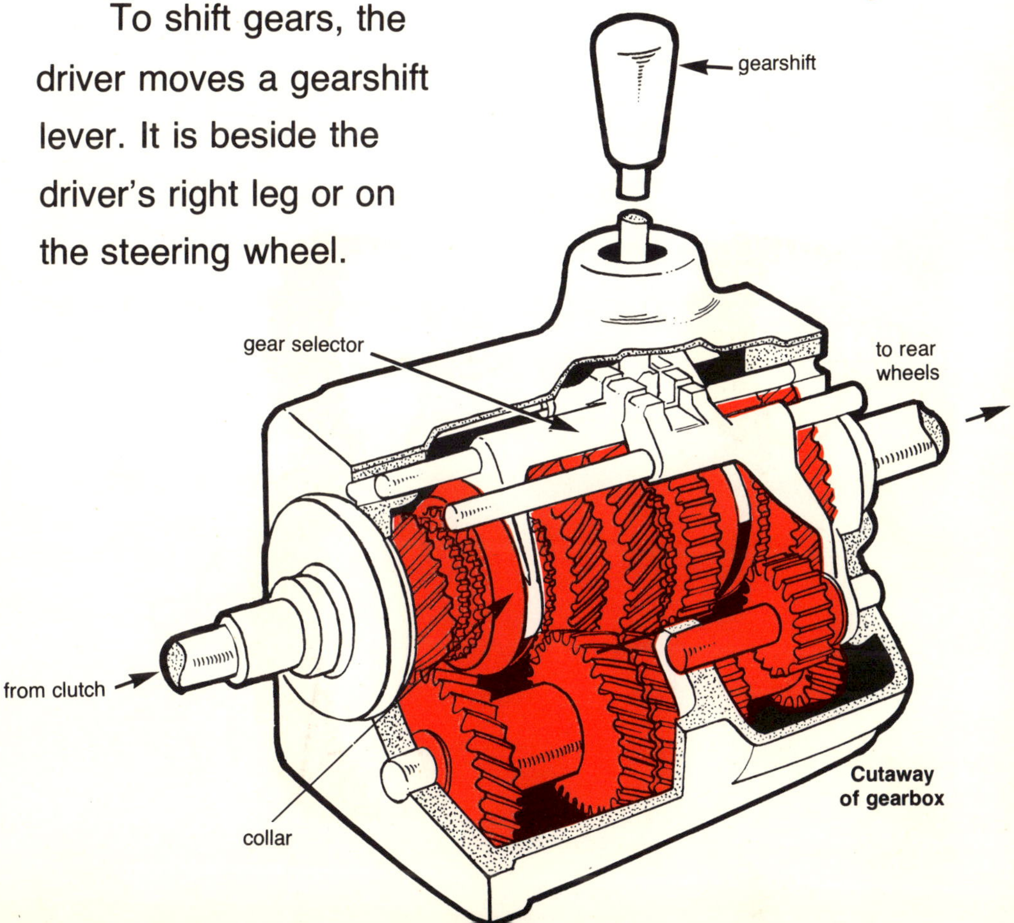

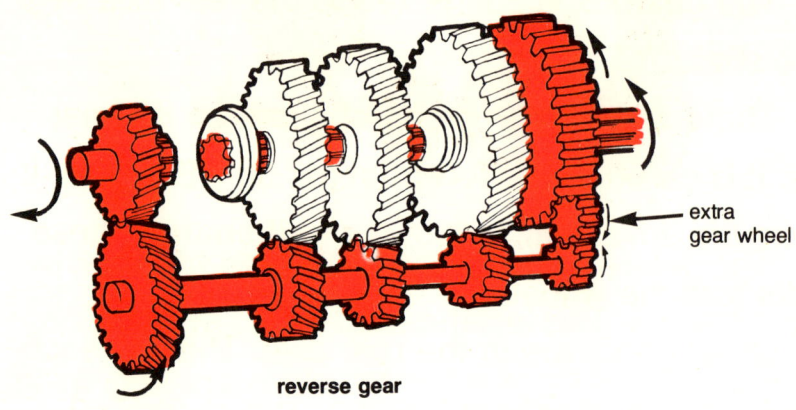

reverse gear — extra gear wheel

The driver makes the car go backwards by shifting into "reverse." An extra gear turns the drive shaft in the opposite direction.

In many cars, the driver does not have to shift gears. These cars have **automatic transmission.** The gears shift by themselves at certain speeds. A car with automatic transmission has no clutch.

The gearbox is connected to the rear axle by a drive shaft.

There is a special group of gears on the rear axle. It is called the **differential** (dif-uh-REN-shul). It allows the drive shaft to turn the **half shafts.** These shafts turn the wheels.

Other gears are in the rear axle. They let each wheel move at a different speed. This is needed during a turn.

A **universal joint** is near the rear axle. It protects the drive shaft and differential.

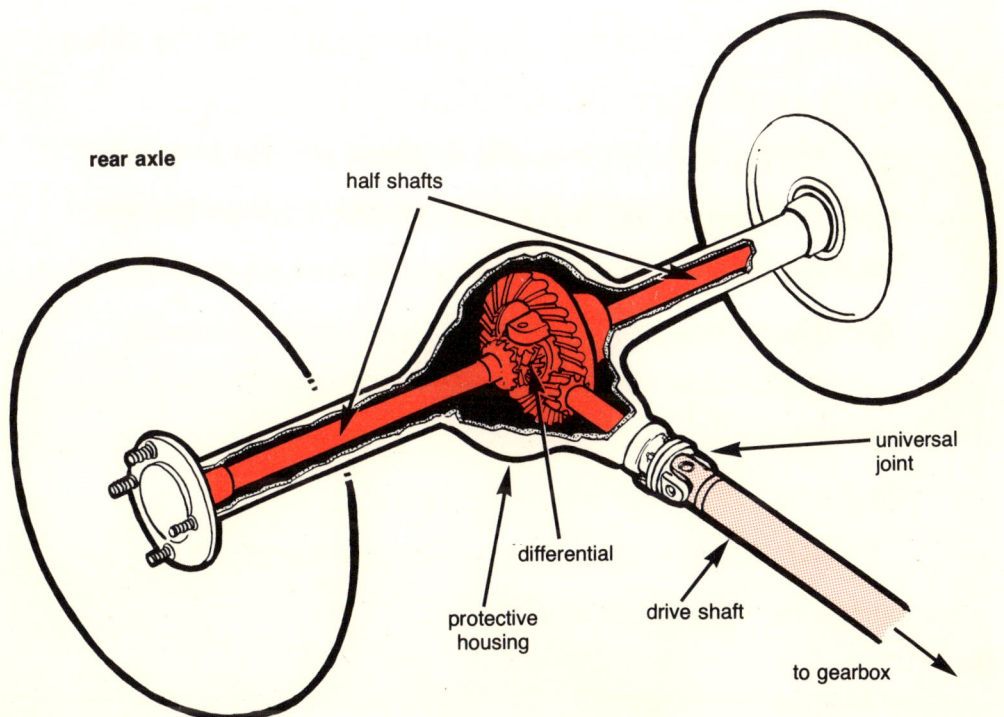

THE BRAKE SYSTEM

A driver uses **brakes** to slow or stop the car. Each wheel has its own brake.

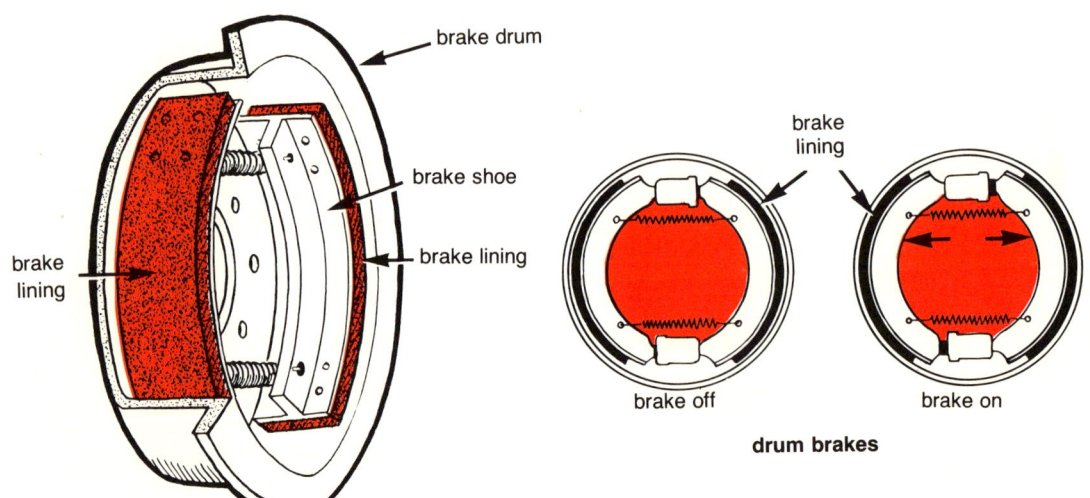

drum brakes

Most cars have **drum brakes** on the two rear wheels. Drum brakes have more power than the front brakes. They play the biggest part in stopping the car quickly.

Inside the wheel is a metal drum. Inside it are two **brake shoes.** They press out against the drum when the driver pushes the brake.

The shoes have a tough **brake lining.** They are not worn down quickly.

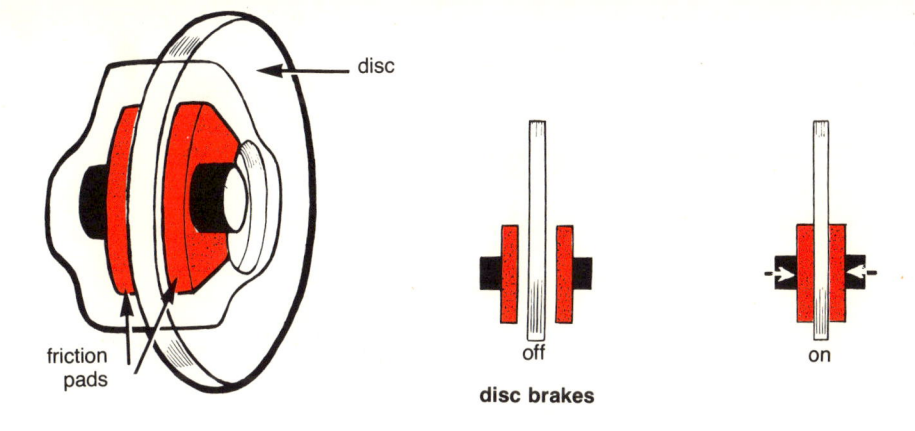

On the front wheels, most cars have **disc brakes.** The disc is attached to the wheel. It turns with the wheel. Two pads press against each disc to slow its turning.

The driver presses the **brake pedal.** This sends liquid (**brake fluid**) to all four brakes. The force of the liquid makes the disc and drum brakes work.

Cars also have a **hand brake.** It locks the rear wheels so that they cannot move. This is used when a car is parked.

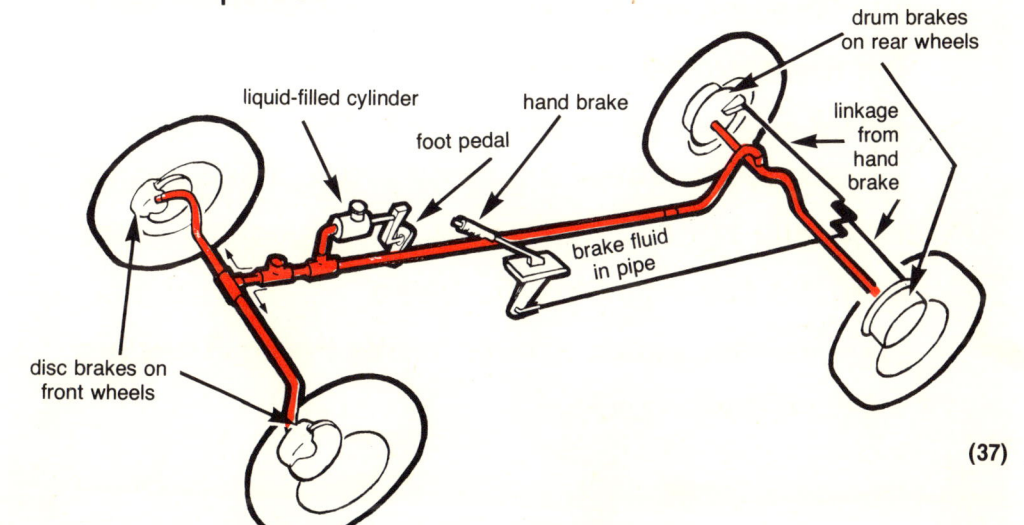

(37)

rack-and-pinion steering

rack

pinion

steering column

steering wheel

THE STEERING SYSTEM

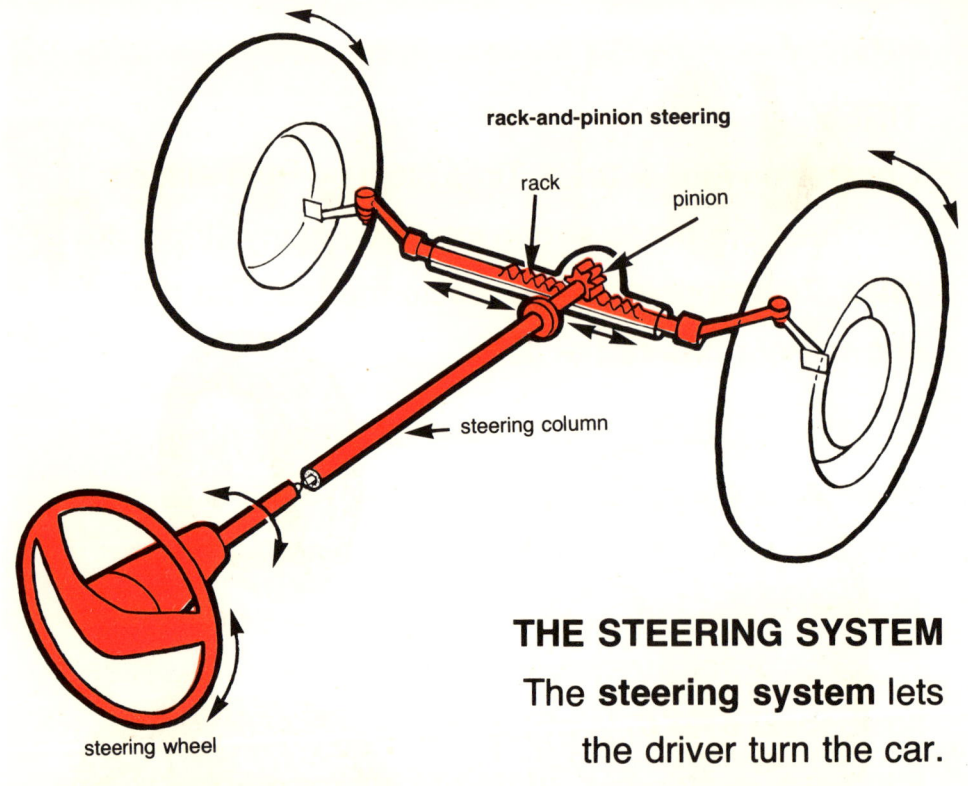

The **steering system** lets the driver turn the car.

All cars have a **steering wheel.** The driver can turn the wheel left or right. The front wheels turn in the same direction as the steering wheel.

The drawing shows the steering wheel joined to the **steering column.** The end of the column has a wheel called a **pinion** (PIN-yun). This fits into the teeth of a **rack** on the front axle. When the column turns, the rack moves and the wheels turn.

straight

turning

TIRES

Cars roll on rubber **tires.** Tires must be filled with air.

Tires are made strong inside by many strips, or **plies.** The strips of rubber circle the tire. The tire shown here has **radial** plies.

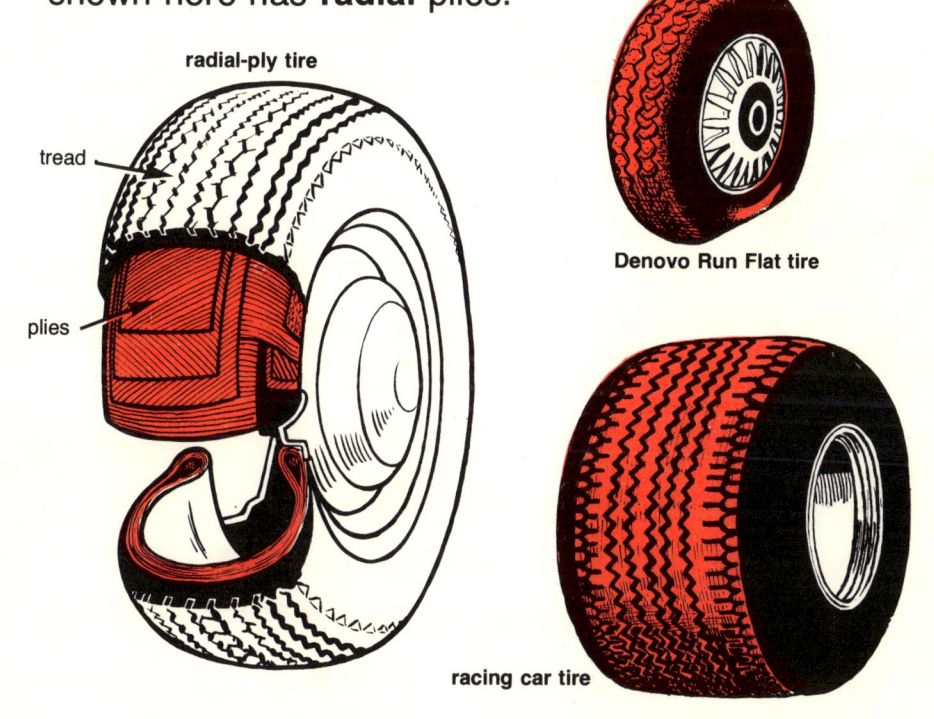

radial-ply tire

tread

plies

Denovo Run Flat tire

racing car tire

The lines on the outside are the **tread.** The tread helps the tire hold the road and stop easier.

Car tires used to have **inner tubes**, like bicycle tires. Today most car tires are **tubeless.** They have no inner tube.

(39)

without suspension

THE SUSPENSION SYSTEM

Tires also help to protect passengers from a rough ride. But the car's most important protection is its **suspension system.**

Without suspension, passengers would have a rough ride. Many parts of the car would soon break down. The picture above shows a car without suspension. The car's body rides along just as the wheels' axles do. This is a hard ride.

With suspension (page 41, top) the car body stays almost flat. Only the wheels move up and down.

car without independent suspension

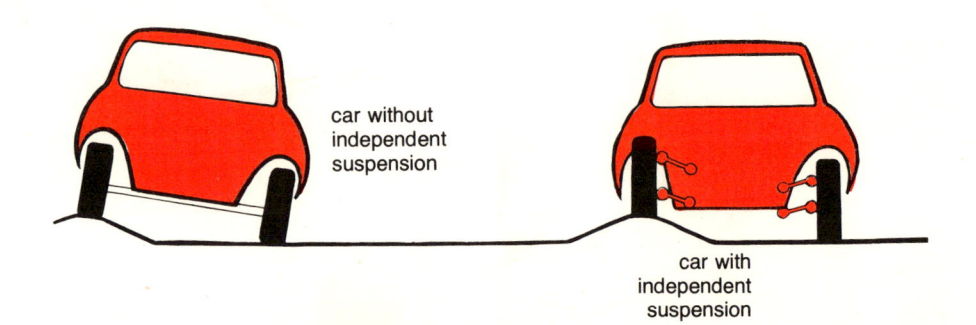

car with independent suspension

with suspension

Most suspension systems are made of **springs** and **shock absorbers.** The air inside the shock absorbers helps protect the car. Other suspension systems use liquids and gases.

Some cars have **independent suspension.** Each wheel is free to move up and down by itself. The picture on the bottom of page 40 shows how independent suspension keeps the car body flat.

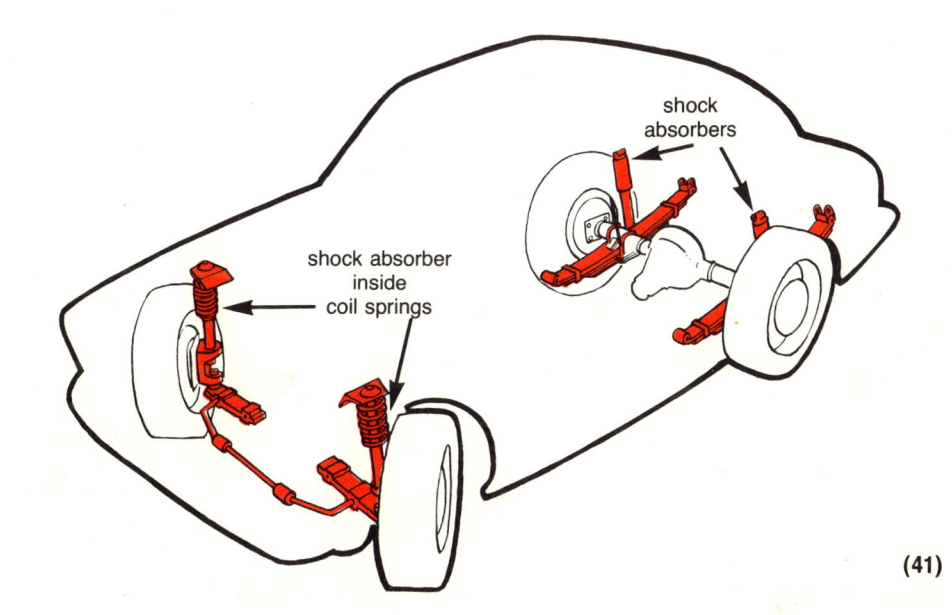

shock absorbers

shock absorber inside coil springs

(41)

body pressing assembly

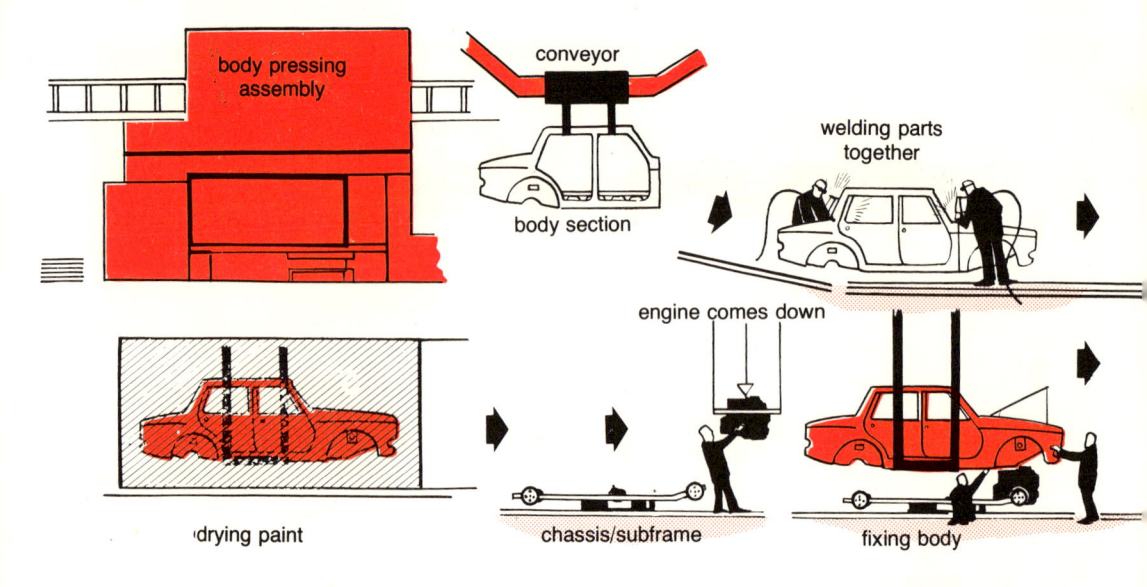

conveyor

body section

welding parts together

drying paint

engine comes down

chassis/subframe

fixing body

There are so many parts and systems inside just one car. How are so many cars made each year?

In 1913 Henry Ford began the car **assembly line.** Cars could be put together eight times faster than before. Ford's company could turn out 1,000 cars a day.

In an assembly line, the car body and its parts move by **conveyor.** Small parts are built into larger parts. Then the larger parts are built into the body.

Each person along the assembly line has only one task. The person might add a tire or a window. Then the car moves to the next worker.

The pictures on these two pages show some of the many steps. Assembly lines are very important.

dipping body

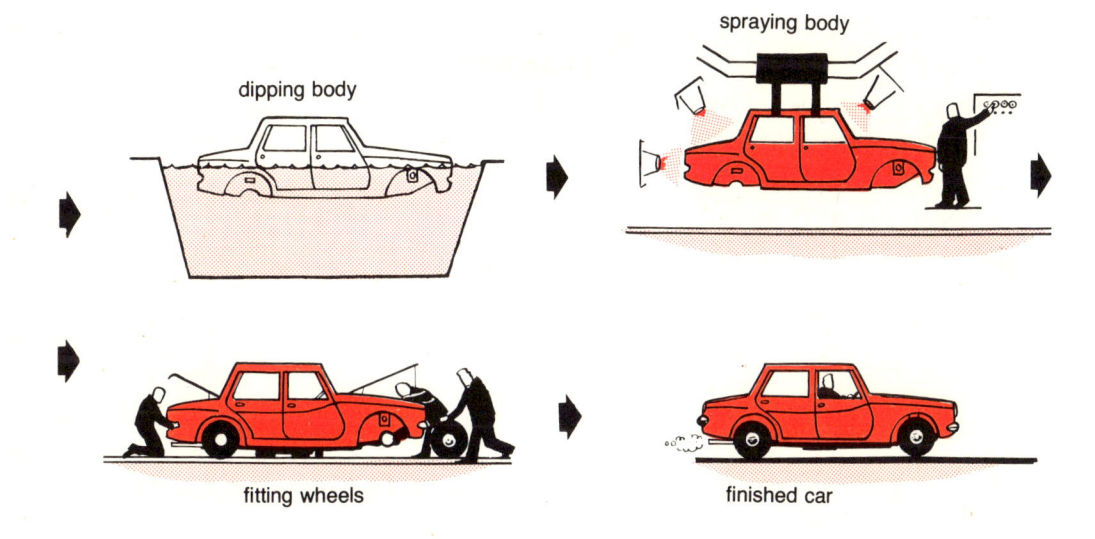

spraying body

fitting wheels

finished car

At the end of the assembly line, the car is complete. It is ready to be shipped to a car sales office.

Car assembly line

No one man or woman invented the car. Rough models were built as early as 1769. Karl Benz and Gottlieb Daimler built the first practical cars with gasoline-powered engines. This was in 1886.

Only rich people could buy cars until Henry Ford's Model T. This car was made between 1908 and 1927.

Early cars looked like the old buggies once pulled by horses. So they were called "horseless carriages."

Many improvements have been made in cars. But auto makers still have a lot of work ahead. They must use engines that burn less gas. Engines must not dirty the air. And car makers must make cars even safer.

The car of the future may run on electricity instead of gasoline. And engineers are designing a car that will steer itself!

Benz, 1885

Daimler, 1886

Lanchester, 1897

Rolls-Royce Silver Ghost, 1906

Model T Ford, 1913

(45)

"Prince Henry"
Vauxhall, 1910

Morris Crowley, 1915

early Bugatti, 1913

Le Mans Bentley,
1920s

Austin 7, 1922

MG K3
Magnette, 1933

(46)

Volkswagen
Prototype PE, 1937

XK120
Jaguar, 1948

Mercedes Benz
300SL, 1952

Citroën DS19, 1955

Aston Martin DB4, 1961

Studebaker V8, 1950

(47)

INDEX

Accelerator, 15, 23
Air-cooled engine, 27
Air filter, 22–23
Alternator, 25
Assembly line, 42–43
Automatic transmission, 34–35
Axles, 12, 16, 35, 38, 40

Battery, 25
Bearings, 29
Benz, Karl, 44
Brake fluid, 37
Brake lining, 36
Brake pedal, 15, 37
Brake shoe, 36
Brake system, 36–37

Camshaft, 20
Car manufacture, 42–44
Carburetor, 22–23
Clutch, 15, 30–31, 34
Coil, ignition, 25
Combustion chamber, 17
Compression, 17
Convertible, 7
Cooling system, 26–27
Crankcase, 29
Crankshaft, 16, 20, 27, 30
Cylinder, 16–18, 21, 27

Daimler, Gottlieb, 44
Differential, 35
Dipstick, 29
Disc brake, 37
Distributor, 25
Drag racers, 9
Drag strip, 9
Drive shaft, 16, 34, 35
Driven plate, 31
Drum brake, 36, 37

Engine systems, 12
 cooling, 26–27
 fuel, 22–23
 ignition, 24–25
 lubrication, 28–29
Exhaust, 17
Exhaust manifold, 17

Fan, 27
Fan belt, 27
Flywheel, 20, 31
Ford, Henry, 42
Four-cylinder engine, 20
Four-stroke cycle, 18
Front-wheel drive, 13
Fuel pump, 23
Fuel system, 22–23
Future, cars of, 44

Gas pedal, 15
Gas tank, 22
Gasoline, 17–18, 22–23
Gearbox, 31, 32
Gears, shifting, 30, 33–34
Gearshift, 15, 33
Grand prix cars, 10

Half shafts, 35
Hand brake, 37

Ignition system, 24–25
Independent suspension, 41
Indianapolis 500, 10
Intake manifold, 17
Internal-combustion engine, 18

Left-hand drive, 14
Lubrication system, 28–29

Model T Ford, 44

Oil, 28–29

Oil filter, 29
Oil pump, 29

Pinion, 38
Piston, 16–18, 20, 21
Pressure plate, 31

Races, 8–10
Radiator, 26–27
Rallies, 8
Rear axle, 12, 16, 35
Rear-wheel drive, 12
Reverse gear, 34
Rotary engine, 21
Rotor, 21

Sedan, 6
Shock absorber, 41
Spark plug, 17–18, 25
Sports car, 8
Springs, 41
Station wagon, 7
Steering column, 38
Steering system, 38
Steering wheel, 15, 38
Stock cars, 9
Suspension system, 40–41

Throttle valve, 23
Tires, 39
Traction, 13
Transmission system, 30–35
Trunk, 6, 12

Universal joint, 35

Valve, intake, 17–18
V-8 engine, 21
Volkswagen, 12, 27

Water cooling system, 26–27
Wheels, 36–37, 38, 40

(48)

Libraries —
inc Hunting   1976

Of Books and Men

Published in Columbia, South Carolina, during the one hundred and seventy-fifth anniversary of the establishment of the University of South Carolina and the two hundredth anniversary of the establishment of the United States of America.

Of Books and Men

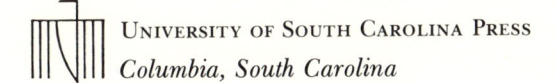

By Louis B. Wright

UNIVERSITY OF SOUTH CAROLINA PRESS
Columbia, South Carolina

Copyright © University of South Carolina 1976

First Edition

Published in Columbia, S.C., by the University of South Carolina Press, 1976
Manufactured in the United States of America

Library of Congress Cataloging in Publication Data

Wright, Louis Booker, 1899–
   Of books and men.

   Includes bibliographical references.
   1. Research libraries—United States—History.
2. Libraries, Private—United States—History.
3. Henry E. Huntington Library and Art Gallery,
San Marino, Calif.—History. 4. Folger Shakespeare
Library, Washington, D.C.—History. I. Title.
Z675.R45W75   026'.8223'3   76-26493
ISBN 0-87249-344-X

For my son Christopher,
who, after years of avoiding
his father's footsteps,
has become a librarian.

Contents

PREFACE	ix
INTRODUCTION:	
Libros Virosque Cano	xi
CHAPTER I:	
The Making of a Bookman	3
CHAPTER II:	
From the British Museum to Paradise Among the Orange Groves	23
CHAPTER III:	
Evolution of a Research Library	49
CHAPTER IV:	
Community of Scholars	69
CHAPTER V:	
An Uncloistered World	96
CHAPTER VI:	
Agony of Decision	111
CHAPTER VII:	
Problems of the Folger Library	119
CHAPTER VIII:	
"Our Enterprise Is First of All a Library"	140
CHAPTER IX:	
Extracurricular Activities: Near and Far	156

Preface

MY PURPOSE IN WRITING this little book has been to describe as succinctly as possible the unique position of privately endowed research libraries in the United States and their potential for exerting an influence on learning. It has been my aim to relate in some detail the evolution of the Huntington and the Folger libraries from ducal collections of wealthy men into active research institutions. The transition from private collections to public institutions was not easy, and perhaps the solutions of problems facing them may have some value to others. I have been particularly concerned to report the purposes of the founders and the way the founders' intentions have been carried out.

If I have been obliged to use the personal pronoun more often than one might wish, it results, not from vanity, but from the necessity of a reporter to indicate his authority for a statement. In many instances, I am the only living person who can recall certain details.

Much information about the Folger Library has previously been given in my collection of newsletters, reprinted in *The Folger Library: Two Decades of Growth. An Informal Account* (Charlottesville, Va.: University Press of Virginia, 1968). The present volume is a sequel to the personal narrative of my earlier experiences related in *Barefoot in Arcadia* (Columbia, S.C.: University of South Carolina Press, 1974).

My debt is great to many friends, living and dead. My wife has served as a memory bank, for she shared many of my professional experiences.

I want to thank particularly my longtime research assistant and collaborator, Mrs. Elaine W. Fowler, who for many years was a

ix

valued member of the Folger staff. She has proved a wise and sensitive editor of my crabbed text, and without her help, the book might never have been written.

November 4, 1975   LOUIS B. WRIGHT

INTRODUCTION

Libros Virosque Cano

I F I MAY PARODY VIRGIL, of books and men I sing. Much of my life has been devoted to helping create research collections in great libraries and to encouraging the use of these collections by imaginative scholars.

As John Milton reminds us in *Areopagitica*, "Books are not absolutely dead things but do contain a potency of life in them to be as active as that soul was whose progeny they are." So it has always seemed to me necessary to remember not only the authors of books but also the purposes for which they were written. Libraries were not meant to be mere repositories of dusty volumes but living sources of knowledge and inspiration. It is about such living libraries and the personalities who helped to make them that I want to report.

Because in the brief compass of a few chapters it is obviously impossible even to mention many of the significant libraries of this country, I shall emphasize only those with which I have had some connection. Thanks to longevity, I am the only person still alive who remembers many of the details of the transformation of the Henry E. Huntington Library and Art Gallery in San Marino, California, into an active research institution. Even some of the early episodes in the development of the Folger Shakespeare Library in Washington, D.C., are fading into obscurity. With these two libraries I was long intimately associated, and a brief account of their goals and development may have some historical value.

The Huntington on one side of the continent and the Folger on the other represent a type of research institution unique to the United States. Libraries from time immemorial have been designed for the preservation of books and documents. Readers were expected to find out about their materials as best they could; traditionally, libraries made no positive effort to induce scholars to utilize their resources. As recently as a decade ago, the *London Times* reported a by-law passed by the county council of West Suffolk making it an offense to sleep in a library, punishable by a fine not to exceed five pounds. This prompted the librarian of Cambridge University to comment: "We welcome sleepers. A sleeping reader is less of a menace to books than a waking one."

Facetious as this remark may have been, it illustrates a traditional view that is the very antithesis of that of a few privately endowed libraries in the United States which, in the twentieth century, adopted the novel practice of supporting scholars in residence to come and use their materials and even of providing stipends for research fellows and visiting scholars. In short, such libraries became active research institutions, not mere repositories. They had no particular axe to grind but wished to encourage learning in significant fields. Nowhere else in the world had founders of libraries arrived at such a concept.

In hardly more than a century and a half, the United States has become a nation of book collectors—book collectors with a purpose. Many have left their collections to universities or private libraries of their choosing. Their benefactions have been so great that booksellers—and some would-be collectors—have complained about their responsibility for the scarcity of purchasable books.

Book collecting, however, is nothing new. The success these Americans have had rests upon a long tradition inherited from the English-speaking world. From colonial times we have prized books, but in an earlier day most of our libraries were strictly utilitarian. Our pioneering ancestors had little room in their luggage for any type of book except those that would be useful in solving the problems of life on the frontier—or those that might help them to a better world hereafter. Households that had no other book might at least have a Bible.

Benjamin Franklin, telling in his *Autobiography* of the founding of the first subscription library in Philadelphia, remarked: "This was the mother of all the North American subscription libraries, now so numerous. It is become a great thing and continually increasing. These libraries have improved the general conversation of the Americans, made the common tradesmen and farmers as intelligent as most gentlemen from other countries, and perhaps have contributed in some degree to the stand so generally made throughout the Colonies in defense of their privileges." Franklin testifies to the zeal shown by Americans of his day for self-education through books bought or borrowed. Books were the means of self-improvement on every frontier as Americans pushed westward, and the possession of books marked a man as above the common run of mortals. If Americans on the expanding frontier had neither money nor opportunity to become book collectors, they bought such works as they could afford and made use of them to the best of their abilities.

Cotton Mather in New England and William Byrd in Virginia both were eager buyers of books. As different as these two men were, and the societies they represented, their libraries were much alike in content. In Philadelphia James Logan, who came to Pennsylvania as William Penn's secretary, was a lover of books and brought together probably the best classical library in the colonies. Thomas Jefferson was one of the most diligent collectors of the early nineteenth century; his books became the nucleus of the Library of Congress. Jefferson was a patron of booksellers and encouraged others to buy books which he believed to be useful in the advancement of learning.

One of the earliest American booksellers to exert an influence on the development of research libraries was Henry Stevens of Vermont (died 1880), who went to London, opened a bookshop, and helped to develop collections of outstanding Americana in the John Carter Brown Library in Providence, the Lenox Library in New York, the Library of Congress, and the Smithsonian Institution. In a preface to his *Recollections of James Lenox of New York and the Formation of His Library*, Stevens signed himself "Bibliographer and Lover of Books." He was one of the first to recognize the importance of photography in adding otherwise unavailable items to a collection, and he was the first bookseller to understand the importance of out-of-the-way items to American historians.

The Lenox Library and the John Carter Brown Library both represent the application of special knowledge and intelligence by the founders—a characteristic of American book collectors—plus the skill and enterprise of a bookseller.

James Lenox deserves credit for setting a precedent followed by many later collector-philanthropists, for he brought together a magnificent collection of rare books and at his death in 1880 bequeathed them to the public to become the nucleus of an aggregate of other fine collections that make up the New York Public Library, one of the important research libraries in the nation. Lenox, son of a wealthy New York merchant of Scotch Presbyterian background, used his wealth for the public good. He enjoyed book collecting and knew what he was about. As a Scripture-reading Scot, he was interested in Holy Writ and first began to collect Bibles. Ultimately he procured a Gutenberg Bible, one of his proudest possessions. Working from the known to the unknown, he proceeded from early Bibles to early imprints of a less sacred nature and gradually collected many fine examples of sixteenth-century presses, both English and Continental. He also bought, with Stevens's advice, valuable early Americana. But his collecting primarily represented his own interest and knowledge of books.

The same may be said of John Carter Brown (died 1874), member of the distinguished family of merchant princes of Providence, Rhode Island. He became an early addict of book collecting, beginning with the fine books that any cultivated man would want. Before long, however, he too became interested in the historical background of his own country, and he settled on the period from the discovery of America to 1801 as the area in which he would collect intensively. The books brought together by the founder and his successors have made the John Carter Brown Library an outstanding collection of early Americana. Like the Lenox Library, the John Carter Brown Library in time became a public research institution, in this instance, as part of Brown University.

The method of collecting, the quality, and the disposition of these two nineteenth-century libraries are symbolic of much rare-book collecting and library development that followed. American book collecting by and large has been remarkably discriminating.

Libros Virosque Cano

The buyers generally have known what they wanted and have not been sold merely a collection of rarities by some enterprising dealer.

During the last quarter of the nineteenth century, and ever since, Americans have been among the most avid book buyers in the world. This appetite for books has grown steadily, and the market for rare books in America has paralleled the increase in national wealth. Philanthropic collectors have created in the United States some of the finest and most effective research libraries in the world. And all of this has come about in a little more than a century.

The recent remarkable expansion of academic research libraries could not have taken place without continued contributions of books, money, and talent by public-spirited philanthropists. One has only to read the annual reports of the Houghton Library at Harvard, the Yale Library, or almost any other university library to see how this development is continuing.

Book collectors usually want to have their collections maintained and used. They have, therefore, frequently placed their books in privately endowed or university libraries where they will have perpetual care and serve the interests of learning. One of the greatest collectors of our time, Lessing J. Rosenwald, who combines an interest in art with his interest in books, continues to give to the Library of Congress early illustrated books of untold value. He has also been a generous donor to other libraries. The du Ponts have created an important library for economic and social history in the Eleutherian Mills Historical Library at Wilmington, Delaware. There they have deposited invaluable manuscripts and business records of the first century of American independence.

Book collectors in America have seen to it that the universities have become increasingly effective in many fields of research. Arthur Houghton has made great contributions to Harvard, for example, and to many other American libraries, and he still gathers books and manuscripts that interest him for his own collection. Wilmarth Lewis, one of the most enthusiastic collectors of this century, has made a magnificent library of eighteenth-century literature and history at Farmington, Connecticut, which he is giving to

Yale. The nucleus of this library was a collection concerned with Horace Walpole. The late James Ford Bell brought together a fine library of travel and geographical works, including the most complete group of the Jesuit Relations, which he gave to the University of Minnesota with an endowment to keep it up. A remarkable rare-book library assembled by Josiah K. Lilly was given to Indiana University and overnight added a new dimension to the research facilities of that institution, particularly in English literature and literary history.

The rare books gathered by Tracy W. McGregor and C. Waller Barrett and presented to the University of Virginia have made that institution an effective place for the study of American literature and history.

Among the special libraries attached to universities, the William L. Clements collection of books and manuscripts concerned with the American Revolution, given to the University of Michigan in 1923, set an example for other donors. That library has become a highly significant resource for the early history of the nation, especially for military history.

One of the more important libraries placed under the control of a university was the bequest in 1934 of the William Andrews Clark Memorial Library to the University of California at Los Angeles. It specializes in fine seventeenth-, eighteenth-, and a few nineteenth-century collections. The most valuable single body of material consists of works by and about John Dryden. This collection prompted the definitive edition of Dryden's works now being prepared and published under the aegis of the Clark Library and the University of California.

The Clark Library, like Wilmarth Lewis's Walpole library, represents a special library that is a part of a university but not swallowed up in the main library collection. Both of these libraries also demonstrate an active initiative on the part of the library to advance learning in a special field. The Clark is vigorously supporting seventeenth- and early-eighteenth-century research and is publishing a definitive edition of Dryden, greatest literary figure of the later seventeenth century after Milton. The Walpole library is actively fostering eighteenth-century research, and the donor himself, a brilliant man of letters as well as an exacting scholar, not only collects books but writes some of the most charming essays on the subject published in our time.

The activities of these libraries, attached to universities but not dominated by them, is paralleled by the development of the independent research libraries. The major geographical sections of the United States now have endowed research libraries of international importance and influence. They are privately supported and cost the taxpayer nothing. They all actively collect research materials, freely make their resources available to accredited scholars, and in some instances provide substantial support for research fellowships and publications.

New York has the Pierpont Morgan Library, one of the most remarkable collections in the world of fine printing, early manuscripts, great examples from the Renaissance presses, rare first editions of English literature, as well as English literary manuscripts. The Morgan Library continues to grow and to add to its resources. It has an active group of enthusiastic Fellows of the Morgan Library who help in its present collecting program, and it is an important resource for research in the fields it covers.

The Middle West has the Newberry Library in Chicago, one of the earliest of the independently endowed research libraries. The Newberry has long had the advice of scholars in the universities of Chicago and its environs, and it has developed remarkably effective collections in American history, American literature, French history and literature, the history of the American Indian, the history and languages of primitive peoples, the history of printing—even an unusual collection on gipsies, the gift of a former chairman of its board of trustees. During World War II the Newberry Library provided invaluable material for the study of Philippine dialects and other languages of exotic Pacific Ocean peoples. During the past two decades it has acquired immense amounts of materials for the study of the history of railroads of the Middle West. The Newberry has had a fellowship program for some years and encourages research in its varied collections.

Among the privately endowed libraries, the two that led the way in fostering research during the past three decades and in publishing the results are the Huntington in California and the Folger in Washington. Because these libraries are peculiar to America in their manifold activities, and because I know most about them, I want to stress in the following chapters their history, characteristics, and significance for the future.

In recent years, librarians and buyers of books for the first time have found themselves on the defensive against foes who predict the end of the book. At the same time, they must answer academic administrators who demand that their librarians find some substitute for the avalanche of printed works resulting from the information explosion. A warning note was sounded a decade ago at a meeting of the American Library Association in New York on July 10, 1966, by Dr. Gordon Ray, president of the John Simon Guggenheim Foundation, who felt impelled to talk on "The Future of the Book." That a distinguished book collector should think it necessary to assure professional librarians that the book does have a future is significant. Dr. Ray made it plain that he himself had no doubt about the durability of books. But he quoted current popular sages who wag their heads and announce the demise of the book as other media for the dissemination of information and entertainment become more popular and omnipresent.

We continue to be told that other media will take the place of the book: television and a variety of "visual aids," plus computerized information on every subject under heaven. By pressing a button we will be able to obtain instant knowledge on any topic. The distant days when the family gathered around a student lamp in the evening and the father read a chapter from Dickens, Thackeray, or perhaps the King James version of the Bible, are almost as remote as the civilization of Minoan Crete. Those days disappeared with the collapse of family unity. It would require a warrant and a sheriff's posse to find a teenage child to be read to in the evening nowadays, even if there were an intact family to instigate the search. As for the use of books in higher learning, some prophets of a new dispensation promise more up-to-date methods of instruction. An official of a company with modern gadgetry to peddle—"teaching machines" and other wonders—commented at a meeting of the American Book Publishers' Council that "We are not in-

Libros Virosque Cano

terested in the book business. We are interested mainly in the information business. I predict that you people will be chiefly information publishers in the future."

An obvious fallacy is apparent in the argument that the book, along with God, is dead. We want more than information, mere facts, and we shall continue to look to the book, to the printed word, for the satisfaction of emotional, intellectual, and spiritual needs. The worship of the book, however, should not blind us to the value of new methods of preserving and disseminating the printed word. The computer can do many things for a library, but it will never take the place of the book.

Efficiency experts sometimes delude themselves into believing that the new technology assures greater speed, convenience, and accuracy in retrieving information than did the ancient dependence upon books. Few will gainsay the utility of computerized information for the hard-pressed physician looking for the latest work on some rare disease. But for general information, especially in humanistic fields, the book remains the most effective instrument for the storage and retrieval of information. A wise bookman recently commented:

> The book has merits as an information-storage-and-retrieval machine that, strange to say, are not nowadays obvious to some people to whom they *should* be obvious: it is very compact and portable, does not have to be plugged in to an electric outlet, is user-paced (the reader turns the pages at his own speed); random access is available (you can flip back to any page you wish); and it can mix verbal and nonverbal information.

Administrators continue, however, to pursue the hope that the computer will help solve the problem of library expansion. The world has always found it comforting to believe in such magic. The late Middle Ages attributed to Roger Bacon the invention of a brazen head which could be rubbed to produce much the same effects as are now popularly assigned to the computer. Many academic administrators are being taken in by brazen heads, and a question for the future may be whose head is brazen.

The inundation of books in our time is the major reason that librarians and others have been looking desperately for rescue.

They would like to reduce books to film, tape, or the head of a pin to keep from being drowned in this flood. Perhaps the Babylonians worried about the same problem, with thousands of writings preserved on clay tablets—mud bricks that clearly presented a space problem for the ancients. At any rate, we are now applying our ingenuity to trying to solve the insolvable. We can rest assured, however, that books of value are immortal, and collectors of such books will share in their immortality.

Higher education in the United States owes an enormous debt to philanthropic book collectors who brought together libraries that became a part of the book wealth of the nation and made possible effective research collections in every section of the country. The creation of vast research libraries at Harvard, Yale, Princeton, Columbia, the University of Pennsylvania, the University of Illinois, the University of Chicago, the University of California at Berkeley and at Los Angeles, and at many other institutions did not come about exclusively from purchases made out of university budgets. The distinction of these libraries results from gifts made by generous donors—collectors who, by their own financial means and their own wisdom, brought together books on special subjects of value to learning.

We are all in the debt of these collectors, and I have learned much from those whom I have known. My apprenticeship as a bookman began at the University of North Carolina many years ago. And that apprenticeship has been a continuing process, for one never ceases to learn about books and book collecting. For many years I was a consumer of the materials preserved in research libraries and I gained an appreciation of their great value—and of the people who created them. The following chapters attempt to show how two great research libraries developed. The account is informal, personal, and nonstatistical—the type of information likely to be overlooked and forgotten. I hope these reminiscences will be of some interest and utility.

Of Books and Men

CHAPTER I

The Making of a Bookman

DURING THE YEAR 1923, I served briefly in Washington as a newspaper reporter. For a provincial representing a country newspaper, life in the capital was new and strange, exciting to be sure, but disconcerting. The year had seen the culmination of a period of "normalcy" proclaimed by President Warren Gamaliel Harding as the ideal of his administration. Much of the year appeared reasonably placid, with just enough excitement to keep the public reading newspapers. On August 2, Harding died unexpectedly in San Francisco, and Calvin Coolidge, a monument of tranquility, was sworn in as president by his father, a notary public of Plymouth, Vermont.

Before Harding's death, as I carried on my reportorial chores around the Capitol, I picked up some of the gossip that was rife concerning scandals in his administration. Soon the Teapot Dome investigations would implicate a few members of his cabinet in gross rascality. My fellow reporters, older, more experienced, and more cynical than I, commented that everything was for sale in Washington except the dome of the Capitol, which no politician could unscrew.

As the year wore on, Harding's vaunted normalcy gave way to events at home and abroad that had significant meaning for the future, if one could have read the portents aright. If I had perceived the future opportunities—and rewards—for investigative reporting, I might have remained a journalist.

On July 19, 1923, Mussolini celebrated his fortieth birthday amid loud acclaim in Italy, while Americans argued pro and con about his reputed "reforms." In Germany Adolf Hitler staged his

3

"Beer Hall *Putsch*" at Munich on November 8, but few yet worried about the demagogic little house painter from Austria. In January we had normalized relations with the German Republic by pulling down our flag and calling home our army of occupation on the Rhine; on December 8 we signed a treaty of friendship with Germany. Ten days later Secretary of State Charles Evans Hughes rejected a petition from the Soviet Union for diplomatic recognition.

The news of 1923 was not all political. Archaeology, inventions, amusements, and sports created even more excitement than politics. Thousands of pages dealt with the feats of Lord Carnarvon and Howard Carter in exploring the tomb of Tutankhamen. Following the death of Lord Carnarvon and a series of mishaps to others, the alleged "curse" upon tomb-disturbers got much attention. The immense treasure from the tomb set businessmen to figuring the accrued value if King Tut's heirs could have invested it at six percent. Fashion designers, inspired by Egyptian art and much free publicity, decked women out like King Tut's concubines in flowing silks, sandals, and scarabs. Howard Carter shuttled between Luxor and Cairo with the fervor of a febrile diplomat negotiating with the Egyptian government about control of the discoveries. In America, the Egyptian research stimulated new interest in Mayan civilization. The Carnegie Institution, having obtained a concession to explore ruins at Petén, Tikal, and Chichén Itzá, announced a ten-year program of investigation.

Advances in science and technology created much public interest in 1923. Robert A. Millikan received the Nobel Prize for isolating the electron. Many years later he was to tell me emphatically that man would never crack the atom—and he had better not! During the year transatlantic radio communication between New York and London was perfected, and the Manhattan Opera Company made its first broadcast by radio. The *New York Times* boasted that it could now deliver a copy of its paper by airplane in San Francisco the day after publication. An "airship" (dirigible) passenger service between New York and Chicago was being discussed. On February 6 a British pilot, Flight Lieutenant Haig, astonished the world by flying a plane to an altitude of 20,000 feet in twelve minutes, twenty-four seconds.

Americans in 1923, as always, found much to entertain them in watching and reading about sports, for this was a veritable golden age of athletes. Bobby Jones won the National Open championship in golf. In September Jack Dempsey knocked out the much-heralded giant from the Argentine, Luis Angel Firpo, in the second round for the heavyweight title. Babe Ruth hit forty-three home runs and was awarded the American League trophy for "most valuable player." The Yankees once more beat the Giants in the World Series. Big Bill Tilden and Helen Wills took the national tennis titles. Gertrude Ederle and Johnny Weismüller (later to become famous as Tarzan) were busy all year breaking world swimming records.

For dramatic amusement, millions of Americans trooped to movie houses throughout the land. Cecil B. De Mille, sensational producer, at the end of the year brought out his spectacular *Ten Commandments*, which had a phenomenal success. Alla Nazimova, a sultry actress by the standards of the period, returned to the stage in *Dagmar*. The "divine" Sarah Bernhardt, who had held audiences enraptured for half a century, died on March 26. Florenz Ziegfeld, creator of the titillating chorus of "glorified" girls in the *Ziegfeld Follies*, was threatening that next season might be his last (it was not). Will Rogers, cowboy comedian and philosopher, was gaining a wide audience with a series of syndicated articles in the *New York Times*. I had first seen Rogers perform between the acts of Ziegfeld's *Follies*. Years later, in California, I got to know and admire him.

Moral problems were of great concern in 1923. A "Clean Books League" enlisted the support of prominent citizens, and an equally ineffective organization, the "Society for the Prevention of Vice," was in the newspapers at intervals with dire warnings of damnation to come. The New York Legislature defeated a "Clean Books Bill," and on May 3 the successful opponents of moral censorship gave a dinner in New York for Horace Liveright, to show appreciation of his labors for freedom of expression, sexual or otherwise. A commentator remarked, however, that defeat of the bill was "a danger deferred." The Women's Christian Temperance Union was especially active, putting its finger on the thirsty and the unwary. Lord Birkenhead, in Sioux City, Iowa, for a lecture, was charged with drinking liquor before his public appearance but denied the allegation. This was the era of prohibition, of course, and the papers reported with a certain relish the ingenuity and impudence of rum-runners and bootlegging.

The *New York Times* reported on April 19 that Dr. A. S. W. Rosenbach, the great Philadelphia book dealer, had sailed for home after spending $1,275,000 for rare books in Europe. He was to sell some of these books to Henry E. Huntington, and I was later to be concerned with his purchases. On April 26 the *Times* reported that Rosenbach had "negotiated by wireless" the purchase of a Gutenberg Bible. Sir Sidney Lee, biographer of Shakespeare and a leading light among English Shakespeareans at the time, lamented in print that "all Shakespeareana is being taken by American collectors." Later, at the Folger Library, I was to try to counter similar charges. On April 23 scholars throughout the world celebrated the tercentenary of the publication of the first collected edition of Shakespeare's works, the Folio of 1623.

Some of the happenings in 1923 were to affect my later life in ways I could not then foresee. But the year brought, also, an immediate change in my career.

I was then completing five years of newspaper work begun while still a student at Wofford College. During my last two years there I had been a proofreader and occasional reporter on the *Spartanburg Herald,* an experience fascinating and sometimes bizarre. The composing room of the *Herald* in those days was populated by printers much given to drink, prohibition not withstanding. On Saturday nights the linotype operators and pressmen were accustomed to hold a midnight oyster stew in the stereotyping room. Full of oyster soup and bootleg liquor, they fell something short of accuracy. A linotype operator named Tinsley, letter-perfect when sober, was assigned to set the editorials. But on Saturday nights he played on the keys of his machine with the wild

The Making of a Bookman

abandon of a drunken pianist, and the editorial galleys came out utterly pied. On many a Sunday morning, sunrise saw us going to press, and we missed all the mails. But printers were scarce, and the *Herald* management suffered in stoic gloom.

At Wofford I had majored in chemistry with a minor in biology, and was determined to be a scientist. My first job was analyzing fertilizer and testing the city water for purity. But a letter in June of 1920 from Harry L. Watson, editor of the *Greenwood Index-Journal*, urged me to return to Greenwood and become city editor. In the meantime I had begun to question my own ability to be the kind of mathematician that science would require in the future—and I was tired of seeing the same precipitate on the filter paper every day. People were more interesting than fertilizer and bacilli. I took the newspaper job and never regretted it.

By the autumn of 1923, however, I was beginning to be a little restive. Not that I found newspaper work boring. In fact, I had developed a macabre taste for murders, or rather for efforts at solving their motivations (unmotivated murder was a rarity in those days). In the course of my reporting I had pried out several curious confessions which explained the crimes, but luckily was never called upon to testify against my informants. What bothered me about reporting was the impermanence of the product. It was discouraging to see the sweat of one's brain being tossed into a waste can before one got home from work. Perhaps another career would provide time for something more lasting than the daily grist of news. I was realist enough to know that the way to starvation lay in simply becoming a freelance writer.

One of my most valued friends at the time was Robert O. Lawton, a Methodist parson by trade, a journalist by instinct, and an exciting teacher of literature at Lander College. Though beset with recurring illness, he made time to write, to talk, to invite his soul, and to observe the world with both benignity and amusement. If a preacher could have so much fun as a teacher of literature and still find time to write, I decided that I might have even more fun and maybe write something more pleasing than accounts of murders and political finagling. The upshot was that I resigned my newspaper job in September 1923 and enrolled as a graduate student in English literature at the University of North Carolina at Chapel Hill.

My choice of Chapel Hill was made after a careful reportorial investigation of other universities in the East. Harvard, alumni of that institution informed me emphatically, was the only place for a self-respecting man wishing to get ahead in the world. "Why, even if you are dumb as an ox," one enthusiastic emigré from Cambridge explained, "Harvard grads will rally around and get you a good job. They have a network that places Harvard men in the best jobs."

To see for myself, I cased the best-known graduate schools in the East, starting at Harvard and working south. In the Widener Library one day I observed George Lyman Kittredge, that university's most famous ornament of erudition, grab a graduate student by the lapels of his coat and shake him like a mouse. What had precipitated the great man's wrath at the poor wretch, who had stopped to ask him a question at the catalogue, I never knew. But I realized that if Harvard's doyen of letters ever treated me that way, I would hit him and have to leave. So I plodded onward.

Yale impressed me in those days as a delightful place for undergraduates, with several charming professors, two or three of whom were possessed of great learning. But the atmosphere was too redolent of ease and academic trivialities, overly filled with elegance and Whiffenpoofery. First impressions may have misled me, for Yale turned out many scholars of my generation who became my respected friends.

Columbia University, I quickly decided, was not for me. Graduate students whom I knew and questioned complained that they rarely saw the important men on the faculty, had no contact with them, and got what little guidance they received from one another and a few junior members of the faculty who deigned to spare them a few moments.

Princeton impressed me favorably as an attractive place to live. It still had the charm of a country town, albeit a better manicured town than any I had ever seen. But undergraduates dominated the place with a rah-rah immaturity that I thought would be hard to take, day in and day out.

Eventually I brought up at Chapel Hill. The University of North Carolina had made Edwin A. Greenlaw head of the English department and dean of the graduate school. He was a no-nonsense type who looked like a prosperous banker and talked like a man of the world. He wasted few words, but was kindly, showed a keen interest in what a potential student wanted to know and do, was decisive, and clearly was devoid of the trivial rigmarole with which academics sometimes envelop themselves. Here was a man whom I could work with and respect. Greenlaw had edited a high-school textbook whose title, *Literature and Life,* was indicative of his point of view. For him literature was a living thing, written by men and women of flesh and blood, localized in a definite time and place. In short, literature was never an abstract puzzle but something vital and pertinent to any intelligent individual.

Associated with Greenlaw on the English faculty were other men of similar calibre: Thornton Shirley Graves, who had served in the American Expeditionary Force in France and won decorations as a sharpshooter. He taught Elizabethan drama and related subjects. James Finch Royster, a salty North Carolinian who had barely missed becoming a professional baseball player, taught Old English and Chaucer. Norman Foerster, who had not yet strayed off after something called "New Humanism," made the Romantic Movement a stimulating subject. And there were others. A little later Howard Mumford Jones joined the faculty to lecture on the eighteenth century—and anything else that might be required. Few teachers ever exceeded Jones in brilliance as an instructor or as a catalyst of ideas. Other departments had able and stimulating men. Howard Odum, for example, already had an international reputation as a sociologist of common sense and wisdom.

My choice of the University of North Carolina was based on the quality of its men, not on the promise of a "network" that would land a job for a graduate. Few students could have had a more profitable experience than those who elected to do their research at Chapel Hill in the 'twenties.

The quality of the faculty and the growing reputation of the University of North Carolina as an institution unencumbered with useless academic folderol attracted a vigorous group of graduate students. Some took their degrees and remained to become distinguished members of the North Carolina faculty; others went to other institutions as teachers, scholars, and administrators. Among my close friends were William Dougald MacMillan, who stayed in Chapel Hill to become editor of *Studies in Philology,* head of the English department, and a renowned scholar in eighteenth-century drama; Russell Potter, who for many years directed the Institute of Arts and Sciences at Columbia University; Frederick Hard, who became dean of Sophie Newcomb College and later president of Scripps College; Almonte C. Howell, who made a name for himself as director of studies for foreign students at Chapel Hill; Hubert Heffner, who went to Stanford University to direct the department of drama there and later was named Distinguished Professor at Indiana University; his brother, Ray Heffner, who contributed enormously to the rejuvenation of the English department at the University of Washington in Seattle; Paul Green, who became a Pulitzer Prize-winning dramatist and the author of nationally famous pageants including *The Lost Colony;* Sterling Stoudemire, student in the Romance languages, who became a noted specialist in the Spanish Golden Age; and others equally competent in their fields.

The significant fact about these graduate students was their camaraderie, their good will toward each other, their seriousness of purpose, and above all the fun they found in the pursuit of learning. Greenlaw's concept of "literature and life" influenced them all and gave them a point of view which they carried to many other institutions. The study of literature and the personalities who created it was not only a professional end but a subject providing solid enjoyment. Greenlaw's course in the Renaissance conveyed to his students a vivid impression of an age infinitely important to the world they themselves had inherited. We all felt that we knew Petrarch, Vittorino da Feltre, Cosimo de' Medici, Erasmus, Thomas More, Leonardo da Vinci, Machiavelli, Rabelais, Ronsard, Montaigne, and countless others as living beings, not as names in a book.

For me the historical background of these men of the Renaissance excited a curiosity that has never waned and turned me to history rather than to literary criticism. I found literature more significant as a matrix of ideas than as an art form to be studied, puzzled over, and admired. Others might concern themselves with the analysis of lyric forms or with the structure of plays or novels, but I found myself more interested in what literature revealed about the social mores of an age and about the living people who had become the theme and substance of literary creation. What men and women had accomplished in an earlier time seemed to me important for an understanding of man's current life. Consequently, though I technically acquired a doctorate in literature, my research from the beginning was oriented toward social history.

Much has been written about the "deadening influence of the Ph.D. regimen" in graduate schools. My own observations lead me to believe that studying for a Ph.D. never made man any duller than God made him. Some men—and women—are born pedants, and the Ph.D. regimen merely serves to confirm a pattern established by their genes. On the other hand, the requirements for the doctorate as we encountered them at the University of North Carolina induced a profound respect for accuracy, facts, and, indeed, for truth as we could discover it. More than that, we learned to be orderly in our assemblage of information and to sort out the wheat from the chaff. Some courses were more tedious than others, but none was a waste of time. I sweated blood over linguistics, for instance, and cursed the day that Jakob Grimm gave up folk tales to foster Grimm's Law. Nevertheless, once I had got through the worst intricacies of philology, I relished even Beowulf's deeds in their guttural Anglo-Saxon, and Middle-English rhythms still ring in my ears. Chaucer proved a pure delight, one of the authors I would hold in most request if I were to be marooned on a desert island.

Graduate students at the University of North Carolina did not expect to be hovered over by their instructors. Study was a business for adults, and we would never have dreamed of going to Greenlaw, Graves, or Royster with minor problems. All the modern pother about faculty-student relations and the belief that even graduate students need to have their hands held, their backs patted, and their egos soothed would have impressed us as an abomination. When we had necessary scholarly matters to discuss, we found all of our professors courteous and helpful. But they addressed us formally in class as "Mr. Wright" or "Mr. Hard," and I cannot remember one of them calling me by my first name. By the same token, we addressed them formally—and politely—by their titles. Good manners prevailed in Academia in those days, and everyone benefitted thereby.

That is not to say that we found the University a stuffy place or that there were no moments of levity and ribaldry. Occasionally echoes even from faculty meetings sent a ripple of laughter across the campus. There was the time, for example, when Archibald Henderson, senior professor of mathematics, tall and pompous, was presiding over a faculty meeting in the absence of President Harry Woodburn Chase. In the midst of the proceedings, Marcus Cicero Stevens Noble, professor of education and somewhat far gone in drink, staggered into the meeting and introduced an incoherent and irrelevant resolution. "Gentlemen of the faculty," Professor Henderson intoned, "you will have to overlook Professor Noble. He is not himself today." Noble pulled himself to his feet and protested. "Mishter President and zhentlemen," he explained, "ish't true I am drunk; tha's a temporary condition. But Professor Henderson, he'sh a damn fool; and that's permanent." And many a colleague muttered to himself, "In vino veritas."

The graduate students of the 'twenties were a well-behaved lot who believed that a scholar ought also to be a gentleman. If they did not come to Chapel Hill with that conviction, they soon acquired it from their fellows and their mentors. That does not mean that any were prudes, but good manners and decent behavior happened to be fashionable. Men dressed as well as they could afford. When they drank, they endeavored to carry their liquor with such gravity as they could muster.

These were the days of Congressman Volstead's lamentable effort to dry out America, but the notorious act was no more successful in Chapel Hill than elsewhere. Illicit distillers in the isolated swamps of Orange County produced copious drafts of "white lightning"—raw corn whisky clear as tap water and sometimes practically warm from the still. The student body and faculty provided a steady market. One of the grave concerns of the university physician, Dr. Abernethy, was to insure the purity of the product. Like many of his colleagues he liked a restorative draught, but he wanted it free of poisonous residues. Once when a known distiller marketed liquor made from a still with lead pipes, Dr. Abernethy sent for him and lectured him roundly. "Unless you throw away that lead still and get you a proper copper still, I am going to turn you in" was his ultimatum. "And get the word out that only copper-still whisky is going to be sold in Chapel Hill," he warned.

One of my graduate-student colleagues who had a studio where he gave violin lessons proved particularly popular because he kept a well-filled charred keg hidden under a couch. For special friends who looked peaked and in need of a tonic, he would roll out the keg and siphon off the needed dram. A surprising number of his friends professed ailments better cured in the studio than in the infirmary.

Everybody with access to a closet or a kitchen nook engaged in home brewing. With a large stone crock or two, one could start operations. Everybody had a favorite recipe for wine, but rice-and-raisins, with an occasional orange or two thrown in to improve the flavor, served as a regular standby. Making beer required a bit more equipment, including bottles and a capper, but few ice boxes were without bottled beer of varying alcoholic or explosive potency. Sometimes fermentation continued after bottling, and explosions could be disastrous for neat housekeepers.

The best brewer in our enclave was Hubert Heffner, upon whom we conferred the earned degree of "Master of Brewing." But occasionally even his mix went wrong. On one notable Saturday night we gathered at Russell Potter's house (he was married and had better facilities than the rest of us) for the sampling of some of Hubert's latest brew. As each bottle was uncapped, the contents geysered to the ceiling and we had to catch it in a dishpan on the rebound. Wine-making and brewing, however—and the consumption of the product—did not hinder hard work by graduate students.

Chapel Hill was still merely a country village. Durham, twelve miles away, on a road partly paved, was the nearest metropolis. The only railway station was at Carrboro, a small mill town two miles away. Early trustees of the university had decreed that no railway should enter Chapel Hill to distract students from their orthodox labors. Organized sports were embryonic and uncommercialized. Football of course was played but with a minimum of commotion. The chief excitement from sports resulted from the annual "Big Game" between the University of North Carolina and the University of Virginia. Most students found their own amusements and entertainment as best they could.

When the weather was suitable, usually in the autumn, we bought rolls and porterhouse steaks (then cheap enough even for a graduate student's purse) and hiked down to Morgan's Creek where we could find a convenient flat rock. Building a fire of oak limbs, we soon had a bed of coals over which we could broil a steak, spitted on a green forked stick. I can still smell the damp leaves of the forest and the smoke of our cooking fires, and recall the taste of those steaks. Good talk and good food sufficed for countless evenings of excitement in the woods. Russell Potter and his wife Dean, Westerners from Colorado, loved the outdoors and shared my own enthusiasm for evenings on the creek.

The University of North Carolina admitted women graduate students and undergraduate daughters of local residents. Among other accomplishments, they improved the social amenities and provided actresses for the Carolina Playmakers, then one of the most noted student theatre groups in the country. Fanny Gray (later Mrs. Frances Gray Patton and author of *Good Morning, Miss Dove*) was the star of several of Paul Green's early plays. In the finale of one of his folk plays called *Fixin's,* Fanny, playing the role of a mountain wife starved for a few ribbons and a pretty dress, swept off the stage declaring, "I'm goin', I'm goin', and I ain't never comin' back." She then collapsed in the wings and was hurried to the hospital with a ruptured appendix. Unmarried graduate students, many of whom were Fanny's ardent if overlooked admirers, spent their last cent sending her flowers. Another coed, Maybelle Penn, enjoyed immense popularity. She was petite, could look like a Christmas-tree angel, and had a wicked wit. She had a repertory of songs that originated in Sunday School but, as rendered by Maybelle, lost something of their original intention. Particularly provocative was one of our favorites, "Jesus Wants Me for a Sunbeam." She could also put unorthodox meaning into "Brighten the Corner Where You Are." Greenlaw's oldest daughter, Dorothy, who affected a leopard coat and swept through the campus with the élan of Nazimova, was too remote for most of us.

A few of the more opulent graduate students boarded out in town but others had to be content with a dormitory room of Spartan simplicity. The luxury of the "Colleges" at Yale and the named "Houses" at Harvard would have exceeded any possible fantasy dreamed by a denizen of Chapel Hill.

The most popular boarding house, one inhabited by the more fashionable bachelors on the faculty and an occasional graduate student, was run by Mrs. Klutz, a woman of formidable mien and proportions. Her husband, by my time known as "Old Doctor Klutz," ran a combination drug and general store. His "doctorate" had been bestowed by the student populace in recognition of his proprietorship of a drugstore. "Doctor" Klutz had an obsessive addiction to playing checkers—in winter by the stove and in summer among the shadows by the back door. One day a would-be customer found the store deserted of clerks but heard a hoarse whisper from Doctor Klutz to his fellow player: "Sh-h-h—be right quiet; maybe she'll go out." On another occasion, when Mrs. Klutz fell and broke a leg, a messenger rushed to the store to inform Doctor Klutz. Deliberately intent upon the checkerboard, not until he had jumped a king did he look up to inquire: "Which one?" Not a man to be bothered with outlandish requests, to a customer who asked about the possibility of getting some grapefruit, a fairly rare commodity in those parts, he explained: "Oh, we got some in last week but folks bothered us so much we decided not to order any more." A saga of stories accumulated about Doctor and Mrs. Klutz. The sight of Mrs. Klutz on a summer Sunday, dressed all in white, marching down the aisle to her pew in the Presbyterian Church reminded me of a merchant ship under full sail.

If anybody bothered about the religious life of students at the University of North Carolina, I do not recall it. The Presbyterian minister, known affectionately as "Parson" Moss, preached sensibly brief sermons and had a considerable following. My friend Fred Hard, an Episcopalian by adoption, nevertheless consented to direct the Methodist choir—for a modest financial consideration. On Sundays I was accustomed to wait for Fred on the stone wall outside the church while the choir droned out the doxology. We would then saunter across the street to Mrs. Cates's Cafeteria for a leisurely if indifferent lunch. One Sunday Fred came out scowling. "I can't stand another one of those sermons," he exploded. "You know what that preacher said today? 'Every man is born into the world with a packtrain of troubles around his neck.'" Not the plight of mankind, but the ludicrous metaphor offended Fred's sensibilities.

The University of North Carolina had the good fortune to be guided by a president, Harry Woodburn Chase, who knew how to take advice and where to seek it. He proved an exceptionally effective administrator. Tall and handsome, with a shock of prematurely white hair, he looked every inch a president and made a good impression on both populace and legislature, which granted essential appropriations. Perhaps Chase's wisest counselor, and a power behind the throne, was Louis Round Wilson, the librarian, a man who was to continue to be an active influence upon the university instead of a bust of himself to the library. Wilson pointed out to educators of his time. For a period he left the University of North Carolina to develop the Graduate School of Librarianship at the University of Chicago, but on his retirement there he returned to Chapel Hill to continue work for the university and its library. Largely through his efforts the university received benefactions of genuine importance. For example, he managed to persuade John Motley Morehead, who had made a fortune in carbide and been an ambassador to Sweden, to give a large sum of money to the university instead of a bust of himself to the library. Wilson pointed out to him that no bust would be big enough really to do him justice.

The Making of a Bookman

Next, however, Morehead proposed a memorial carillon on top of the library. Wilson begged for books but Morehead kept repeating, "I want to hear the bells." This noisy benefaction Wilson evaded by suggesting something more imposing—a campanile halfway between the library and the athletic field. For its dedication Morehead brought over from Belgium a master carilloneur to ring out his two favorite tunes: "Sweet Genevieve" (his wife's name) and "How Tedious and Tiresome the Hour." So pleased was the benefactor with this philanthropy that he later contributed a planetarium and an endowment of several millions. In these negotiations, as in many other matters affecting the university, Wilson proved an adroit diplomat.

Wilson's main concern was the university library, which he was determined to make adequate for graduate research. In his efforts he had the enthusiastic support of Greenlaw, Graves, J. G. de Roulhac Hamilton of the history faculty, and many others. Hamilton, who was responsible for building the great collection of Southern history, personally foraged through the entire South wheedling or buying letters, diaries, and documents of all sorts contributing to a knowledge of Southern history. Wilson had been one of the first to receive a North Carolina doctorate in literature with a dissertation in Middle English, and he was personally interested in adding material in the early periods. Considering its slender financial resources, even by 1923 the library was astonishingly well equipped for graduate study.

My own indoctrination in book buying came early in my career at the University of North Carolina. Graves, who served as bibliographical advisor for the English department, asked me to help read secondhand book catalogues and pick out items needed by the library. From that day to this, I have found it hard to throw away any rare-book catalogue, and the mere perusal has provided me with both entertainment and information. Although my purse was slender, I began buying for myself items of interest and making suggestions for the development of the university library. Fate, as it turned out, would make me a book collector—not for myself but for research libraries. At this time, of course, I did not dream of what the future held.

17

Graves was a cold-blooded scholar who expended no energy on trivialities. Enormously helpful to students who elected to work under him, he maintained an attitude strictly of business and wasted neither their time nor his own. I liked his businesslike approach to learning and chose to write my dissertation under him. Early drama was his primary field of interest, and I picked a lowbrow subject but one that I thought would reveal something about popular English taste for theatrical amusement in the medieval and Renaissance periods. My subject was "Vaudeville Elements in Elizabethan Drama," but I began with the mystery plays and ended with the Puritans' closing of the theatres in 1642. To accomplish my purpose, I read every extant play from the earliest known dramatic performance in English to the end of the period. Before the job was done I was to rue the decision to take such a big bite of drama, and vowed to erect a monument to Henry VIII and the antiquary John Warburton's cook, because they had destroyed an appreciable amount of early literature, thus happily eliminating it from my task.

During my second year of graduate study, I was appointed a teaching fellow. With a stipend of $100 per month, a fellow could do little else except devote himself to high thinking and avoid yearning after flesh pots. But the necessity of instructing a gaggle of callow freshmen in English composition had intangible benefits. It placed upon a youthful instructor a responsibility to try to make the subject both interesting and effective. Because we did not cynically believe that our efforts would be wasted, the struggle to induce literacy in such obdurate material put us on our mettle and made competent teachers of some of us.

Before I had finished my dissertation Graves died of influenza in the spring of 1925, leaving me a literary orphan. Greenlaw gave as his optimistic opinion that I had absorbed enough of Graves's information and methods to carry on. Greenlaw himself had received a call from the Johns Hopkins University and was leaving Chapel Hill. With little further advice from anyone, I finished the dissertation and managed to pass the examinations in time to receive my degree in June of 1926. Not all readers of my thesis enthusiastically approved. One precise and solemn professor was suspicious of anyone dealing with a subject so unacademic as vaudeville and stated in his report, "Humor has no place in a doctoral dissertation."

The University desperately needed someone to take over Graves's graduate courses in drama, and to my vast surprise I was offered the job. Rarely has anyone been so conscious of academic responsibility. Graves had been so efficient, especially in his knowledge of books, that students used to say that he "had a bibliography instead of an alimentary canal." I was less well equipped. To try to step into Graves's shoes was awesome for a neophyte. At a memorial service for this learned man Greenlaw had said: "He was an explorer, not in the realm of Nature, but in those rich provinces which are inhabited by the spirits of the mighty dead. His own work, and the work that he directed as the leader of his small group, was the essence that distinguishes the university from a fitting school." To try to carry on the ideals of learning set forth by Greenlaw and Graves was my goal.

At the same memorial service Greenlaw had emphasized his belief that humanistic learning must have meaning for the present. "I think," he said, "that a man who, minutely, with no preconceived notions, free from prejudices . . . studies the subject of county and state government in order to go out and apply his knowledge to the glory of God and the relief of man's estate is infinitely superior in his conception of scholarship to the man who writes a thesis on the sources of 'The Pardoner's Tale' or the dialect of the Moral Ode or the Platonism of Henry More merely for the acquisition of a Ph.D. in order to get a job as a college professor. We sometimes try, mistakenly, to make a distinction between pure scholarship and a scholarship that is, I suppose, impure. . . . A scholarship that is too bright and good for human nature's daily food is no scholarship at all, but an impostor, no matter how seductive in appearance." This belief that scholarship ought to have genuine validity and utility coincided with my own ideas and motivated much of my future work.

Teaching proved a pleasure. I liked my students and they seemed to reciprocate. Like Greenlaw and Graves, I was concerned with living people behind the printed word, and it was fun to try to bring to life another set of conditions and another age. By this time I knew that I was committed to a life of scholarship, but not the dry-as-dust vocation practiced by a few devotees. For the rest of my academic experience—more than forty years in various parts of the world—life proved an exciting adventure. A frequently expressed notion that research and teaching in some strange way are antithetical seemed to me a blatant heresy. Intelligent research, research that seeks fresh information and fresh interpretations, vitalizes instruction. Some of the dullest professors I ever encountered were those who proclaimed their "devotion to teaching" and abhorrence of research, and consequently, over the years, played the same old cracked record to their classes. But, as Greenlaw had implied, some so-called "research" is merely the pot-boiling busywork of impostors. Too often, especially in the field of literature, dull men spend their days picking up unconsidered trifles and labeling this activity "research." They give true learning a bad name and convince a skeptical laity that college professors are little better than ineffectual whittlers. Sometimes they are.

Having inherited Graves's courses, I was also handed the job of serving as bibliographer for the English department. That is, I was expected to consult with my colleagues and make out lists of books that we hoped the library could buy. I redoubled my labors over book catalogues and suggested countless volumes for purchase. Surprisingly, we procured many of these items. I took pride in a growing collection of scarce books.

Greenlaw was now at Johns Hopkins University and during the summer of 1927 he invited me to come to Hopkins for the academic year of 1927–28 as Johnston Research Scholar. My duties would be to conduct one graduate seminar and to devote the rest of the time to my own research. The University of North Carolina gave me leave—one of many to follow, so that some of my colleagues sourly referred to me as the department's "traveling representative."

By this time I had married a kindred spirit, Frances Black of Spartanburg, South Carolina, and we set out for Baltimore in a Model-T Ford. Life during the next year was full of fresh stimulation. Hopkins was stirring with new energy, for Greenlaw had already attracted another group of intelligent and spirited students. My friend Fred Hard had followed him there, as had a former roommate, Stanford Webb, a charming Lincolnesque type, of the family who founded the famous Webb School at Bell Buckle, Tennessee. There we met for the first time Leon Howard, later to become a force in American literary scholarship, Ernest Strathmann, already turning his attention to the Renaissance in which he would later distinguish himself at Pomona College, and Kathrine Koller, whose charm was only exceeded by her scholarship.

During the year, Greenlaw, who had just become a member of the Selection Board of the newly created John Simon Guggenheim Memorial Foundation, suggested that I apply for a fellowship. The head of the Foundation was Frank Aydelotte, President of Swarthmore College. I was already working on what I hoped would be a book on social aspects of Elizabethan drama, and the thought of a year at research centers in Europe set my wife and me to building castles, if not in Spain, at least in Bloomsbury.

Having duly filled out application forms, I was presently visited by Henry Allen Moe, a man who was to become a fast friend, one of the most remarkable men I have ever known. He had been appointed Secretary-General of the Guggenheim Foundation and was personally investigating candidates for fellowships. Having read law at Oxford after service in the United States Navy during World War I, he was a skilled interrogator. I remember thinking that he knew more about my proposed subject than I did. After a good lunch at one of the Baltimore hotels where we had talked at length about Elizabethan drama, we parted. Each passing day thereafter, as we watched an empty mailbox, our tension increased. Finally, after three weeks, we got a notice of my appointment. Greenlaw met me outside his office. "You had very little proof of your scholarship to submit," he pointed out. "But the committee took my word about you. Don't let me down."

In June of 1928 we sailed for England on a sturdy old craft, the *Minnekahda* of the Atlantic Transport Line. It was the first time either my wife or I had crossed the Atlantic, and no sixteenth-century explorers could have anticipated higher adventure. I would not have imagined that, in the years to come, I would cross the great ocean so often that I would lose count of the times. Even less could I have foreseen that one day I would succeed Greenlaw on the Guggenheim Selection Board and, indeed, preside in Aydelotte's place as chairman for twenty-one years. At any rate, that June seemed golden though we did not know what the future might hold.

CHAPTER II

From the British Museum to Paradise Among the Orange Groves

TO A PROVINCIAL AMERICAN, London in 1928 was a city of excitement and enchantment, a city where nearly every street carried some echo of history or literature. England was in the grip of a depression, it is true, and in the seamier streets a visitor was depressed by the sight of undernourished children and adults who also bore evidences of malnutrition and misery. Yet to Americans conditioned by the reading of Dickens, this too was a part of the expected picture of London. If one met Bob Cratchit around the next corner, it was not a matter for surprise. Nevertheless, the visual evidence of distress aroused compassion and sometimes indignation; street musicians playing for a few pennies, blind and crippled veterans of the Great War asking for alms, and sallow, rickety children in rags with outstretched hands kindled the sympathy of even the toughest among us. No one would have dreamed that England in a few decades would have so altered the condition of the poor that children even in the grimy East End would bloom with health.

In addition to the honest poor, the streets teemed with impostors, a type common from medieval times. We soon learned to detect them. Paul Green, the dramatist, who had also won a Guggenheim Fellowship, turned up in London after a miserable stay in Berlin, where he and his family nearly died of influenza. A beggar whom some of us had already spotted as a fraud encountered Paul near the British Museum and told a doleful story of having a wife and children starving in a garret in the St. Pancras district. Paul replied with a vivid account of his own sorrows in

23

Berlin. So touched was the beggar that he offered Paul a sixpence.

Thanks to the good offices of Kemp Malone of Johns Hopkins University, we took a flat at 19 Little Russell Street, a stone's throw from the British Museum. Malone and his wife had spent their honeymoon in this flat, and the aura of bliss must have obscured from them the dust of centuries that had settled into the corners. We managed to endure the winter there before moving to less antiquated quarters in Taviton Street below Gordon Square.

Our landlord at Little Russell Street stepped straight out of Dickens. A Welsh schoolmaster named Evans, he snooped about, rubbing his hands and expatiating on the vintage quality of each piece of decrepit furniture. The old housekeeper, Mrs. Collins, who lived in the basement with her cat Peter, explained: "Mr. Evans, 'e's a strange un. People don't like 'im; 'e's always arskin' questions and lookin' about. 'E takes a bit of knowin', 'e does. But I always say, let 'im go on and pay 'im no mind."

Evans, it turned out, was deeply read in the works of James Fenimore Cooper and had an insatiable curiosity about Indians. So tediously inquisitive was he about our relations with "the natives" that I finally satisfied him with a lurid account of red men, dwelling in the woods outside Baltimore, who hung scalps to dry from their tipi poles. Actually, the Baltimore and Ohio Railroad had brought to town during the previous year an encampment of Blackfoot Indians to lend color to a railway fair.

The flat at 19 Little Russell Street, completed, I was told, during the reign of George IV, had undergone few alterations since. But one "improvement" was the installation of a bathtub in a recessed nook off the bedroom, a space too low for standing but adequate if one slithered horizontally into the tub. A fearsome contrivance called a geyser (pronounced "geezer" by the English) supplied a modicum of tepid water. A match struck under a gas burner caused an explosive roar and sent flames around a coil of pipe in the geyser. Gradually a trickle of hot water spattered into the tub. But steam, condensing on the cold ceiling a foot above one's head, dripped icy drops upon the victim in the sarcophagus below. Because the winter of 1928–29 was the coldest in the memory of man, bathing invoked a troubling debate between present comfort and traditional hygiene.

The election of Herbert Hoover as President of the United States on November 7, 1928, was received with mixed feelings by the British. Remembering his efficiency in the administration of Belgian relief after the war, English newspapers expressed fear that he would further American commerce to the detriment of British competition. When he made a trip to South America soon after his election, *The Morning Post* lugubriously predicted loss to British firms competing with Americans for Latin trade. So desperate was the economic situation in Britain that politicians engendered considerable anti-American feeling by blaming the United States for a desire to collect war debts. Because *The Morning Post* reflected this anti-American spirit, I read it sedulously during the winter to raise my blood pressure and thus help me to endure the climate.

No walls in the world could encompass a more fascinating space than the British Museum reading room, then or now. But in 1928 it contained an especially curious lot of the species *Homo sapiens*, for not yet had the authorities revoked lifetime cards of many eccentrics who inhabited the place. Near the entrance door, for instance, a self-appointed specialist in antiquities known as "Egyptian Jack" dozed behind an elephant folio devoted to hieroglyphics; he kept this volume standing open on his desk to provide a screen for his slumber until an accomplice hurried in to tell him that gullible tourists outside might use his services as guide. He would then bustle out, solicit their patronage, and lead them through the Egyptian gallery dispensing dubious information about mummies and monuments. Another habitué, an ancient black man with a thatch of woolly white hair, spent his days sleeping over a mound of books piled on a desk near the entry. Although the Museum by American standards was colder than the tomb of Rameses II, it was warmer than the outside, and some of these "readers" used it as their dormitory. Another ever-present denizen of the reading room was an enormous fat man in clerical garb, reputed to be an unfrocked priest, whom we called Friar Tuck. Frequently seated next to me in the reading room was a furtive Latin type who read exclusively books on murder. I wondered if his "research" had a practical motivation. At intervals he would sneak an orange out of his left pocket and take a surreptitious swig of juice. On the way out at night he would snare a pigeon or two, evidently the makings of his dinner.

Americans carrying on research in the British Museum formed a small enclave of congenial spirits. Among those whom we frequently saw were Gerald E. Bentley, Robert Spiller, Helen White, and William Haller. At this time the American University Union, a useful institution since defunct, had as its director for the year Noel Dowling, professor of law at Columbia University. With a wide acquaintance in England, Dowling saw to it that American students made valuable contacts with English scholars. At the American University Union we met a charming couple, Frank and Katherine Dehler of Baltimore. Frank was then European representative of the Davison Chemical Company with professional connections in every European capital. We spent many pleasant evenings at their hotel off St. James Street comparing notes on the state of the world.

The Museum reading room provided an opportunity of seeing—and sometimes meeting—famous scholars whom one knew by reputation. There I first encountered Professor R. W. Chambers, biographer of Sir Thomas More. At 11:00 A.M. at University College, a short distance away, Chambers lectured on Beowulf or Middle English prose or some kindred subject. Then he would hurry over to the British Museum. A little man, dressed conservatively for his lectures in a long-tailed morning coat, Chambers would go bobbing about among the catalogues filling out slips for the books he wanted. After depositing these with an attendant, he would seat himself at a desk, fold his hands in front of him, and take a little nap, looking for all the world like the dormouse in *Alice in Wonderland*. Attendants would tiptoe past or deposit his books gently so as not to wake him.

The officials of the reading room were efficient, courteous, and, in some instances, picturesque. One of the supervisors, a specialist in Russian literature, used to sit at the elevated desk in the center of the circular room wearing a high silk hat. I never saw him sukiyaki in a big brass bowl. A Chinese restaurant in High Holborn also proved a godsend, though it took a bit of experimentation to learn to love their sweet onion fritters. We also explored Soho, a region where I have dined well ever since.

The winter of 1928–29 was so cold that the Thames froze over from bank to bank, and students rode bicycles on the river's surface from Oxford to London. Although nobody organized a full-fledged "Frost Fair" in the manner of the seventeenth century, the Thames at London was alive with skaters and with children and adults pulling sleds. For several weeks the cold held its iron grip over Europe, and reports from Venice said the Grand Canal was blocked with ice. Gas lines in London froze and outside pipes burst. When Americans met they compared notes on when they last had experienced the luxury of a bath.

The wealth of material in the British Museum more than offset its bone-chilling temperature, and though we might grumble about the cold, we got there early and stayed until the reading room closed each night. Every day brought what to us was an exciting discovery as we read books available nowhere else. My own topic had expanded from a study of social aspects of Elizabethan drama to a more comprehensive investigation of the whole of the Tudor and Stuart literature—to discover, if possible, the writings that reflected the interests of the rising middle class from the accession of Henry VII to the death of Charles I. This research resulted ultimately in the publication in 1935 of a book entitled, somewhat inaccurately because of the time span covered, *Middle-Class Culture in Elizabethan England*. "Elizabethan" was merely a term of convenience for the Tudor and early Stuart periods.

No precise bibliography existed for books and pamphlets that might throw light on my subject. In the stacks of the British Museum lay some sixty percent of the output of the printing press from the introduction of printing in England until the end of 1640. Pollard and Redgrave's *Short Title Catalogue* contained abbreviated titles of most of the books published during these years. By systematically going through the *Short Title Catalogue* and drawing out every title that sounded even remotely like something of interest, I accumulated a body of useful data, not only for my book but for many peripheral subjects. To this day, that body of notes proves of value.

Once in a great while I would run into a snag with the British Museum's own catalogue, but an appeal to Arthur Ellis, Superintendant of the Reading Room, invariably brought courteous and effective assistance. Once when I could not find listed anywhere in the Museum catalogue an anonymous playlet entitled *Canterbury His Change of Diet* (1641), which was supposed to be there, I went to Ellis with the problem. He searched everywhere in vain and finally asked, "Who was Archbishop of Canterbury in 1641?" "William Laud," I replied. In two minutes he had found the item in the catalogue. "It's in Laud's appendix," he explained, and so it was, a playlet satirizing the unfortunate prelate.

Experience in the Museum stirred my interest in book collectors responsible for the treasure hoards that we were now privileged to use. A research library like the British Museum represents dedication and devoted interest of many individuals. A layman familiar only with the local library where his wife may draw out novels or books for the children may think that a library can be assembled quickly by appealing to a few competent booksellers and publishers. But every serious student knows that research libraries must grow by accretion, by accumulating rarities preserved by the care and diligence of many collectors over the years.

The British Museum is endowed with countless great collections brought together by bibliophiles dating from the sixteenth century and before. Inevitably users of rare books draw out items once owned by early benefactors, and only an atrophied imagination could keep one from experiencing a thrill at handling a book from the library of Sir Robert Cotton, Archbishop Thomas Cranmer, George Thomason, or some other ancient worthy.

Early in my reading in the British Museum I happened upon a copy of *Philobiblon,* by Richard de Bury, first printed in Latin at Cologne in 1473. The author, Bishop of Durham and Chancellor to King Edward III, was the first Englishman to write a treatise on book collecting, a book both entertaining and informative. De Bury, an avid collector of ancient manuscripts, cunningly used his position to acquire priceless items, for he gave out that anyone craving an audience with the King could more easily gain access if he came to the Chancellor bearing in his hand some precious document. Thus de Bury gathered a library, which he piously declared of value in the propagation of the faith, for he said: "More precious than all wealth are the libraries of wisdom, and all the things thou canst desire are not to be compared unto her (the third chapter of Proverbs). Whosoever, then, confesseth himself zealous for truth, for happiness, for wisdom, or for knowledge, even for the faith, must needs make himself a lover of books."

Because de Bury died in debt, his library was sold and scattered, but two of his volumes survive in the British Museum. Though later bibliophiles lacked his peculiar opportunities for accumulating books, they nevertheless made notable collections.

An Elizabethan benefactor of the nation was Lord Lumley, son-in-law of the Earl of Arundel, himself a collector who gained possession of Nonsuch Palace and established his own library there. Arundel had acquired the books of Thomas Cranmer, Archbishop of Canterbury, as well as books from important contemporaries. In the course of time he turned over the palace and all his books to Lumley, who brought to Nonsuch his own books from the family seat at Durham and consolidated the two libraries. Although Lumley deeded Nonsuch Palace to Queen Elizabeth, he held on to his books until the next reign, when he gave them to Henry, Prince of Wales, to become a part of the royal library. Four years after its founding, the British Museum acquired from King George II in 1757 the Arundel-Lumley collection and many others that had gone to make up what is now known as "the King's Library." Hardly a day passed during my time in the Museum that I did not walk by the shelves of the King's Library and marvel at the riches that previous book lovers had accumulated.

Every historian of the seventeenth century has reason to bless the diligence of George Thomason, a bookseller who died in 1666, for between 1640 and 1661 he made almost a daily round of the other booksellers, buying the latest books and pamphlets. In many cases he dated them and wrote down the names of authors of anonymous works. His collection, numbering 22,761 printed pieces and 73 manuscripts, came ultimately into the hands of King George III, who passed it on to the British Museum.

Going through the Thomason Tracts, deciphering Thomason's scribbled comments, was like a journey into the England of the Puritan Revolution. That journey also brought me into contact with William Haller, one of the wisest chroniclers of Puritanism, for Haller was also devoting long hours to Thomason's collection, and we sometimes found ourselves wanting the same title. My friendship with Haller, begun in the British Museum, continued until his death in 1974.

From Thomason I learned a principle useful in building a library of value to historians, for his tracts illustrate the value of saving for posterity not merely rarities but ephemera. Some of these apparently trifling items often throw a vivid light upon the life of the times.

The British Museum and other libraries in Great Britain—and subsequently many American libraries—became the beneficiaries of collectors who began accumulating books and manuscripts on a grand scale during the later eighteenth and nineteenth centuries. As money poured into England from the far corners of the British Empire, hundreds of men—noblemen, merchants, parsons, and even plain tradesmen—developed hobbies of book collecting. Some noble families already had distinguished libraries which nineteenth-century heirs augmented. Book collecting became fashionable, and English nobles and gentlemen were sometimes as proud of their libraries as they were of their stables. More than one country gentleman confessed to both loves, and found it hard to decide which gave him more pleasure, his prized folio or his promising filly.

What went on in this period profoundly affected the course of American book collecting—and, as a consequence, American learning. For American collectors in the twentieth century acquired many rich libraries gathered by Englishmen in the eighteenth and nineteenth centuries. With the inexorable shift in economic power to America in our century, books flowed to the United States.

Some of the English collectors of the eighteenth and nineteenth centuries were remarkable personalities who devoted their lives to the accumulation of books. Thomas Rawlinson, for example, who died in 1725, filled his house so full of books that he had to sleep in his hallway. And he remained a bachelor until the year before his death to give greater scope to his hobby. When he finally married, he took to wife his servant maid, in order, gossips said, to insure better care of his books. At his death the books were dispersed and have become a part of many modern collections. In No. 158 of *The Tatler,* Joseph Addison satirized Rawlinson under the name of Tom Folio.

Another man who devoted his whole life to making a collection of books was the Reverend Clayton Mordaunt Cracherode, who died in 1799. He too remained a bachelor, and since he hired a curate to perform his ecclesiastical duties, he had full time for prowling in the bookshops on a regular daily schedule. Once a week he went to a watchmaker to have his watch adjusted so that he could maintain a precise timing of his visits to the London booksellers. Four days before his death the old man made a last visit to a favorite London shop, and on his deathbed he was concerned about a purchase which he had empowered an agent to make. Cracherode bequeathed his books, a princely library, to the nation, and they are now in the British Museum.

Asceticism was not a requirement of book collecting, but nominal celibacy apparently helped. At any rate neither Rawlinson nor Cracherode could have so crowded their houses with books if they had had wives to worry about neatness and order.

Richard Heber outdid all his contemporaries in accumulating books, which were so numerous that at his death in 1833 he owned eight houses, in England and on the Continent, filled with books. Unlike the ascetic book collectors, Heber had a cellar as famous in its time as his book collection. Sir Walter Scott called him "Heber the Magnificent, whose library and cellar are so superior to all others in the world." One might remark in passing that the relationship between fine books and fine vintages is a subject worthy of investigation. George Saintsbury, who wrote more about English literature than any other man in the nineteenth century, was also famous for his palate and his cellar.

Heber insisted that one copy of a book was not enough. "Why, you see, Sir," he once explained, "no man can comfortably do without *three* copies of a book. One he must have for his show copy, and he will probably keep it at his country house. Another he will require for his own use and reference; and unless he is inclined to part with this, which is very inconvenient, or risk the injury of his best copy, he must needs have a third at the service of his friends."

I found that the mere handling of books brought together by famous collectors of the past made a lasting impression and gave me a curiosity about these benefactors that I retained. But valuable as were these resources, not all the books that I needed were to be found in the British Museum, and in the spring we went to Oxford for a period of research in the Bodleian Library.

Oxford in the spring has stirred the lyric impulses of more than one poet responsive to the waving daffodils in Magdalen's meadows. But though daffodils can stand the chill of an early English spring, Americans are less hardy, and we shivered both in and out of doors. We found quarters in St. John Street. Our housekeeper, a Mrs. Ing, regarded the burning of more than one scuttle of coal per day as an extravagance bordering on immorality, though England at the time had a surplus of coal and we were ready to buy any amount for warmth. Mrs. Ing also had a culinary obsession with something called "college pudding" which she urged upon us as a traditional Oxford "sweet." At intervals we would have to succumb to college pudding, a heavy concoction of dough, suet, and raisins covered with a lava-flow of pallid sauce. Mrs. Ing, we decided, was descended from a long line of seafarers nourished on plum duff. Somehow we survived both the chill and the cuisine, and soon found the books in the Bodleian as exciting as those in the British Museum.

Discovering what one wanted in the Bodleian catalogue in those days was an exercise in patience and ingenuity. Like most British library catalogues at the time, the Bodleian's was in book form. Paper slips containing the author, title, and other necessary information were pasted into large folio-sized scrapbooks in something approaching alphabetical order. Unfortunately, however, sometimes a page would be filled with slips and later acquisitions would be listed out of their proper alphabetical sequence. Many of the entries, on tissue paper, written with an indelible pencil that dampness had caused to run and blur, were hard to decipher. Pamphlet volumes containing a dozen or more items were catalogued only under the title of the initial pamphlet. Thus, drawing out such volumes proved to be something of a lottery. All of this, of course, produced a sense of adventure with an added thrill on each capture of a rare and unexpected prize.

Americans wise in the ways of the Bodleian had advised against attempting to work there during the winter, for it then lacked artificial light and the heat was minimal. On short dull days natural light was not sufficient for reading until ten in the morning and was lacking after three in the afternoon. That made a very short working day.

It was my fortune to be in the oldest portion of the Bodleian, the part known as Duke Humphrey's Library, on the day that workmen began installing the first electric conduits. Bodley's librarian stood by as two carpenters raised three-inch-thick oak floorboards, boards that had been there nearly five hundred years, and began to install the electric lines. Distress showed in the librarian's face as if he had suffered some personal indignity. A year later, I was told, he was mad. The shock of desecrating Duke Humphrey's Library with electric light was evidently too much for him.

Despite inconveniences and discomfort, research in the Bodleian was a rewarding experience. Like the British Museum, the Bodleian had received over the centuries the accumulations of many learned bibliophiles. Not a day passed that a reader of sixteenth- and seventeenth-century books did not find on his desk volumes from the library of some early collector.

Oxford from an early time enjoyed a reputation as a bibliographical center. The various colleges are proud of their individual libraries, some of them too little known to this day. The library of Humphrey, Duke of Gloucester, came to the University in the fifteenth century, and the "good Duke Humphrey" (1391–1447) is remembered today less because Shakespeare made him a character in his plays of *Henry V* and *Henry VI* than because of the library room over the Divinity School that bears his name.

The personality, however, who most fascinates every reader at the Bodleian Library is, of course, the founder himself, Sir Thomas Bodley. No bibliophile or librarian should fail to read Bodley's letters describing his concept of a university library and his method of developing it. So entranced was I with this man that I spent time when I should have been pursuing my specialty reading about Bodley and the founding of his library. His story undoubtedly influenced me later, and some notice of him is pertinent here.

Thomas Bodley was an extraordinary man—a scholar and diplomat of distinction as well as a philanthropist. Born in 1545 and dying in 1613, he served Queen Elizabeth ably as an ambassador to Denmark, France, and the Netherlands. Learned in Hebrew and Greek, as a young man he lectured at Oxford. A contemporary of Shakespeare's, he despised his fellow Elizabethan's profession and would not permit the library that he founded at Oxford to harbor plays by Shakespeare or any other Englishman. By a strange trick of fate this man, whose foundation has done so much to preserve the records of English civilization, has gone without an adequate biography. Perhaps he has not needed one. His foundation, like the architectural creations of Christopher Wren, sufficiently proclaims him. An Oxford professor to whom the suggestion was made that someone ought to do a modern, full-length biography of Bodley looked rather puzzled and asked why. "Everybody knows about Bodley and the Bodleian," he pointed out. "Anybody really interested can read his letters," he added; "they have been published." Nevertheless, it is worthwhile to repeat a few facts about this greatest friend of Oxford's library, gathered from his letters and other scattered sources, including references from his brief autobiography, the manuscript of which is preserved in the Bodleian. In this document Bodley takes great credit to himself as a diplomat, and plumes himself on his skill as an ambassador. But probably not one person in a thousand of the users of his library knows anything of Bodley's diplomatic successes. His reputation is based on his benefaction to his university.

Perhaps some credit for Bodley's philanthropy ought to go to an obscure person of whom scarcely anybody has ever heard. She was Mrs. Ann Ball, the rich widow whom Bodley married. Without

Ann Ball's fortune Bodley could not have done so much for Oxford.

Like every patriotic Elizabethan, Bodley believed that he had an obligation to serve the state; when, therefore, at the age of fifty-two he decided to give up politics and diplomacy, or, as he himself expressed it, to keep "out of the throng of court contentions," he looked about for some other service in which he might "do the true part of a profitable member of the state." With infinite wisdom, he elected to found a great library in his name at Oxford. In 1597, the very year that other philanthropists were formulating a national plan for the relief of the poor, he made an offer to the vice-chancellor of Oxford to refit the rooms previously occupied by the library founded by Humphrey, Duke of Gloucester. By Bodley's time only the bare and somewhat ruinous shell of Duke Humphrey's library remained. Bodley's offer of restoration was gladly accepted, and by 1600 he was ready to begin gathering books for the shelves that he had installed. He was not the kind of benefactor who thinks a fine building makes a library.

Bodley's experience in the world of affairs had given him a shrewdness and wisdom which he now put to practical use by enlisting the interest of prominent persons in his foundation. He thought up a plan for having "Friends of the Bodleian Library." Perhaps it was not an altogether original idea with him, for nearly two hundred years before, in 1412, an attempt had been made to encourage gifts of books to the University. To this end the University chaplain had been ordered to say yearly masses for the souls of benefactors. But Bodley, being a practical-minded Protestant, hit upon a better method of encouraging givers. He had prepared a handsome Register of Donations, in vellum, in which the name of every benefactor should be written down in a large, fair hand so all might read. And he kept the Register prominently displayed so that no visitor to the library could escape seeing the generosity of Bodley's friends. The plan, as it deserved, was a success, for the Bodleian found that "every man bethinks himself how by some good book or other he may be written in the scroll of the benefactors." The responses to Bodley's suggestions were immediate.

Large gifts came from such important people as the Earl of Essex, Queen Elizabeth's ill-starred favorite, Lord Buckhurst, Lord Hunsdon, Lord Lumley, and other noblemen. Their gifts were chiefly classical texts and works of the Church Fathers. So eager was Bodley to gather a valuable collection as quickly as possible that he employed a London bookseller named John Bill (later printer to King James) to travel on the Continent and buy books.

The next year, 1601, was equally successful. Bodley rounded up still more friends and procured some gifts of money. The Bishop of Hereford was persuaded to give £20, with which were bought thirty books, printed and manuscript, including a rare Anglo-Saxon text of the four Gospels. If these purchases were put on the market today they would bring several hundred times the original £20 invested by the good bishop.

Perhaps the most useful friend acquired in 1601 was a young man named Thomas James, who became the first librarian of the Bodleian and the donor of several manuscripts and sixty volumes of printed books. Where James got these works is a little uncertain. Anthony à Wood ungraciously says he stole some of them from various college libraries in Oxford. At any rate, they found a permanent home in the Bodleian, and we may hope that James received proper absolution for bestowing them so wisely.

Unlike some founders of similar institutions, Bodley took a personal interest in every detail of administration. As a result, Librarian James's lot, we can well imagine, was not all sunshine and roses. Evidently James thought so, for no sooner had he become settled in his job than he wanted his salary raised to the munificent sum of £30 or £40 per year. (It was then fixed at £22 13s. 4d.) And he wanted to get married. Bodley, who had a notion that a wife was a bad thing for a librarian, wrote into his statutes a command that librarians should be celibate. James insisted that the intolerable burdens of the Bodleian could not be borne without the woman he loved at his side. So, after many angry expostulations at his librarian's "unseasonable and unreasonable motions," Bodley gave in; but he made an exception only in James's favor, and not until 1856 was the restriction finally and completely removed.

Though Bodley's personal fortune was not large, he determined that Oxford should have the finest university library in existence. To achieve this result it was necessary, as he expressed it, "to stir up other men's benevolence, to help furnish it with books." Generous friends responded to his first appeal, as we have already noticed, but Bodley had no notion of letting enthusiasm die out with an initial burst of giving. With the help of his new (and now married) librarian, he prepared for a long campaign among potential "Friends of the Bodleian."

By the summer of 1601 the books then collected, amounting to about 800 volumes, were placed on the shelves. When Bodley looked at the meager display they made, he ordered the library closed until sufficient volumes should be gathered to insure a more favorable first impression on visitors. He was taking no chances that any prospective friend should be discouraged by the apparent insignificance of the collection. Thereupon he and James again solicited friends, in all parts of the country, for books and funds. Bodley wrote innumerable letters and called on everybody who conceivably might aid his cause.

Every donor had his reward. Bodley ordered his librarian to see that each volume presented should be carefully described—even though that proved a tedious task—"lest the goodness of men's gifts be not made apparent to the full content." No device was neglected in the effort to interest friends in Oxford's growing library. Careful of the impression that chance visitors might get, Bodley gave strict instructions that the librarian should greet them, and, if they were important people, he was advised to make them a set speech, with the hope of inducing them to come back and bring proper gifts. Less important people might be met by the underkeeper, who was required to be adequately trained to entertain foreign visitors as well as Englishmen. Sometimes Librarian James's pride in his library ran away with his diplomacy, for on one occasion he boasted to visitors that, though some shelves might seem bare, all books "of any worth are almost bought already." When Bodley heard of this tactless utterance, he bluntly told James that such a statement was not only false but tended to discourage gifts—a more serious matter in Bodley's eyes than boastful lying.

Eager as Bodley was for gifts and for patrons who would help the library consistently, he was not willing to accept just any sort of book. To him, a book to be worth preserving had to be a worthy book. Repeatedly he refused what he called "riffraff" books. For example, in 1612, when the librarian had catalogued certain books, sent up from London, that did not meet the founder's approval, Bodley wrote with some indignation: "Sir, I would you had forborne to catalogue our London books, till I had been privy to your purpose. There are many idle books, and riff raffs among them, which shall never come into the library, and I fear me that little, which you have done already, will raise a scandal upon it, when it shall be given out, by such as would disgrace it, that I have made up a number, with almanacs, plays, and proclamations: of which I will have none, but such as are singular." Two weeks later, apparently after a mild protest from the librarian, Bodley wrote again:

> I can see no good reason to alter my opinion, for excluding such books, as almanacs, plays, and an infinite number, that are daily printed, of very unworthy matters and handling, such as, methinks, both the keeper and underkeeper should disdain to seek out, to deliver unto any man. Haply some plays may be worthy the keeping: but hardly one in forty.... The more I think upon it, the more it doth distaste me, that such kind of books should be vouchsafed a room in so noble a library.

When this was written in 1612, some of Shakespeare's greatest plays were lying in booksellers' stalls. But Bodley would have none of them. In this connection, we might remember that the Bodleian Library hesitated to accept the collection of pamphlets bequeathed by Robert Burton. They were merely riffraff in the eyes of the authorities. The collection, however, is now a valuable asset to the social historian, for in it are many rare and unique items that give an insight into the literary taste of plain people.

Bodley's attitude toward gifts of what he considered trash was perfectly logical and intelligent. A university library is dedicated to learning, and the learning of the seventeenth century did not take into its view contemporary belles-lettres. Whether a university has any need to concern itself with modern literature is still a vexed question. Bodley was building a library for the use of scholars of his own day and for the service of scholarship in the years to come. It never occurred to him that later generations would study Shakespeare and his fellow dramatists as Bodley's generation studied Plautus and Terence.

Among influential friends captured by Bodley was King James, who visited the library in the fall of 1605. For weeks ahead Bodley feverishly wrote instructions to his librarian about the impending visit. He was no blind worshiper of his royal majesty, but he coveted many of the royal books. Since King James had on several occasions given ample demonstration of his distaste for boring speeches, Bodley devoted infinite care to the librarian's address of welcome. His order was that the speaker should pronounce his Latin in the Scottish manner of the king; and he and the librarian put their heads together to compose a speech which, as Bodley insisted, should be "short and sweet, and full of stuff."

The librarian himself had a bright idea. He suggested that King James's own works should be bound handsomely and placed in a conspicuous place, where they would catch the monarch's eye. To this Bodley objected. He was willing to flatter his sovereign but he was not willing to spend money binding up works which he probably secretly despised. So he countered with a better plan. The librarian was instructed to hide King James's works so that nobody could find them. If his majesty should ask about them, he was to be told that the books had been sent away to be bound in fine velvet. Thus, Bodley said, "all will be excused that can be objected." The ruse succeeded. If his majesty asked about his own books, he was doubtless pleased to learn that they were especially treasured. At any rate he was sufficiently impressed to promise, under his hand and seal, that Bodley should have the choice of any books in the royal houses and libraries. But back in London he was persuaded by favorites hostile to Bodley to forget his promise, and Oxford never got the royal books.

Undiscouraged by an occasional failure to obtain books from this or that patron, Bodley cultivated the great and improved his opportunities so well that many rich gifts found their way to Oxford. In 1603 Sir Walter Raleigh gave £50, but, more important than this, he was responsible for the bestowal on Oxford of a valuable library which he and the Earl of Essex captured in Portugal in the naval foray of 1596. To the literary tastes of the English buccaneers, that library, which had been collected by the famous Bishop Osorius, was worthy booty. Fine folios of the Church Fathers thus reached the Bodleian Library by a method only a shade better than piracy.

In season and out, to prospective friends of his library Bodley drove home the idea that learned books were wanted. Though contemporary literature was spurned, he accepted works in any foreign language, if they seemed sufficiently scholarly. A university was a place for the highest studies, he insisted, and Oxford's scholars would know what to do with the books. When in 1606 Lady Katherine Sandys gave £20 to the library, Bodley bought eight volumes in Chinese. In the same year John Clapham, who had written a *History of Great Britain,* gave Bodley £5. He was rewarded by having his own work purchased, but the rest of the sum went for two more Chinese books. To Bodley, Chinese probably represented the uttermost reaches of erudition, and he was therefore convinced that his library ought to have works in that tongue. Interest in the Orient was stirred at this time by the activities of the Levant and the East India companies. That fact may account for the accumulation of books in other Oriental languages, partly as a result of gifts from friends in foreign countries. In 1611, for instance, the English agent at Aleppo, to whom Bodley had written three years before, sent a quantity of Persian, Arabic, and other manuscripts. Throughout the world, wherever Englishmen had gone, Bodley sent letters soliciting works that would be useful in his library.

One set of professional friends enlisted by Bodley was responsible for the wisest provision ever taken for the preservation of books. In 1610 the Stationers' Company of London voluntarily formed an agreement with Bodley to supply his library with a perfect copy of every book published. But, though the Stationers' Company sent a copy of every book, Bodley did not relax his rules of selection, and such trash as printed drama was promptly rejected.

To the end of his life, Bodley himself proved the greatest friend of Oxford's library. In 1612, the year before his death, he borrowed money and pawned his plate for his beloved institution. When his will was read it revealed that he had left £7,000 to his foundation—a large sum in those days; but his relatives and servants were disappointed. The children of the widow who had brought him all his wealth felt uncharitably neglected. A gossip of the day wrote that "he was so carried away with the vanity and vainglory of his library that he forgot all other respects and duties almost." Whatever his motives, the singleness of purpose displayed by Bodley enabled him to create the finest and most enduring monument any man could have. But his foundation has been more than that. The influence of the Bodleian Library upon the minds and spirits of more than three centuries of students and scholars has been immeasurable. Nevertheless, the greatest university library of all time could not have been built, even by so zealous an enthusiast as Bodley, without generous friends. The habit of contributing to the riches of the Bodleian—a habit that Bodley was wise enough to fix upon the imaginations of his contemporaries—grew into a tradition. In the centuries since the founder's death, thousands of books, and thousands of pounds, have been given by friends who believed that this form of generosity became them best.

In Bodley's time, as in ours, heavy pressure was exerted to induce philanthropists to contribute to humanitarian causes. In 1597 the unemployed of England were crying for bread; the sick were suffering for lack of hospitals; widows and orphans were destitute. Bodley might have founded hospitals and orphan homes, as did some of his contemporaries; he might have made a little provision for the unemployed. If he had, a trifling number would have called him blessed, but his name would have died with him, and the good would have been interred with his bones.

To Bodley there was a higher service to his state than caring for a few broken bodies that would soon be dust. The preservation of the living thought of great men who had gone before, and the transmission of this thought to future generations, seemed to Bodley more important than making easy the hard lot of widows and orphans or giving crusts to the poor. Measured in sentimental terms of human sympathy, Bodley was doubtless a hard man—callous, selfish, and vainglorious, some of his acquaintances said.

But if he had not turned a deaf ear to pleas of human charity and given all his energy and means to the collection and care of books—objects that must have seemed inanimate and dead to unthinking sentimentalists—our civilization would have lost a potent influence that has made it better and finer.

My own research in the Bodleian Library led me to many of what the founder would have called riffraff books, for I was trying to determine the literate interests of the average sort of Englishmen in Bodley's time. Despite his strictures against such works, I found much grist for my mill and enjoyed the search. Although the reading room sheltered fewer picturesque "characters" than the British Museum, famous scholars haunted the place. A young instructor like myself, interested in Elizabethan drama, found a certain fascination in working across the table from E. K. Chambers, greatest scholar of the day in this field. A serious man, intent upon some erudite problem, he did not look up from his books, and I could merely admire him in silence and wonder what thoughts were coursing through his brain. Countless times in the years to come I would find use for his works and remember his scholarly concentration.

As the Guggenheim Foundation enjoined its fellows to take a vacation, in the early summer we left Oxford for a journey to the Continent, a busman's holiday, for I wanted to visit European libraries. Paris was our first stop, and the Bibliothèque Nationale my first acquaintance with French library administration.

After the helpfulness of officials in the British Museum and the Bodleian, the bureaucratic rigmarole of the Bibliothèque Nationale was an astonishment. In many instances I wanted merely to look at a book briefly, not to study it in detail, to see whether it had any value for my project. To the officials behind the desk, however, the difficulty of producing a dozen or more books in the same forenoon for a single reader appeared to be insurmountable. If the books happened to be folios instead of quartos, the problem became even more complex and onerous. Books, it appeared, were to be preserved and protected and used as little as possible. For my project, luckily, only a few rare titles were to be found exclusively in the Bibliothèque Nationale, and, having seen those, I could turn my attention to less time-consuming and more exciting activities in Paris.

The rate of exchange in the 1920s was in our favor, and for a few francs one lived well. We had quarters in a modest hotel on the Left Bank in the rue Monsieur le Prince and we soon spotted excellent restaurants in the neighborhood—not famous on the grand tour but the sort, alas, now extinct, of fabled little places with red-checked tablecloths where Madame looked after the cash and Monsieur was the chef. One place near the Odeon was famous for its *mousse au chocolat,* and another in the rue St. Jacques favored us with delicious omelettes.

The cafés of Montparnasse were the haunts of literati and those who aspired to letters, many of them obvious phonies. But the drinks were good, the company sometimes amusing, and Montparnasse a reasonably interesting spot. For my pragmatic tastes, however, too many of the American habitués appeared to be merely wastrels giving a bad name to their country. Perhaps I was not sufficiently inoculated with the notion of what it takes to be a man of letters. We were told that we were the "lost generation," and some of the hangers-on in Montparnasse were lost beyond rediscovery.

Paris in the 'twenties still retained elements that seemed reminiscent of the Middle Ages. For instance, an old woman regularly each morning led a couple of goats down our street to provide milk for customers who heard her call and ran out with cups or pitchers for her to fill as she milked the patient animals beside the curb. They stood undisturbed by infrequent motor cars, which were still relatively scarce. Every weekday just at dawn we were wakened by a squadron of cavalry cantering by from a barracks not far away. In the gray mist they looked like the ghosts of crusaders off to Palestine. The romance of Paris had its appeal, to be sure, and I could imagine the city in the days of François Villon or Abelard, but it left me without the enthusiasm that London has always aroused from then until now. Latter-day Paris, grasping and greedy, overrun with tourists, I have managed to avoid whenever possible. I always find myself wishing that the Louvre, with its infinite attractions, were somewhere else.

A modern tourist cannot imagine the nonchalance of an American traveling on the Continent in the 'twenties, for hotels were uncrowded and often inexpensive, railway accommodations comfortable and cheap, and reservations usually unnecessary. We traveled through provincial France, Switzerland, southern Germany, Holland, and Italy with never a hotel reservation a day in advance. These were not the days when students swarmed to Europe to stay in hostels and cheap facilities. Even an American student on a fellowship was expected to choose a decent hotel and enjoy the ordinary comforts of life.

The narrative of a research worker's vacation travels has no place in this book except as it relates to libraries and scholars. To a youthful provincial, museums and art galleries, as well as libraries, were a daily revelation of civilizations previously known only through books. Old streets, ancient buildings, busy markets, and the varied people one met, whether in Breton villages or the center of Rome, were equally fascinating. A few fossilized libraries, like the collection of manuscripts at St. Gallen in Switzerland and the Biblioteca Laurenziana in Florence, provided a new conception of the beauty and rarity of old books and manuscripts. The Vatican Library impressed me as a treasure house of untold—and unfindable—wonders.

By late summer we were back in London feverishly trying to complete tasks in the British Museum that demanded attention before departure for the autumn session at the University of North Carolina. To helpful officials in the Museum and to various British scholars I owe a great debt. Particularly kind was Ronald B. McKerrow, then editor for the publishing firm of Sidgwick and Jackson with offices in a nearby street. Though I was then totally unknown as a professional scholar, he welcomed me to his office, helped me solve a difficult bibliographical problem, and treated me with the kindness and courtesy that he might have shown the most distinguished scholar from Harvard. He provided an example that I have tried to remember.

My classes at the University of North Carolina that fall and winter, two undergraduate and one graduate, were stimulating, at least to the instructor. Each day presented a fresh problem of trying to make interesting the life and times of the Renaissance as reflected in literature. The students were an appealing and well-mannered group, and to this day I have kept up with a few who became fast friends. Teaching and research never appeared to me incompatible but rather complementary functions for a university teacher.

During the spring quarter, the University of North Carolina let me go "on loan" to Emory University to fill temporarily a vacancy caused by the death of James Hinton, an able professor who taught the Renaissance. The quarter at Emory was a delightful interlude. The students were a select group, the schedule was light, and the Emory campus in spring gleamed in a white mantle of blossoming dogwood. My associates were charming, and friendships made then continued for years afterward. Later I was to return to Emory at intervals to serve as a visiting consultant concerning problems of the graduate school.

A renewal of my Guggenheim fellowship brought us back to the British Museum for another period of intensive research in the summer of 1930. By this time my book was beginning to take shape—at least in my head—and on my return to Chapel Hill in the fall, I had a definite outline and a few tentative chapters written. But several much needed items were in the Huntington Library at San Marino, California. The prospect of crossing the continent to consult a few books was dim. I had never been west of Asheville, North Carolina, and all I knew about California was derived from an occasional Mack Sennett comedy. Microfilming was then in its infancy, and I reconciled myself to doing without the material in the Huntington Library.

In the autumn, however, Max Farrand, then director of the Huntington, unexpectedly turned up in Chapel Hill. At a called meeting of the English and history departments of the University, he described the resources of the Huntington and its program for future development. It happened that I had planned a hiking trip along Morgan's Creek with Russell Potter that afternoon, and we debated whether to go as planned or stay to hear Farrand's talk. Reluctantly, I decided to give up the hike and listen. On such frail decisions does destiny sometimes hang. The morning following the lecture I called upon Farrand, and we chatted about scholarly problems. He showed interest in my study of middle-class culture—he had once been attracted to a similar subject in American history—and expressed the hope that I would come some day to the Huntington. I assured him that nothing would give me greater pleasure. It all seemed a pleasant conversation and nothing more.

In the late winter, however, a letter arrived from Farrand inviting me to come to the Huntington Library for the academic year 1931–32 as Visiting Scholar, with a stipend that I then thought munificent. It was exactly double my Guggenheim stipend of $2,500! With some hesitation, I asked for another leave from the University of North Carolina, which was granted—not without grumbling from several colleagues tired of adjusting schedules to take care of my absences.

So it was that, in the following summer, my wife and I departed in a Model-A Ford that took us, across what we considered the wilds of America, eventually to the orange groves of California.

CHAPTER III

Evolution of a Research Library

THE MONTH OF AUGUST, 1931, was unusually benign to a tenderfoot who had never been west of Asheville, North Carolina. Believing that we would probably never make another trip so far afield, we planned to see it all if possible by driving diagonally across the continent from Spartanburg, South Carolina, my wife's home town, to the upper reaches of British Columbia and then down the rim of the Pacific coast to Pasadena, California. We accomplished this formidable undertaking in our Model-A Ford without a puncture, with no serious car trouble, and with sunny skies between late July and the end of August. Our good luck gave a distorted notion of weather in the country through which we passed. I remember the puzzled look on the face of a Seattle resident when I asked if it ever rained there. We managed to visit the principal national parks en route: Rocky Mountain National Park, Yellowstone, Mount Rainier, Yosemite, and lesser sites along the way.

The Great Depression was already troubling the land, and we were not planning to spend much money on this hegira. Consequently we had prepared for an economical trip by packing blanket rolls and camping equipment. In those days motels were not luxury hotels but frequently provided only bare beds on which the customer spread his own blankets and sheets. They were invariably equipped with a primitive stove, gas, electric, or wood, on which one could prepare meals. The best accommodations of this type were found in the national parks. Despite the number of unemployed plodding along the roads or beating rides on every freight train, crime was not yet a problem; at least we had no fear of

49

robbery or mayhem. With a minimum of expense and no anxiety, we managed to see the vast stretches of the West and Northwest and to marvel at the wonders.

On August 28, late in the afternoon, we drove into Pasadena and were welcomed with a rare thunderstorm, one of the few we encountered during the whole journey. After one night in a hotel we set out to find an apartment. We discovered what seemed to us an ideal solution, something called a "motor court" on Sierra Bonita Avenue. This was a little house in a garden setting: three rooms and a garage. Identical little houses lined each side of a closed-end street, with just enough room between for oleander, azaleas, and other flowering shrubs. We were pleased with such comfortable and inexpensive quarters.

The next day, August 30, I reported for duty at the Henry E. Huntington Library and Art Gallery, and was greeted by the secretary of Max Farrand, the director. She had instructions to help find housing for Visiting Scholars and to see that they were comfortably cared for in every way. When I explained that we were already settled on Sierra Bonita Avenue she looked a bit pained and remarked that a Visiting Scholar at the Huntington Library ought to have a "better address."

For the first time in my life I had encountered the notion that a "good address" mattered. Coming from the provincial South, where one lived where one's ancestors had lived (or in an academic community, where one could), I found the idea of determining one's habitat according to fashion a bit absurd, but I was to learn that Pasadenans and others like them laid great stress on such matters. Nevertheless we retained our little house on Sierra Bonita Avenue. After all, we had been invited for only an academic year, and it did not seem worthwhile to move to satisfy the *amour propre* of the director's secretary.

To one used to the green hills of the Carolina Piedmont and the heavily forested mountains of the Blue Ridge, the California landscape at the end of August looked forbidding. The hills were brown and dry; the Sierra Madre Mountains were sparsely stuck with pines and littered with a tangle of underbrush. Streaking across the mountains were what looked like dirt roads but were in

Evolution of a Research Library

reality fire-breaks. These mountains on first acquaintance looked unkempt and unshaven, tramps of nature. I decided that by taking the maximum amount of vacation allowed at the end of my stay, I could endure California. It all looked like a Hollywood stage-set, and I expected to see it moved away the next morning. I could not yet foresee that I would learn to like the brown hills and the ragged—and rugged—mountains.

My first day at the Huntington was devoted to discovery. All the scholars whom I had looked forward to seeing were absent on holiday. Farrand, the director, was at Bar Harbor, Maine, where he spent every summer. A few male members of the library staff who happened to be around at this unpropitious season were polite but cool. I soon discovered that they were suspicious of scholars coming to disturb their bibliographical Eden. But women secretaries of one sort and another buzzed about, fitting up my study with files, typewriter, and supplies; they showed me everything I needed to know except the whereabouts of the washroom, discreetly hidden. A lunchroom reached by a pleasant walk under a rose arbor saved the reader from straying from the grounds at noontime.

The library was housed in a building separate from Huntington's magnificent residence, already turned into an art gallery. The buildings occupied an idyllic setting in an estate of 207 acres, a portion of a large ranch and orange grove previously owned by J. de Barth Shorb, who had named it San Marino after the tiny Italian republic of that name. Huntington saw the ranch for the first time in 1892 and was captivated by it. In 1903 he had bought all 600 acres of San Marino Ranch and ultimately developed a third of it into the gardens that I found on arrival.

So fascinating were the Huntington grounds that it was difficult to settle down to inside work. A garden of cactus and desert plants looked like something Dante might have dreamed up for a landscape in the *Inferno*. A Japanese garden, complete with arched wooden bridge and tea house, provided a gentler view. The residence sat upon a bluff overlooking lily ponds; the bluff was the upper rim of an earthquake fault—a long-dead fault, it was hoped and believed. Exotic plants, shrubs, and trees surrounded the

51

house, and a long vista dotted by Italian garden statuary pointed to the Sierras to the north. Farther away were more prosaic citrus and avocado orchards.

But I had come to work in one of the greatest collections of rare books in the western world, not to marvel at serpentine cacti and other natural wonders, and I soon buried myself in the reading room.

What manner of institution was this that invited scholars to use its materials and paid them for doing so? No other library that I had ever heard of showed such generosity. The story of the founding of the library and its subsequent history has been adequately told by Dr. John E. Pomfret in *The Henry E. Huntington Library and Art Gallery from Its Beginning to 1969* (San Marino, 1969), and statistical details need no repetition. Members of the library staff, celebrating the fiftieth anniversary of its founding, published four essays in the *Huntington Library Quarterly* in August 1969, giving fresh interpretations based on a search of the archives. I merely want to provide my personal recollections of the development of a remarkable and in many respects unique institution of learning.

By the time of my arrival, the shaping force in the library's development was Max Farrand, a former history professor at Stanford and Yale and more recently a foundation executive with the Commonwealth Fund. He had visited Pasadena in 1926 and had been enlisted by Dr. George Ellery Hale, astronomer and director of the Mount Wilson Observatory, to help crystallize plans for making the Huntington Library into a great research institution, a scheme that Hale had been promoting since 1906. Farrand showed immediate interest in the possibilities, made an excellent impression on Henry E. Huntington and his trustees, and was appointed director on February 5, 1927, only a few months before Huntington's death on May 23, 1927.

The account of Hale's persistent efforts to persuade Huntington to create and endow his library, as related by R. A. Billington in "The Genesis of the Research Institution," *Huntington Library Quarterly* (August 1969, pp. 351–72), has the suspense and excitement of an adventure story. Basing his narrative on the Huntington archives, Billington tells of Hale's first meeting with Huntington in 1906 at a dinner in Pasadena, when Hale extolled Southern California as a future cultural center; Huntington was already planning his San Marino mansion, and Hale urged him to bring his magnificent collection of rare books from New York to Pasadena. For the next twenty-one years Hale was never to let Huntington forget the glory that would redound to him—and to Southern California—if he founded and endowed a great research institution. In the end, Hale's plan, with Farrand's help, won Huntington's acceptance, though the final transfer of securities to the endowment fund was not accomplished until a few months before the founder's death, and even then a codicil to his will cancelled a $4,000,000 additional bequest that Hale and Farrand hoped to get.

Billington emphasizes that Huntington himself envisioned an institution of learning and was willing to accept those aspects of Hale's plan that appealed to his common sense. Hale had soaring schemes for research in the whole history of civilization, including expeditions to Egypt and Mesopotamia, but Huntington himself was convinced that investigations in the history of British and American culture would be enough. Billington suggests that Huntington was not impressed by Hale's scheme for building a replica of the Parthenon in Pasadena. Whatever extravagant visions Hale might have had, he clearly was the driving force that at last induced Huntington to create something more than a repository of rare books and manuscripts.

He shrewdly enlisted persuasive allies, the earliest being George S. Patton, father of General George S. Patton, whose ranch bordered San Marino on the west. A close friend of Huntington's and a legal counselor, Patton proved an ideal vehicle of Hale's ideas (at least those that seemed viable), and Huntington listened. By 1919 he had decided to establish the Henry E. Huntington Library and Art Gallery at his San Marino home; he had drawn up a deed of trust and had appointed a self-perpetuating board of five trustees consisting of: William E. Dunn, an attorney, as chairman, George S. Patton as vice-chairman, George E. Hale, Howard Huntington, son of the founder, and Archer M. Huntington, adopted son of Collis P. Huntington. Between August 20, 1919, when the deed of trust was signed, and 1927, he would alter his plans many times.

By the autumn of 1925 he had in his hands a plan for a research institution that Hale had drawn up during the previous summer. The scheme had been worked over by Patton with the advice of Robert A. Millikan and Henry M. Robinson, by this time members of the board of trustees. On October 14, 1925, Huntington signed the document with this notation: "I approve the adoption of this policy." The scheme provided for the continued acquisition of research material, the appointment of a distinguished scholar as director, the gathering of a group of research associates, and publication of the results of research.

Details for implementing this program came after Farrand's selection as director and his subsequent influence upon Huntington. At a meeting of the trustees with Huntington on February 5, 1927, Farrand's appointment was formally ratified, and the founder agreed to endow a "Research Department" with a separate budget of not less than $400,000 a year. According to Billington, Huntington turned to Patton as they left the meeting and declared: "Patton, I never had any idea of doing anything of this kind." But he had made possible a unique institution of learning even if he cut $4,000,000 from the endowment a little later. The value of the ultimate endowment was estimated at approximately $10,500,000.

When I arrived, the "Hale Plan," as it was then called, was regarded as the fundamental constitution on which the institution would be developed. Hale himself had called his proposals the "Huntington Scheme." Huntington had altered his deed of trust to create a "free public research library," and research was to be the primary emphasis in the years to come. By 1931 Farrand was already bringing to San Marino for brief periods senior scholars from the great universities of the United States and Europe. These could provide counsel and suggestions about all aspects of development. He was inviting for a year's study a few younger men who might have promise.

Farrand's first appointment of a research associate was Frederick Jackson Turner, the great historian of the frontier, recently retired from Harvard; he joined the staff in October 1927. Billington, in his *Frederick Jackson Turner, Historian, Scholar, Teacher* (New York, 1973), describes Turner's delight at the opportunities offered by the Huntington Library, his useful advice to Farrand about developing research facilities, the demands upon him as a speaker by Southern California—and the distractions that kept him from completing his life work on western history.

Turner's office at the Huntington was next to mine, and I had the privilege of talking with him during the few months before his death on March 14, 1932. Though he was an ill man, his mind was alert, and to the end he was revising his magnum opus. A fatal desire for perfection kept him from finishing it. Farrand once remarked that if Turner had lived forever, he would never have finished this work. In the end Avery Craven, an admiring young friend, and Merrill H. Crissey, Turner's devoted secretary and amanuensis, utilized Turner's few complete chapters and miscellaneous notes to put together *The United States, 1830–1850: The Nation and Its Sections,* published in 1935. At a memorial service for Turner at the Director's House on March 19, 1932, Farrand read a moving eulogy prepared by Craven as we all paid tribute to a great historian.

In 1930 Farrand made an important appointment to the incipient permanent research staff, Godfrey Davies of the University of Chicago, an historian specializing in seventeenth-century England. Almost immediately Davies was asked to serve as editor of publications being prepared by other scholars invited to the library on a temporary basis. For many years to come Davies was to serve as a meticulously careful editor. As proofreader and aid, he had Merrill Crissey, the most eagle-eyed proofreader and editorial assistant I ever encountered. On one occasion Professor Oscar J. Campbell, then of the University of Michigan, submitted a seven-page manuscript for publication in the *Huntington Library Quarterly* and got back nine pages of suggested changes. Crissey was shy and deferential, but he never let an author get by with a repetitive expression or a dangling modifier.

My invitation to the Huntington was for one academic year, and I never dreamed that I would be there longer. My time was spent in collecting material in the library's rich Renaissance sources for my book, *Middle-Class Culture in Elizabethan England,* and in actually writing the book. In the spring of 1932 I received an offer of a professorship at the University of Michigan and asked Farrand's advice about it, since he had recently received an honorary degree at Michigan. At lunchtime he suggested that we take a walk in the cactus garden and, to my complete surprise, told me that the Huntington wanted me to join the permanent research staff. My principal obligation would be to carry on my own research in English and American literary history, but I would be asked to help in the development of the research program. Opportunities would be available for teaching at neighboring universities and colleges if I cared to do so. I would also be free to spend part of the year in research elsewhere if that seemed desirable. Farrand explained that he intended to build up a research staff that would have the same relation to the library as a faculty served in a university. I thanked Farrand but told him that I would have to take time to think over his generous and much appreciated offer.

In the 1930s academic life in a university appeared to me the most attractive form of existence, and I hesitated to give it up. A telegram and letter from my friend and former teacher, Howard Mumford Jones, warned me to think twice before turning my back upon a great university for the gamble of a library post that he feared might prove sterile without the stimulus of students. I liked teaching, and Howard's messages gave me pause. The decision was a hard one, but at last I decided to take the gamble. As it turned out, I managed to attain the best of both worlds, for many opportunities came in the next seventeen years for teaching and for a variety of academic interests.

Farrand was bringing together a small nucleus of scholars who would help develop several significant fields of the library's strength. Davies would look after English history before 1800. Farrand himself would cover most American history. I would be responsible for English and American literary history, with particular emphasis on the English Renaissance and colonial American history and literature. To develop the history of English art of the eighteenth century, a field represented by a magnificent collection of English portraiture of that period, Farrand invited C. H. Collins Baker, Keeper of the National Gallery of Art in London and Surveyor of the King's Pictures, to join the staff in 1932. At the beginning, we were the "faculty," the academic cadre, entrusted with transforming an incredibly rich collection of rare books, manuscripts, and pictures into a new sort of institution of learning.

The Huntington Library was a pioneer in shifting from a repository of books and artifacts to a living institution dedicated to the active utilization of its materials. Within a few years other privately endowed libraries would be following similar plans, but the Huntington paved the way. Our little group set to work with enthusiasm. In theory, we were there to carry on our own research, to write our own books, and to give our recommendations on those who might be invited to the library on a temporary—or even a permanent—basis. Actually all of us were soon involved in a multitude of administrative responsibilities. Davies and I, being the youngest, shouldered the heaviest loads. Davies had already begun editing publications that were in the works. I soon found myself concerned with academic personnel, and served for the duration of my stay at the Huntington as chairman of the fellowship committee. It was my business to know the people best equipped in this country and Europe to make the most effective use of the resources of the Huntington Library.

The transition of a private ducal library of infinite riches into a public institution freely serving the academic world is a more difficult shift than most laymen can conceive. That was the problem that our research staff faced. The examples we had to follow were few or none. The British Museum and the Library of Congress, to be sure, had distinguished scholars working on their staffs. The great university libraries like Harvard and Yale had members of their library staffs who were contributing to learning; the same was true of some of the historical societies like the American Antiquarian Society and the Massachusetts Historical Society; but no other library had the particular problems—and opportunities—of the Huntington. Our research staff had to be trail blazers like the explorers of the old West.

Our first task was to allay the fear of the inherited library staff brought out from New York that the new academics would be throwing their weight around and running over them roughshod. That may now sound absurd, but it was a very real problem in the early days. Huntington had moved most of his own library staff along with his books and manuscripts to Pasadena, and they had continued their accustomed routines of checking, collating, and cataloguing. A few had become set in their ways and saw no reason to change—to shift, for example, to a catalogue of standard library three-by-five cards from the much larger size they had previously used. Some odd practices came to light. Collations of rare books costing thousands of dollars were sometimes inserted in the books written on the backs of old envelopes. This was one of the small economies of Henry Huntington. His even richer uncle Collis had been an inveterate string-saver. William Hertrich, Henry Huntington's ranch superintendent and later curator of the Botanical Gardens, told in his *The Huntington Botanical Gardens* (1949, p. 80) of how, during the unpacking of goods for the house, Huntington had sat by the kitchen door carefully smoothing out the larger pieces of packing paper and rolling up string into balls. "It's not so much the value of the paper and string as the example it sets for the men, to impress on them the fact that nothing is too small or too insignificant to save," Huntington explained. His library staff had learned their lesson almost too well. In the early days it had been harder to get a $5.00 dictionary than a $10,000 quarto, and the skepticism about acquiring too many inexpensive reference books carried over into later times.

Gradually the older New York staff came to accept the newcomers and to cooperate fully with their endeavors to transmute the collection into a working library open to scholars. Sometimes the instinct for preserving a rare book in its pristine state collided with a scholar's demand to use it. Once when someone wanted to read an "unopened book" (a volume whose leaves had never been cut), the curator thought it would be a desecration to spoil the book's value as an artifact by cutting the leaves. Could not the scholar hold the book up, make a sort of tunnel of each fold, and read it that way? To the curator, the problem seemed all but insuperable. It was finally solved by disbinding the book, photographing the text, and rebinding it with the leaves still uncut. Such problems were rare, however, and in time disappeared.

Huntington had gathered a group of able bibliographers and

bookmen. When I arrived, Leslie E. Bliss had become librarian; for many years he proved a knowledgeable and helpful colleague. Even after his retirement he continued to be an indefatigable collector of Californiana. One of the most versatile, hard-working, and useful members of the staff was Robert O. Schad, who had been with Huntington since boyhood. Although Schad had never darkened the door of a college, he was one of the best educated men on the place. During my time he served as curator of rare books, as head of exhibitions and public relations, and wherever else he might be needed. The curator of manuscripts was an Englishman who had once worked for Sotheby's and had served in the English army in Africa during World War I. He insisted upon retaining his military title of "Captain" R. B. Haselden. He regarded the manuscripts as a private preserve over which he was lord but was gradually reduced to cooperation, especially after Professor Conyers Read of the University of Pennsylvania began to dig into the hoard of papers preserved by Sir Thomas Egerton, Lord Keeper to Queen Elizabeth I, and his heirs.

The art gallery was presided over by Maurice Block, an ebullient, friendly, and cooperative man. Block served as curator, while Collins Baker devoted his talents to research. How to incorporate a fabulous collection of English portraits by Reynolds, Gainsborough, Romney, and lesser lights into a research program was Baker's problem, but we gradually solved it by concentrating on the history of art as revealed by thousands of engravings, lithographs, and manuscripts in the library. Baker catalogued the pictures and set to work to write a book on the eighteenth-century Duke of Chandos as art patron, based on our manuscript sources.

Eighteenth-century portraiture apparently represented Huntington's concept of the kind of aristocratic society that had given England stability and strength. He liked the stately ladies and gentlemen painted by Reynolds and Gainsborough. On one occasion, according to James Thorpe ("The Founder and His Library," *The Huntington Library Quarterly,* October 1929, p. 301), Huntington once turned down Sir Joseph Duveen's offer of a version of Reynolds's "Strawberry Girl" because, he said, he had "no doubt but that the picture is fine in color, but it is not one that I would care to purchase: the girl is too simple." Years later, when the new gallery was built and opened to the public, I was standing near a visitor who looked earnestly at Romney's portrait of Jeremiah Mills, a complacent English gentleman resplendent in gold satin breeches and waistcoat, then turned to his wife and said, "That would have been a vote for Hoover."

One of the most difficult portions of the art collections to assimilate into a coherent contribution to the research program was the Arabella Huntington Memorial established in the west wing of the library; the founder had decreed that this must be left in perpetuity as it was set up. Any material alterations required a court order. Early in 1927, shortly before Huntington's death, Sir Joseph Duveen had arrived in the San Gabriel railroad yard with two express cars crammed with objects of miscellaneous art, some of great monetary value: Italian primitives, French sculptures, tapestries, etc. These he sold to Huntington for the Memorial. Hertrich comments drily that this deal "involved the acceptance by Sir Joseph of a large tract of land as partial payment" and was "the last and definitely the largest transfer of art goods between Mr. Huntington and Sir Joseph Duveen."

William Hertrich was one of the most extraordinary and valuable members of the inherited staff. A German landscape gardener who began to work for Huntington at the age of twenty-six, he remained a forceful personality at the Huntington Library until his death at the age of eighty-eight in 1966. Hertrich was responsible for the important Botanical Gardens and became their first curator. In the general effort to develop the research program of the entire institution, Hertrich demonstrated imagination and enthusiasm for incorporating the gardens into the plan. Before his death the Botanical Gardens had become world renowned for experimentation and hybridization of exotic plants, especially camellias.

The transition of the Henry E. Huntington Library and Art Gallery from the greatest private collection of rarities in America to a working institution was accomplished with less stress than might have been expected, partly as a result of the good will and imagination of most of the inherited staff and partly as a result of the understanding and sympathy displayed by Farrand and his recruits. The changes required were psychological and emotional as well as material.

A great collector, of necessity, gathers about him a devoted staff who come to share his instincts for rarities that are not always of great utility. Fortunately, Huntington's collections were of such magnitude and diversity that there could be no question about their value in any context. Because utility does not necessarily inspire zeal in a collector, his supporting staff must adapt to new purposes when the collection "goes public." Since nearly every book has an intrinsic value in itself, the collectors of books, whatever their personal motivations, usually bring together something worthwhile. The instinct for collecting, however, can sometimes result in strange aberrations. For example, I once knew an old bachelor at the University of North Carolina who was an avid collector of baby caps. Book collectors do not fall into such absurdities, but they do become victims of the desire to possess a work because of its unique "points"—an upturned letter on the title page, let us say. That may add to the price of the volume but it has little more significance for scholars than the points scored by a poodle at a dog show. Huntington was rarely if ever moved to seek a book just because of its points. He bought vast collections that included works of unusual scarcity but was invariably prompted by significance as well as by beauty and rarity. Even so, it was difficult at first for some of the collector's staff to envision the continued use of priceless volumes by academics who had little comprehension of an item's value in the auction room—or to other connoisseurs.

The shift from any important collection of rarities to a research institution nearly always creates administrative difficulties as bibliographers employed by the original collector, because of their special knowledge, change intellectual gears. Sooner or later this is accomplished, and the collection becomes a working library.

Academics, on the other hand, are not remarkable for their patience and are sometimes highly critical of measures taken by private libraries for the protection of their treasures. This attitude is especially noticeable during transition periods when staffs are adapting to new conditions, when catalogues must be compiled, and when items must be prepared for use. Occasionally readers are unreasonable in their demands. They may arrive on a holiday or just before closing time, demand special service, and become irritable when they don't receive it with alacrity. Small wonder that members of library staffs sometimes show less patience than Chaucer's Griselda. But, however sorely tried, they usually keep their tempers and confine their swearing to some remote corner of the stacks.

The academic attitude hardest for a collector's staff to comprehend is the lack of appreciation of sentimental values inherent in books or manuscripts. Occasionally a scholar will speak disdainfully of the provenance of a book: it makes no difference to him whether the work once belonged to Cosimo de' Medici or to Napoleon Bonaparte, unless the previous owner had annotated it. Others will sneer at the premium put upon limited editions, fine printing, or beautiful bindings. The expression "mere collector's item" will be spoken pejoratively. Collectors and bibliophiles look upon such unappreciative users of libraries as mere barbarians, and they take to their bosoms those library directors who understand the deep emotional instincts that induce men and women to pay big prices for works that make no discernible contribution to literary or historical knowledge.

In practice most librarians sympathize with collectors because they know that any motivation that induces them to purchase books results in money well spent. Sometimes librarians themselves become converts to bibliophilia to such an extent that they squander budgeted sums unwisely, but most of them keep a delicate balance between values, however emotionally tempted they may be.

One bibliophile appreciative of all aspects of library development is Lawrence Clark Powell, retired director of libraries of the University of California at Los Angeles. He has often been vocal in his defense of sentimental values, which has encouraged friends to bait him. At a library conference several years ago someone suggested that computers might one day substitute for many books. Larry rose and asked sarcastically how a computer would supply the delectable smell of old leather bindings. "Just spray the tapes with synthetic perfume," was the reply. The barbarian rejection of extraneous values had reached its peak. If no such heresy was thought of in the transitional days at the Huntington, now and then an academic suggestion was almost as painful.

Convinced bibliophiles, long indoctrinated in the ways of Henry Huntington—the most spectacular spender for rare books in the first quarter of the twentieth century—found it as hard to comprehend the scholar's desire for an avalanche of cheap books as the academics did to appreciate the emphasis on fine printing and provenance.

On my arrival at the Huntington in 1931, the library possessed less than twenty percent of the reference works that a scholar would need to complete any task. A legend bandied about in the early days asserted that if a visitor wanted to read Benjamin Franklin's *Autobiography* he would have to use the author's original manuscript, because no modern editions were available. That, of course, was an exaggeration, but it was true that fundamental critical editions, biographies, and needed interpretations of older works were lacking.

One of the first duties of the research staff was to direct the search for reference works to remedy this condition. We asked visiting scholars to suggest titles for every reference book that they needed and did not find. Over the years this proved a remarkable source of information, and in the next seventeen years the Huntington acquired a remarkably efficient reference library, with little waste. So effective was this library that when I left the Huntington in 1948 to become the director of the Folger Library in Washington, D.C., I photographed the pertinent section of the Huntington's reference catalogue to use as a buying list.

Farrand received advice from Frederick Jackson Turner and other scholars who visited the library to continue to "build to strength." The great problem at the Huntington was to decide which fields represented the greatest strengths, for the founder had bought some of the finest libraries in the world and fused them into his own. These libraries ranged in time from the Middle Ages to the twentieth century. What fields were we to emphasize in the new dispensation?

An analysis of the most important of Huntington's acquisitions was made by George E. Sherburn, then professor of English at the University of Chicago, who compiled a list for publication in the first issue of the *Huntington Library Bulletin* in May 1931. To describe the principal collections that Huntington had bought in merely a paragraph or two required seventy-three pages. The story of Huntington's uncanny shrewdness—and luck—in acquiring great English libraries like that of Bridgewater House has been often told and needs no extended reiteration. The financial stress in Great Britain during and at the end of World War I made it necessary for many families to sell their family libraries and archives. Huntington was ready to outbid any other buyer—and did. Sound principles of business, learned in his career as a railroad and real estate magnate, he now applied to book collecting. When the opportunity arose to acquire a desirable library property, Huntington did not bargain or quibble, but plunged. The Bridgewater Library, begun by Sir Thomas Egerton in the reign of Queen Elizabeth I and continued by his heirs for over three hundred years, cost Huntington a cool million dollars in 1917. A facsimile of the purchaser's letter, setting forth the terms of payment, was published in the *Huntington Library Quarterly* for August 1969, though Huntington himself was always reticent about making public the cost of his acquisitions. He preferred to buy libraries *en bloc* by private treaty, before they reached the auction rooms; because he was willing to pay a premium, dealers soon learned to give him the first option.

Huntington learned a great deal about books and was appreciative of their intellectual values. Farrand observed that Huntington would quickly turn a conversation about business matters to comments on books. The collector, however, was wise enough to use the best professional aid available in making his deals, whether with private owners or in buying at auction. Only amateurs ever attempt to bid for themselves. Myron Hunt, architect of the San Marino residence and the library building, once told me that he was startled to see Huntington bidding at a New York book auction. "Mr. Huntington, I never knew you placed bids in person," Hunt exclaimed. "Ssh, I am not buying, I'm *selling*," the magnate explained. Would-be purchasers would see Huntington ostensibly buying and would run the price up. He would then drop out and let them have the items. Huntington sold off thousands of duplicates acquired in *en bloc* purchases of libraries, sometimes for almost enough to amortize the original cost, and then fused the choice items into his library.

The two agents who represented Huntington in making his biggest purchases were George D. Smith and Abraham S. W. Rosenbach, both of New York. Smith, a colorful figure who preferred race tracks to personal contact with the insides of books, was nevertheless one of the canniest book dealers of his time. He managed one of Huntington's most important early acquisitions, the purchase in 1911 of the entire library of American and early English books brought together by an American collector, E. Dwight Church. Catalogued by George Watson Cole in seven handsome and beautifully illustrated volumes, five of Americana and two of early English literature, the whole lot was acquired by Smith for Huntington, who then hired the cataloguer as his librarian. Until his death in 1920, Smith continued to represent Huntington. After that the collector turned to Rosenbach, a Ph.D. in Elizabethan literature from the University of Pennsylvania, who rejoiced in his title of "Doctor." Already, however, Huntington had acquired a princely library through the agency of Smith: the Kemble-Devonshire plays (1914), the Britwell Court Americana (1916), and other valuable collections of English and American works in history and literature. Rosenbach had an eye for rarities and guided Huntington in the purchase of incunabula and other scarce items. Sometimes he bought books for himself and resold them to Huntington at astounding markups. On one occasion, an assistant carelessly enclosed the original invoice in a book shipped to the collector. Horrified at the thought of his patron finding out how much he had increased the price, Rosenbach overcame his distaste for flying to reach San Marino ahead of the parcel. A check for $1,000, slipped to Huntington's male secretary, insured the retrieval of the invoice, and Rosenbach had to be ruefully content with this "business expense." Huntington, of course, knew that he was being taken by Rosenbach but probably was not aware to what extent.

When Huntington was in a Philadelphia hospital for surgery in 1925, Sir Joseph Duveen, the picture dealer, and Rosenbach both managed to get into his room at the same time and were sitting on opposite sides of his bed. Huntington looked up, turned to Dr. Ernest A. Bryant, his San Marino physician, and commented: "This is the perfect time for me to die; here I am being crucified between two thieves." Dr. Bryant's daughter, Mrs. Susannah Bryant Dakin, told me the story and vouched for its accuracy.

The magnificent libraries bought by Huntington and merged to create his own institution left a puzzling problem for his successors in deciding what fields to stress in their future development. In practice, few areas were neglected, but the English Renaissance, colonial America, and the history of the Far West attracted the greatest attention of scholars. Turner had expressed the opinion that the history of Western America would be a primary interest. As it turned out, the English Renaissance quickly attracted scholars because of fresh resources for literary study in numerous collections rich in Elizabethan works. Hitherto unavailable materials for the study of English drama also brought literary scholars to San Marino: the mass of Kemble-Devonshire plays; the hoard of play texts submitted for approval to the Lord Chamberlain and preserved by John Larpent, deputy to the Lord Chamberlain from 1778 to 1824; and other valuable pockets of drama gave the Huntington nearly ninety percent of all English plays before 1824. One of our first efforts was to collect in some form, originals or photographic copies, the remaining ten percent of extant texts. Within a few years the valuable collections of books and manuscripts on the history of California and the Southwest lured many students of Western history to the Huntington. Farrand was accustomed to say that he dared not tell a scholar, in any field of English or American civilization, that the library had nothing for him because investigation was likely to bring to light unexpected treasures that he could use. Our decision, therefore, on what areas to concentrate upon in the continued program of acquisition was complex. We tried not to neglect any field, but we emphasized those subjects that were attracting the most demanding scholars.

When a collector bequeaths his library to a board of trustees and leaves an endowment for its support, however generous, the institution henceforth has to operate on a fixed budget. That means that it can never again engage in the freewheeling purchase of rarities that had characterized the policy of the original donor. Booksellers long accustomed to dealing with wealthy collectors find this obvious fact hard to grasp. For many years after Huntington's death (as also happened when Henry Clay Folger died), dealers who had battened on sales of high-priced items to the founder complained that the Huntington Library had "gone out of the market," and a few engaged in carping criticism of a management no longer cognizant of treasures that Huntington in his lifetime would have plunged to buy.

Actually the Huntington Library never ceased to look for books and manuscripts that filled gaps in the inherited hoards. The libraries that the founder had fused with his own were so incredibly rich in rarities that we had little need to seek such things; and we could therefore direct our attention to supplementing the rare books with needed secondary works. In the transition to a research library, that policy would have been essential even if we had possessed the wealth of Golconda.

Yet dealers and even trustees sometimes found it hard to understand the purchase of material of no interest to collectors. On one occasion a trustee asked sarcastically why the Huntington was buying such trash as ordinary sermons, not knowing that seventeenth-century English sermons were valuable sources of information about social history. Even librarians are sometimes tempted to equate the value of a book with its monetary price. Actually, many books of earlier periods, extremely valuable to scholars, were cheap when the Huntington opened its doors. Seventeenth-century pamphlets, of no interest to collectors then, could be bought for two or three dollars apiece—sometimes for much less, if bought in quantity. Historians were eager for them, and we acquired large numbers. Sermons, devotional books, controversial works, manuals of ethics, and similar publications a few years earlier had sometimes been sold for waste paper. We began to salvage such material, and the price started to rise. From the invention of printing until 1641, religious literature made up 43.7 percent of the total output of the English printing presses, and historians could not ignore these significant works. Yet until fairly late in our own century, few rare-book libraries bothered with such uninteresting stuff. Fortunately the libraries that gathered great masses of such ephemera served the interest of social historians; for their forethought, they had to endure the sneers of a few snobbish collectors and booksellers for their "lack of taste."

To fill gaps in source materials, the Huntington began a campaign to acquire photographic reproductions (microfilms and photostats). Because in the early years nearly fifty percent of our readers were working in the English Renaissance, we felt an obligation to procure every text available of books printed in England before 1641. We needed to round out the collection already brought together by Huntington, one of the three largest in the world for this period. In a few instances we could buy the originals, but most of our additions were by photographic reproduction. This procedure met with the approval of scholars, pleased at finding in one place such a large proportion of the books they needed. The policy, most of us thought, was dictated by good sense, but again a few bibliophiles complained that the Huntington was wasting its money on "valueless" items. In their opinion, a book that had almost any sort of pedigree or sentimental association—let us say, a tract once held in the hands of King James I—was worth all the microfilms procurable. But we were a working research library, and we continued our policy of growth by photographic accretion.

In a few short years, the Huntington Library became one of the most efficient places in the world for the study of virtually any aspect of British and American civilization. The transition was complete. Of course we gloried in our beautiful rare books; we put many on view in the Exhibition Gallery and bought a few others when we could afford them; but we placed our emphasis on the sources of literary and historical knowledge and bought the tools that a scholar would need to recreate the past.

CHAPTER IV

Community of Scholars

As one looks back from the troubled world of the 1970s, the first fifteen years of the Huntington Library's existence as a research institution was, for academics gathered there, a time of halcyon peace, years retrieved from the Golden Age. During part of this time, it is true, the Great Depression cast its shadow over Southern California, as it did over the whole nation, but despite concern over some of the Huntington's investments and the curtailment of income, no essential programs had to be abandoned, and we gathered a community of scholars diverse in interest and vivid in personality. Boccaccio's companions who took refuge from the plague outside Florence, to while away the time telling stories that went into the *Decameron,* enjoyed a life no more idyllic than did the men and women who came to the Huntington Library between 1927 and 1942. Only the coming of World War II interrupted the steady growth of the research program and altered the activities (and the careers) of some of the research staff.

A constant stream of scholars from the United States and Europe poured through the Huntington Library, a few on their own initiative but most on our invitation. In addition, literati of various sorts found Pasadena a congenial resort and sometimes foregathered with us for lunch, tea, or dinner. For instance, Robert Frost spent a winter in the neighboring town of Sierra Madre and was frequently on hand. Hugh Walpole (later Sir Hugh) entertained us with fascinating off-the-record stories of Galsworthy, D. H. Lawrence, and other contemporaries. St. John Gogarty, the Irish physician, senator, and writer, liked to wander through the Huntington Gardens and tell stories or expostulate on the folly of trying to make Gaelic the national language of Ireland. "How can you teach medicine in an obsolete language like Gaelic?" he once exploded. We worked hard, but we never lacked entertainment and intellectual stimulation.

In selecting additional members of the permanent research staff, Fellows, and Visiting Scholars, we tried to choose individuals who knew the difference between significant learning and pedantry. We may have made a few mistakes but our batting average was high. Rarely have so many learned men and women shared so congenial an atmosphere, engaged in literary and historical enterprises so exciting to them and their colleagues, and found life so enjoyable. Some of us were young in years, all were young in spirit.

Within a few years four new members greatly strengthened the permanent research staff: Edwin F. Gay, an economic historian and former dean of the School of Business Administration at Harvard; Allan Evans, a highly competent medievalist from Harvard; Dixon Wecter, a promising young scholar with a Yale and Oxford background, interested in both eighteenth-century England and American literature; and Robert G. Cleland, a distinguished historian of California and dean of Occidental College. All these men proved stimulating and delightful companions as well as productive scholars of eminence.

Mr. Gay was senior to us all in years and experience. One of the most learned men I ever knew, he was disarmingly modest and utterly devoid of any pretentiousness. Although he knew more than most of us about fields in which we specialized and was ready to offer helpful suggestions, his comments were always given with informal ease, often with a glint of humor based on some observation he had made or some passage in an obscure author he had come across. Conversation with him was both a pleasure and an education. He himself was studying the English industrial revolution, a theme that had occupied his interest for most of his adult life. He was planning a definitive book on the subject but, like Turner, he was a perfectionist; two weeks before his death he was still avidly taking notes for the book he never wrote. His daughter Peggy, a scholar in her own right, was the only one who could translate his notes, written in a distinctive but illegible hand. Gay was so enthralled by his explorations of the library's hoard of English family papers, covering centuries of social history, that he let his correspondence pile up unanswered. He occupied Turner's old study, next to mine, and I watched with some apprehension the accumulation on his desk grow ever larger. At intervals, however, Peggy would come over, sort through the letters, and rescue dividend checks or other important communications. "If you wait long enough, most letters won't need answering," Gay once commented a bit apologetically.

The Battle Abbey Papers were a valuable but difficult collection of historical documents, with virtually complete records of a great manorial establishment from the eleventh century to the nineteenth. The monks who conducted the affairs of the Abbey and its estates meticulously recorded an infinite amount of detail highly useful to later historians. After the disestablishment of the monasteries by Henry VIII, the Abbey estates passed into private hands, but family bailiffs continued to keep careful records. Someone remarked that the social history of England in little could be reconstructed from the Battle Abbey Papers. But only a skilled medievalist could interpret the difficult Latin and even more difficult financial accounts in the records. Allan Evans was well equipped for the task and had a detective's genius for ferreting out abstruse information. With the outbreak of war, his research abilities were recognized by the State Department, and he left the Huntington for Washington, never to return. In time he became head of the State Department's division of intelligence research. But in the meantime the Battle Abbey Papers were left unexploited. The war was to prove that the scholarly training of many of the Huntington's specialists had practical utility, and some of us devoted much of our time to classified war work.

Robert G. Cleland's concern with California history went back many years. While still serving as professor and dean at Occidental College, he became a Research Associate and was constantly at work in the Huntington's manuscripts on Western history. In 1943 he joined the permanent research staff. Cleland knew how to write entertainingly without sacrificing historical accuracy, and he had the respect of the general public as well as the professionals. One of his books, *Cattle on a Thousand Hills,* first published in 1941 and reprinted several times, describes the California cattle industry in Spanish and subsequent times. It provides an excellent background for later social history of the state. Cleland organized a program for systematic research in the history of the Southwest, obtained a substantial grant from the Rockefeller Foundation, and brought a number of Western historians to the Huntington. He also encouraged the collection of papers of pioneer families as well as pertinent documents of the later developers of California and the Southwest. The vigorous efforts of Leslie E. Bliss, the librarian, and of Lindley Bynum, a library staff member appointed for this specific purpose, resulted in the accumulation of a remarkable collection of documentary material for the history of the whole of the Southwest. Cleland's use of this material, demonstrated in several of his own books, set an example for other historians of the Western United States who found the Huntington a hospitable and effective place to work.

Cleland was a remarkable man: an excellent historian and writer, a leader in higher education in California, a speaker in great demand, a cooperative colleague, and an enthusiastic outdoorsman and fisherman. He first introduced me to the grandeur of the High Sierras and the joy of trout fishing in mountain streams. He and three of his friends, Dan Hammack, a Los Angeles lawyer, A. W. Buell, a Long Beach physician, and Frank Rush, head of the Pacific Telephone Company, were long-time fishing companions. In the summer of 1936 they invited my old friend Frederick Hard, Huntington Fellow from Tulane, and me to join them on a fishing trip to Arcularius Ranch on the Owens River. For one who had known only worm-fishing in muddy Carolina streams, this induction into the art of dry-fly fishing in crystal-clear mountain torrents was the beginning of a new outdoor life. We became seasoned companions of Cleland and his friends on many a fishing expedition. In 1944, after Fred Hard became president of Scripps College, we contrived to share as many holidays as possible in the High Sierras. No sport equals whipping a mountain stream with a dry fly in the hope of luring a rainbow or speckled trout to strike. To this group of fishermen, who became my fast friends, I shall ever be grateful for days of pleasure in the high altitudes, for good fishing, and for hours of stimulating talk around camp fires.

The Huntington Library sought to establish a special relationship with the neighboring colleges and universities by providing their faculties with research facilities equalled only by those in the greatest universities of the East. While the library welcomed faculty members, it did not open its doors to undergraduates or even to graduate students until they had exhausted resources elsewhere. The deed of trust stipulated that the library was founded for the advancement of learning and the promotion of the public welfare, but that did not mean becoming a "public library" in the sense of admitting the general public to read anything that came to mind.

As interpreted by the trustees and research staff from the beginning, the advancement of learning meant learning on the highest levels, through the encouragement of research by those best equipped to take advantage of the opportunities offered. The trustees realized that they were the custodians of invaluable resources for learning that could never be replaced if destroyed or worn out. They respected the founder's wishes that these treasures should be protected and preserved for future generations. Consequently the library was adamant in refusing admission to dilettantes, casual readers, or undergraduates merely wishing to find easy material for a term paper. The Huntington Library has wisely adhered to this intellectual priority even though from time to time some well-meaning do-gooder has wondered why it did not "encourage bright students to appreciate the fine books in its possession." Enlightening youth, even those with a glimmer of intellectual curiosity, was not the Huntington Library's vocation.

The popular notion of a library is that of a local repository of reading matter for the general and nonspecialist public. The concept of a *research* library is exceedingly hard for most citizens, even those with above-average intelligence, to grasp. Occasionally trustees of such institutions have been abysmally ignorant of the contributions their institutions were making and of the necessity of restricting their activities to specialists who had genuine need of their materials. Fortunately, the Huntington Library had a governing board aware of the folly of trying to be all things to all men;

other libraries have not always been lucky enough to avoid little-wits inspired with large ideas of having their institutions perform miscellaneous services to the community. Given control of an institutional budget, such well-meaning trustees feel obligated to prescribe washing the feet of the poor as a blessed contribution to social uplift. But a research library has no more obligation—or right—to waste its substance in such activities than a medical school has to open its doors to every passerby who would like to learn a little something about the treatment of headache. The Huntington Library, with scientists and scholars as well as enlightened businessmen on its board, was able to set an example of restriction of its resources—a restriction that other institutions could point to, sometimes with envy.

From the day it opened its doors, the Huntington became a haven for scholars, not only from nearby colleges and universities but from many American and European institutions and, now and then, from as far away as Australia. One of the earliest of the local scholars, and one of the most distinguished, was Lily Bess Campbell, professor of English at the University of California at Los Angeles. Possessed of a doctorate from the University of Chicago, Miss Campbell was a learned and acute student of Elizabethan literature, especially Shakespeare, and stage history. She became interested in the contemporary impact of an early sixteenth-century anthology of narrative "tragedies" entitled *The Mirror for Magistrates*, and in 1938 published a definitive edition of that work with an illuminating commentary.

Miss Campbell was a delight to have around. Our lunchroom was becoming an informal forum for all sorts of discussions at noontime, and Miss Campbell added immensely to the gaiety and the illumination of those occasions. Never one to bear fools gladly, she took pleasure in deflating pomposity, albeit with the rapier wit of a lady who was always a stickler for good manners. She could not tolerate pedantry, and her deft criticism of scholarship that fell in this category put up red flags for workers in the vineyard who were inclined to belabor unconsidered trifles snapped up in their reading. In short, Miss Campbell was a fine and influential scholar who, as a Visiting Scholar for many years, made important contributions to the Huntington's program and to the world's store of enlightenment about the Elizabethan period.

No dry-as-dust recluse, Miss Campbell frequently invited other Visiting Scholars and members of the research staff to charming dinner parties at her house just off the University of California campus. Her culinary talents equalled her distinction as an explorer of Elizabethan byways, and the trifles she produced were never unconsidered, nor surpassed by any English cook. Rarely have blanched almonds, raspberry jam, angelica, lady fingers, sherry, and whipped cream been combined into so delectable a dish. From her own English department she frequently included Kay and Franklin Rolfe, Tom and Elizabeth Swedenberg, and Ada Nisbet—all to achieve eminence in their fields. One hazard of a visit to Lily Bess's house was her noisy fox terrier, who once took out the seat of a dignified Princeton scholar's pants.

Among a galaxy of scholars from many universities, one of the most stimulating, ebullient, and uninhibited was Oscar James Campbell (not related to Lily Bess) of the University of Michigan, later of Columbia. Working on problems in Elizabethan drama, he spent several consecutive summers in Pasadena. At that time the rare-book reading room was presided over by a lady of sedate dignity who regarded learned men from great universities as objects of awe and respect. She was also highly religious, and was occasionally shocked by the comments of some of her charges. To Avery Craven of the University of Chicago, working on Civil War history, she remarked, on his arrival one day: "Jesus came into my life this morning," to which Craven briskly replied, "I hope you were up and dressed." Campbell also proved a shock to her. At that time, the reading room closed promptly at twelve noon so that everybody could go to lunch at the same time. Campbell had a talent not to be expected in a professor: he could imitate almost any animal noise. On his first day in the reading room he rose on the stroke of twelve and loudly cuckooed, for all the world like a German cuckoo clock. Readers grew accustomed to wait for this signal for lunch, and the presiding lady somehow survived without apoplexy.

Each year saw the number of scholars increase, some coming at their own expense, others on the invitation of the library. Historians were represented by such distinguished names as Carl Becker of Cornell, Conyers Read of the University of Pennsylvania, Merle Curti of Smith College, later of Wisconsin, Sir Maurice Powicke of New College, Oxford, and many others. Literary scholars were more numerous still. From Princeton came Hoyt Hudson and William Ringler, then a graduate student; Dean R. K. Root was so pleased with the atmosphere of the Huntington that he spent several summers in residence. Known at Princeton as a formidable man, he relaxed in California and proved a congenial companion. He joined a group from the Huntington who went to Laguna Beach every Sunday and was as carefree as the youngest graduate student. Few Princetonians would have recognized the stern dean of the faculty as he sat barefooted in bathing suit at a beach restaurant table. On one occasion the waitress apologized for nearly stepping on the dean's bare toes. "Mind your tootsies," she cautioned. "Wouldn't Princeton students be surprised at that," Root mused.

From Columbia University came a constant stream of men of great distinction. Harry M. Ayres, a specialist in Chaucer and early Elizabethan authors, was one of the first to arrive. Pleased with the benign winter climate and clear crystalline days—then completely free of the smog that would later become an affliction—Ayres worked hard at his research but took time out to renew acquaintances with retired people whom he had known in New York. "You know," he remarked one day, "I have the weird feeling of having gone to heaven. Everything is pleasant and delightful here, and I meet people in Pasadena I thought had died twenty years ago." A more cynical description of Pasadena, sometimes voiced by envious journalists, had it that Pasadena was dedicated to adding twenty years to useless lives.

Another Columbia University man, actually a professor in Barnard College, was William Haller, whom I had known in London when we were both in the British Museum reading through the Thomason Tracts, that interminable collection of pamphlets throwing light on the period of the English Civil Wars. At the Huntington and later at the Folger, Haller continued his excellent work on the history of Puritanism. He proved a wise counselor in the development of both these research libraries.

Several distinguished men from the University of Chicago joined the staff for brief periods. The much respected dean of Chaucerian scholars, John Matthews Manly, already retired, spent a few months at the Library. He was an excellent raconteur and had many anecdotes about scholars he had known. About him an even greater number of colorful legends had gathered and were given fresh circulation by his presence in Pasadena. C. R. Baskervill, who had followed Manly in the English department at Chicago, spent a season at the Huntington. Baskervill was somewhat saturnine and could be devastating in his criticism. An Englishman had recently arrived to accept an important professorship in this country. When someone asked what he had written, Baskervill replied: "A whole wastebasketful of books." A young scholar from Chicago whom I had known when he was a graduate student at the University of London was Gerald E. Bentley. He did a great deal of research at the Huntington for his great multi-volume work on the history of the Jacobean stage.

The history of Elizabethan science proved an attractive field and drew several scholars of distinction: Francis R. Johnson of Stanford University, Sanford Larkey of the University of California at Berkeley, later of Johns Hopkins, and Frederick Kocher of Pomona College, later of Stanford. All three produced books or articles that made genuine contributions to learning.

The borderline between the history of literature and the history of art was an area to which Frederick Hard of Tulane, later president of Scripps College, devoted his attention. His work on the influence of visual art, especially scenes in tapestries, upon the poetry of Edmund Spenser was original and highly significant.

Few scholars had so many diverse interests as Howard Mumford Jones of Michigan, later of Harvard. One day he would be discovering a hitherto unrecognized work of Edgar Allan Poe; the next day he would be excited by speculation about some philosophic influence of eighteenth-century England or France upon colonial America. Companionship with Howard Jones was stimulating and provocative and sometimes stirred those around him to highly productive research. How many books resulted from Howard's offhand suggestions, no one knows, but he had a profound influence, then and later, upon American scholarship.

Two friends whom I had made during my year at Johns Hopkins University came to Pomona College and were frequent readers at the Huntington: Leon Howard in American literature and Ernest Strathmann in Elizabethan studies. Strathmann made important contributions to our knowledge of Sir Walter Raleigh and his circle before the duties of a deanship curtailed his time for research. Howard, who later moved to the University of California at Los Angeles, was a creative scholar whose works in colonial thought, and later in eighteenth- and nineteenth-century literature, became classics in their field. Early in his career, students found him a sympathetic counselor, and in time he became one of the country's most influential directors of graduate studies in American literature.

Kathrine Koller, then a professor at Bryn Mawr, later head of the English department at the University of Rochester, spent many summers at the Huntington. A popular and vivacious personality, friendly and merry, she was engaged in a study of the Elizabethan attitude toward death. Another charming scholar was Helen White, professor at the University of Wisconsin, whose works on Elizabethan devotional literature brought her fame on two continents. She and I had been appointed Guggenheim Fellows the same year, and we have slaved away in the same section of the British Museum reading room, sometimes exchanging books or notes of interest to the other.

Several literary scholars of eminence came from England early in the development of the research program: R. W. Chambers, professor in the University of London whom I had met at the British Museum, soon famous for his life of Sir Thomas More; A. W. Reed of the University of London, interested in Tudor drama; F. P. Wilson (known to his friends as David) of the University of Leeds and later professor at Merton College, Oxford; and David Nichol Smith, Merton College. Of these, Wilson was to come back often to the Huntington and later to the Folger Library. He was working on various aspects of Elizabethan drama and Elizabethan prose works. He arrived in late August on one of the hottest days of the year, having driven from Las Vegas where he had picked up a car. Clothed in a heavy English tweed suit, he was the picture of misery. I took him home, urged him to take off his coat, and gave him his first mint julep—which he described as an act of mercy and frequently mentioned thereafter. Wilson was a man of great urbanity and wisdom who made many friends on this side of the Atlantic and set an example of careful, unpretentious scholarship that others were wise to emulate.

Chambers was a reserved and shy little man but utterly charming. At first during lunch he had little to say, but he gradually warmed up and began to participate in the give and take of repartee. He would frequently contribute some pertinent anecdote, usually something illustrative from a medieval saint's legend encountered in his reading. Reed, a genial man with a red beard, looking a bit like Bernard Shaw, took pleasure in gently ribbing his colleague from London. During the summer of their visit, two carloads of Huntington Library scholars went on a three-day visit to Yosemite. Reed was in the first car, and Chambers came behind in a long rakish white Packard, driven by George Parks of Washington University, St. Louis, then working on Renaissance travel literature. At the two or three filling stations where the cars had agreed to stop, Reed tipped the attendant a dollar and told him to tell the little man in the following white Packard that he had overheard someone say that Professor R. W. Chambers was in the next car. Would the professor mind telling him how he was getting on with his life of Sir Thomas More, which Americans had heard so much about? On our return to the library, Chambers marveled aloud: "I never dreamed that this was such a literate country."

Nichol Smith, a specialist in eighteenth-century literature, came to the Huntington to check on hitherto unavailable documents. At the beginning of his stay he was stiffly British but gradually began to relax in the warmth of the winter sun—and in the unknown luxury of central heat. By summer he had become so disarmed that he deigned to experiment with iced tea, corn on the cob, and sweet potatoes. Sometime later his mother-in-law confessed to me in Oxford that Nichol came home "a ruined man": he put in a furnace for central heat.

An English girl, Jean Robertson of Oxford, later Mrs. John Bromley, wife of a history professor at Southampton University, added to the vivacity of the scholars for two semesters while she studied the Elizabethan genre of literary letters. She too was later to continue her research at the Folger. A sprightly nun, Sister Mary Louise Beutner of the Sisters of Loretto, who joined the group for several summers, added variety to the diverse personalities who were carrying on research at the Huntington. She brought a new point of view for many of the readers, was always ready with a cogent observation, and bubbled with good humor. She announced that in addition to her Elizabethan research she was writing a book called "It's Fun to Be a Nun." We believed she exemplified the title.

Among the more staid of scholars was Hardin Craig, professor of English from Stanford. Craig was working on a book that he published under the title, *The Enchanted Glass*. Among other things it dealt with Elizabethan philosophic concepts and was ponderously learned, so much so that it has become a minor classic of Elizabethan scholarship. Written in prose somewhat less than scintillating, it elicited from one of Craig's colleagues the observation that its title really ought to have been *Through a Glass Darkly*. Craig fascinated me, for he had two distinct personalities. Sitting at lunch or tea, gossiping informally with people he did not need to impress, he could be entertaining and had a great fund of anecdotes about people he had known. But when he felt called upon to act the part of the learned man he was, he drew around him a cloak of solemnity, avoided any hint of humor, talked in sesquipedalian words, and thus impressed the impressionable with the dignity of learning. Craig had an enduring influence upon the profession, for after retiring from Stanford at age sixty-five, he taught at the University of North Carolina, the University of Missouri, and Stephens College.

Contemporary with Craig at the Huntington was Frederick Morgan Padelford, professor of English and dean of the graduate school at the University of Washington. He was a Spenser scholar of eminence and joined Ray Heffner, another Spenserian, to continue work on Spenser that the late Edwin Greenlaw had not been able to complete. Heffner, then of Johns Hopkins University, soon was induced to take a professorship in Padelford's department. Padelford, the very essence of a scholar and a gentleman, had the unusual distinction of being sued for alienation of the affections of the wife of one of his graduate students. This student, a perennial candidate for the doctorate at the University of Washington, had been supported in his academic endeavors by a long-suffering wife who worked that her husband might earn a Ph.D. Wondering whether her spouse would ever finish his work, she wrote to Padelford to ascertain whether her husband had any chance of getting the degree. Padelford replied that in all honesty he was obliged to inform her that the possibility seemed slight. With that she left her husband to his own devices. And with that he sued the dean, a suit that a wise judge threw out of court.

Ray Heffner's brother Hubert, who had achieved national recognition with the Carolina Playmakers at Chapel Hill, came to study an extensive collection of melodramas available only at the Huntington. Hubert was later to become a distinguished professor at Stanford and then at the University of Indiana.

For two years, W. Dougald MacMillan, professor of English at the University of North Carolina, analyzed the library's collection of eighteenth-century plays and prepared a catalogue, *Drury Lane Calendar, 1747–1776* (1938). Katharine Balderston of Wellesley College also devoted herself to eighteenth-century research and edited the journal of Mrs. Thrale, friend of Dr. Samuel Johnson.

Merely to list the distinguished scholars who found both profit and pleasure in working in the Huntington Library during the years of its development would require the space of a monograph. I have named only a few, but their names will serve to show what a contribution to learning the library made during these years; all of them became leaders in their respective institutions and exerted a positive influence upon advanced education. Henry Huntington would have been pleased at the contribution to "research and the public welfare" if he could have known of the activities of his institution.

In the meantime the publication program of the library had proceeded apace and had made possible the printing of catalogues of special collections, documents and edited texts, and monographs written by members of its permanent staff and by Visiting Scholars. The first books were published in cooperation with the Harvard University Press, but later the library became its own publisher. Many books and monographs originating in the library, however, were published by university and commercial presses. The occasional *Bulletin* was succeeded by a regular periodical, *The Huntington Library Quarterly.*

Stirred by the enthusiasm of scholars working at the Huntington, the research staff in 1937 undertook to make an appraisal of the opportunities for a more systematic investigation of English cultural history for the Tudor and Stuart periods. During the summer of 1937 we met regularly for conferences in which we analyzed prepared papers dealing with almost every aspect of life in the period from 1485 to 1660. Discussion was lively and provocative, and no participant failed to gain new insights from his colleagues. At the end of the summer's conferences it fell to my lot to prepare a summary which the library made available for internal use in a mimeographed document dated March 12, 1938. A few paragraphs from the introduction to that report may be worth noting:

> By far the largest number of scholars has come to the Huntington to work in the field of the English Renaissance, and the pressure for publication in this field has been greatest.
>
> For some time past the Huntington Library has realized that further accentuation of research in English Renaissance studies must result logically from these developments. The research staff of the library has therefore studied the problem, especially for the span from about 1485 to about 1660, with the aim of formulating a program of research that would make the most effective use of the materials here available and that would also contribute best to a study of the ideas and institutions of an era in which much of our modern life germinated.
>
> To make tentative plans for such a program of Renaissance studies, a committee of nine men representing various aspects of the period held a series of conferences at the Huntington Library in the summer of 1937. The members of this group were: Charles

H. McIlwain, institutional history, Harvard; Edwin F. Gay, economics, Huntington Library permanent research staff; Oscar James Campbell, English literature, Columbia University; Edwin Hubble, the history of science, Mt. Wilson Observatory; Samuel E. Thorne, the history of law, Northwestern University; C. H. Collins Baker, history of the fine arts, Huntington Library permanent research staff; Godfrey Davies, English history, Huntington Library permanent research staff; Louis B. Wright, English literary history, Huntington Library permanent research staff; and Max Farrand, director of research of the Huntington Library. Special reports were made by Frederick Hard, Tulane University, on the relation of the fine arts to literature; by George B. Parks, Washington University, on travel literature; and by Miss Lily B. Campbell, the University of California at Los Angeles, on problems in Elizabethan historiography. Certain important fields were not represented, as, for example, the history of education. Only a cursory survey could be made of the extremely important subjects of religion and philosophy.

The committee investigated the resources of the library and also surveyed the state of Renaissance scholarship with a view to suggesting studies which must be made before an adequate understanding of the English Renaissance can be reached. These conferences, with the diversity of approaches there represented, demonstrated the fundamental nature of the common interest. The interchange of ideas furnished a striking evidence of the underlying unity in the manifold expressions of life in a given historical period. Although it is a truism to say that such longitudinal sections of a people's development as the histories of economic life, of science, literature, politics, religion, and art should not be studied in mutually exclusive compartments, the conference survey emphasized once more the need of Renaissance studies which would deepen our understanding of that stage of civilization as a complex of mutually dependent forces. At the same time, it was recognized that the notion of the unity of cultural phenomena must not be oversimplified or carried to logical absurdities.

The committee realized that such an interrelated history cannot be written until many exploratory studies have been made. The reports of the conferences contain numerous specific suggestions for detailed studies requiring investigation. No single institution could undertake to foster research in all the problems suggested by the committee. But the exceptional resources of the Huntington Library, developed logically since its foundation, warrant its undertaking more systematically a series of studies of Renaissance culture.

George Ellery Hale had dreamed of some great history of civilization that learned men gathered at the Huntington Library might produce. But our conference on Tudor and Stuart cultural history showed that a study limited even to one country and less than two centuries was of greater scope than we ought to undertake until many more monographic investigations had been completed. But at least our summer of exploration had revealed possibilities for further useful research. We emphasized that great areas in the Tudor and Stuart periods needed fresh study and that research should not be confined to conventional and overworked areas. Too much research, we felt, was carried on in barren fields and was simply marginal farming. We wanted to excite the imaginations of scholars, especially younger people, to explore neglected areas. Since that time, many monographs have been written on themes that we then discussed.

Further to advance learning, the Huntington Library in those years periodically organized research conferences and seminars at which both graduate students and seasoned scholars presented topics for discussion. Typical of the type of conference that we held was the Renaissance Conference on August 19, 20, and 21, 1940, which brought some sixty scholars to discuss their problems. We tried to avoid the reading of routine papers of the sort a professor might present at a Modern Language Association meeting. Instead, we required participants to talk informally and tell what difficulties they had encountered, what problems needed solving, and anything else of general pertinence.

The Huntington Library Quarterly for January 1941 (pp. 134–37) printed a summary of the discussions at the August conference and included opening remarks in which I tried to emphasize useful types of research:

> The subject of the conference is the English Renaissance, which at the library is a convenient term for the period roughly from 1485 to 1660, the Tudors and early Stuarts. In fostering the study of the Renaissance the Huntington Library has tried to develop a broader concept of research, particularly literary research, than is sometimes found in the graduate schools. In the fellowships awarded and in the research projects subsidized, the concentration

has been on projects that will illuminate the history of civilization.

The late Professor Edwin Greenlaw, one of the great teachers of our times, used to stress the importance of literary students' always remembering that literature is related to life. He never let the graduate student forget that his thesis, however esoteric it might be, must deal with something significant and vital. Here at the library we want research to center upon something that is really significant in the interpretation of the life of the times, of the whole complex of the social structure. We try always to remember that the material we use was once a part of the living thought of the time. If we have made any contribution to a philosophy of literary research, it is that literary history can not be written in a vacuum, and that literature must be related to other cultural manifestations before its full significance can be realized. Literary research at the Huntington Library enjoys a great advantage because in the related fields of history there are always scholars working here with whom the literary student can discuss his problems. After all, literary students, for the most part, are historians, and their research is good or bad in direct proportion to the soundness of their historical sense.

Literary research in the Renaissance has reached a critical position. Certain kinds of literary research in the Renaissance period have been exhausted, and there is too much marginal farming in the graduate schools. German scholars were the first to approach Elizabethan literary research scientifically. Under their influence, in the latter part of the nineteenth century, a systematic effort was made to establish the canon of the writings of various authors and to prepare critical texts. There was a great emphasis on strictly philological problems, and language occupied the attention of many students. The methods of biological science were taken over, and literature was treated genetically. This was the period of source study and the study of the influence of one author upon another. The scientific or pseudoscientific method was tremendously useful. But, in time, the means frequently became confused with the ends. Graduate students mistook the method for the thing itself. Year after year literal-minded students have pedantically studied the sources of some trivial writer, or written learnedly to show the influence of one third-rate author upon another. Much of the triviality and aridity of Elizabethan literary research has resulted from a lack of historical perspective and historical orientation.

One of the most profitable fields for research, now, is the study of Renaissance literature as an expression of the life of the times. To understand the literature of the Elizabethan age, for example, the student must know what the literature meant to the Elizabethans. Literary historians have perpetuated errors from generation to generation because they have looked at the literature as their own age understands it, not as the Elizabethans understood it. Not even the greatest of the Elizabethans, Shakespeare and Spenser, can be properly interpreted without an adequate understanding of their milieu. And we cannot understand the literary milieu of the period without an investigation of the works of minor authors. Studies of minor authors have, too often, taken a wrong direction. The approach has been from the point of view of belles-lettres, and has led to an attempt to bolster the reputations of long-dead minor authors and inflate them so that they can masquerade as little Shakespeares and little Spensers. The truth is that no amount of archeology will make them readable. Yet they do represent certain literary tendencies of their age which must be known if Shakespeare and Spenser are to receive their proper setting and proper historical interpretation....

There is also a great need for investigation of genres neglected because of the emphasis up to the present time upon belles-lettres. Some of the neglected literary genres are no longer popular but were extremely important in the Renaissance. The most obvious example is religious literature, to be discussed later. In part as a result of Professor Helen White's example, many scholars have been reading Elizabethan sermons and making some significant discoveries.

Over the years, the scholars gathered at the Huntington Library were men and women inspired by a tremendous zeal for learning, possessed of enthusiasm for what they were doing. I do not remember any who were cynics or mere plodders working to get ahead in their universities. We were a community of scholars excited by the opportunities before us. None of us probably has achieved all he dreamed of but we tried—and we enjoyed what we were doing.

One secret of the Huntington Library's success in the first two decades of its existence was the opportunity it provided for the exchange of ideas between scholars of varied interests. "In my university," a professor once commented, "I see people from my own department, or a few from other disciplines on academic committees, but we rarely take time to relax and talk informally about our research. Out here it is different. Every day around the lunch table, we hear about what someone else has found, and we don't mind giving and taking advice in such a congenial atmosphere." A Harvard professor added that talk about one's own activities back home at the faculty club would be unthinkable—"about like a dentist advertising." But we were uninhibited by traditional reticences; we learned from one another; and we had our minds stretched by daily contacts with some of the most acute scholars in the land.

Another factor was the genuine hospitality that the library extended to scholars, both officially and unofficially. One must add that the Huntington was not open to every Tom, Dick, and Harry who imagined he would like to hold a rare book in his hand. But no advanced student working for the doctorate, and no adult who could demonstrate that he needed our resources to complete a work of any importance—whether an academic, a journalist, or a freelance writer—was ever refused admittance. Now and then someone turned up with a chip on his shoulder, ready to believe that a research library was a suspicious place more intent on hiding books than on providing service to readers, but these rare types quickly changed their attitudes when they experienced both efficiency and courtesy.

The director of the library, Max Farrand, set an example of hospitality that we all tried to follow. The director's house, on the grounds in a setting of orange trees, was ideally suited for entertaining, and Farrand had frequent dinner parties for members of the community and the research staff. Late in life he had married Beatrix Cadwalader Jones of New York, a member of the oldest New York aristocracy (for New York still had an aristocracy in Mrs. Farrand's youth), and Max once told me that after his marriage he had consciously tried to mold himself into the kind of gentleman that she would want him to be. A niece of Edith Wharton, with vivid memories of her aunt's social milieu, Mrs. Farrand retained an instinctive formality that left some people ill at ease, but she was genuinely kind, and I liked her. A landscape architect with a national reputation (designer of the gardens at Dumbarton Oaks in Washington, for example), she was frequently away from San Marino, but when she was in residence she gave dinner parties that included a galaxy of fascinating people.

Mrs. Farrand's Christmas dinners, always at eight o'clock on

Christmas night, followed a tradition long established in her family. Because we were among the younger group, she depended upon me to act as a sort of lieutenant, to take charge in case of any emergency and to look after any of the ancients who always sprinkled the guest list. The task was not always easy. One Christmas night an 84-year-old retired United States senator, sleepy from champagne, decided to go back to the Hotel Huntington long before his driver was scheduled to pick him up. I undertook to get him home. When we stopped at a red light on Lake Avenue, he wanted to be assured that we were on the right road to his hotel. Opening the car door, he called to a policeman on the sidewalk to come over and direct him. His speech was a bit thick, and I had visions of delivering him to the police station instead of the hotel, but the cop was understanding and we made a safe landing.

These Christmas dinners, though very formal, were nevertheless great fun. Invariably there were sugar plums sent by a convent in Lisbon because at the time of the Lisbon earthquake in 1755 a seafaring ancestor of Mrs. Farrand had rescued the nuns. We were also served Madeira that had come around the Horn. The Madeira went down easier than the sugar plums, encased in a candied shell as hard as cement.

The guests included a variety of personalities, some famous and all interesting. One Christmas night George Arliss, the actor of stage and screen who had recently achieved a great reputation in the role of Disraeli, and his wife were among the guests. Whether Mrs. Farrand knew it, I do not know, but the Arlisses were strict vegetarians, and the roast goose served that night was not to their liking. Seated on Mrs. Farrand's left was Carl Becker, the historian, then suffering some digestive difficulty so that his Christmas dinner consisted of a bowl of warm milk and crackers. Between Becker and me was Mrs. Arliss. During a lull in the conversation I heard her talking with Mrs. Farrand about what one should serve after the soup, and her voice rose to comment: "And I suppose then you serve some poor murdered thing." Unhappily the lady on my right chose that moment to say something, and I never knew what Mrs. Farrand replied. Becker, thinking deep thoughts and observing the silence of a Trappist monk, afterward claimed not to have heard the remark, and my curiosity has remained unsatisfied.

Mrs. Farrand had an excessive sense of propriety. Late one afternoon she came to call and to tell me about going over her Aunt Edith's papers preparatory to giving them to Yale. She confessed that it had been a wearing experience, for she had to read everything and decide what to destroy. "I have burned those papers Aunt Edith would not want the public to see," she said matter-of-factly. I was horrified, but the task had been finished and I held my peace. One day, I thought, some facet of Aunt Edith's life will be revealed by somebody else's papers, and Aunt Edith will have no document in rebuttal.

My wife and I enjoyed Mrs. Farrand's friendship, and we were privileged to share some of her pleasures in Southern California. She liked an open car and owned an old Lincoln, ponderous as a freight car, driven by a chauffeur long in the family service. On a crisp winter's day she used to tuck us into the car with her, cover us with a buffalo robe that some ancestor had doubtless bought from the Indians, and take us to Midwick Club to watch polo. Midwick itself was an experience. Populated with both old and new-rich of Los Angeles and Pasadena, it had vast snob appeal for some. Not for Mrs. Farrand, of course; she and Mr. Farrand just liked to watch polo. But when Midwick fell on evil days financially and was bought at public auction by an Italian neighbor who had made his money selling bananas, a guffaw shook the region.

The social life of Pasadena and San Marino (its fashionable suburb) was sedate but time-consuming for those who had the inclination to accept all attractive invitations to dinners, luncheons, symphony concerts, and theatre parties. Retired people of wealth seemed to like academic people as dinner guests. An amused neighbor of mine, himself a man of wealth and position, commented: "Anybody who can be addressed as 'Doctor' is a prized catch in the eyes of Pasadena hostesses." A newspaper reported that Pasadena in those years had a population of eight thousand rich widows. An unattached male with a dinner jacket could live well and sometimes keep his freedom.

To avoid too much waste of time, we made a resolution to restrict our acceptance of invitations to two a week. That schedule was necessary if I was to get my own writing done. Social pressures did not always permit us to keep so strict a schedule but that was our goal—then and later in Washington when I became director of the Folger Library. One has to choose among activities and decide which are essential or desirable.

On every Tuesday afternoon we had tea at our house for any scholars working at the Huntington who might care to come. They all knew that we kept open house on that day, and for years we had a constant stream of guests. Our Spanish-type house at 580 Berkeley Avenue, San Marino, was well suited for the purpose, for both living room and dining room opened upon a red-tiled patio in the center of which grew a gnarled olive tree; a fountain at one end gave the patio a Moorish touch. In good weather on Tuesdays, the whole lower floor and patio teemed with guests chattering about their work and their adventures, for many were in Southern California for the first time. We made many friends whom we have treasured through the years.

The Huntington Library was one of a triumvirate of institutions that included the California Institute of Technology and the Mount Wilson Observatory. We all shared a faculty club, the Athenaeum, on the fringe of the Caltech campus. That gave the humanists at the Huntington an opportunity to meet some of the great scientists of our generation. When Einstein came to Caltech, for example, many of us got to know and admire him.

All sorts of professional people converged on Pasadena in the prewar days, including an extraordinary number of admirals who had business with scientists at Caltech. I remember sitting by Admiral James O. Richardson at one luncheon when he remarked that if we ever got into a shooting war with the Japanese, every man, woman, and child in the United States would be affected before it was over. That was at a time when most Americans were convinced that we could whip the Japanese with one hand tied behind our backs.

The three institutions tooks turns providing popular lectures at the Athenaeum, not with invariable success. On one painful evening, when a pedantic philosopher was droning along about "The Metaphysics of Physics," a deaf man on the front seat with a hearing device like a box camera reached over and turned it off with a loud click. Never did an audience so envy a deaf man or applaud his wisdom more heartily. On another evening Odell Shepard, a professor from Trinity College, Connecticut, and a poet, had offered to read an epic poem of his own entitled "The Bow and the Arrow," the bow being the impulse that sent emigrants to Connecticut, and the arrow being the settlers themselves. Shepard also had much to say about the preservation of Connecticut's natural environment. Reading the announcement, the head of the Southern California Edison Company, a collector of books on archery, drove over from Los Angeles in a torrential rain to be instructed on his hobby. As Shepard read interminably, the archery enthusiast got redder and redder and finally stalked out in the midst of a stanza castigating the wickedness of builders of power dams, the spoilers of purling streams.

At intervals Caltech gave a great banquet at the Athenaeum for donors known as the Associates of the California Institute of Technology. Many of the guests were wealthy old ladies who turned out in all their finery to gaze on world-famous scientists and other folk who might be worth noting. At one of these soirées I found myself in a corner with Will Rogers, who was as bored as I. He looked around at the roomful of women, most of them garlanded with bandoliers of orchids, and commented: "Ain't a one of 'em can milk a cow." He thus dismissed an element of society that he regarded as useless.

When the war came with the attack on Pearl Harbor, the Huntington Library staff found itself busy with a variety of duties. We supplied a surprising amount of information useful to the armed services, ranging from studies of whalers' log books to determine the depths of harbors in the South Pacific to detailed information about the terrain of the highlands of New Guinea. Some of us sought active duty—in my case, in vain. The Navy turned me down because I was two inches too short, the Marines because I was too old, and the Army cancelled a captain's commission because of "a history of hayfever for life." As it turned out, I probably served more usefully as a civilian consultant and in various intelligence operations. These duties brought me to Washington with wearisome frequency during the war years when I shuttled between Pasadena, the Pentagon, and the State Department.

The governance of the Huntington Library requires some comment. The founder had provided that control would be vested in five trustees who would be self-perpetuating. The five appointed by Huntington would serve for life; later trustees would be elected for ten-year terms but could be reelected.

When I came to the library the trustees were Henry M. Robinson, the chairman, a banker and financial adviser to President Herbert Hoover; Robert A. Millikan, chairman of the Caltech Executive Committee, its governing body; Henry S. Pritchett, of the Carnegie Institution; George Ellery Hale, of the Mount Wilson Observatory; and Archer M. Huntington, whose primary interest was the Hispanic Institute.

Robinson, the dominant influence on the board at this time, was a wise and far-sighted trustee. He was convinced of the value of the research program and needed little "education" about what that included. As a man of business he also realized the value of public relations, and he saw to it that the Huntington utilized its grounds, gardens, and exhibitions to serve the general public. Thousands of visitors were admitted and made to feel welcome. But Robinson was never willing to sacrifice the intellectual side of the institution to cater to the general public. He insisted upon keeping both programs in balance.

Interested in books, Robinson had a particular liking for the English seventeenth century. One of his favorite authors was Samuel Pepys, the diarist. When he was in the Huntington Hospital during a long illness that eventually proved fatal, Farrand asked me to write a daily account of activities at the library in the style of Pepys's diary, to keep Robinson informed and also amused. Probably no chairman of a board of trustees ever received so unusual a report.

When Pritchett resigned at the age of eighty in 1936, the board elected ex-President Herbert Hoover. On the death of Robinson in 1937, Millikan became chairman, and William B. Munro, formerly professor of history at Harvard and then head of the humanities division at Caltech, was elected to the board. When Hale died in 1938, Edwin Hubble, the astronomer at Mount Wilson, succeeded him. On the resignation of Archer Huntington in 1945, James R. Page, a Los Angeles banker, was elected in his place. These were the men who controlled the library in my time.

During these years the board always had some dominant figure who stood ready to defend the research program that had been developed by Farrand and his staff. But a board that met once a month—or oftener on occasion—composed of local residents who took an almost parental interest in what was going on, had its liabilities. Trustees were not always willing to establish policy and leave day-to-day operations to the administration; they sometimes insisted on meddling in affairs that were not properly the business of trustees.

Farrand retired in 1941, and Millikan, as chairman of the board, objected to the appointment of a director to succeed him. Caltech was administered by an executive committee with Millikan as chairman, and he believed that a similar administration would be suitable for the library. So that was the procedure until I left in 1948 to go to the Folger. Members of the research staff took turns serving on the executive committee. In addition to serving as chairman of the fellowship committee, which required much correspondence as well as personal interviews, I soon found my own administrative duties multiplying. The appointment of a director would have saved some of us an immense amount of time. I was frequently required to come East on official business, and during my last two years at the Huntington I often journeyed to New York to consult Mr. Hoover, at times our most alert trustee.

Because of illness, the frailties of age, and frequent absences of a busy scientist like Hubble, we occasionally had difficulty rounding up a quorum of trustees to legalize actions of the executive committee. Hubble often had to be away for long periods on essential war work, and his absences were a great loss to the library, for he had both brilliance and wisdom. But somehow we muddled through. The Huntington trustees had no mandatory retirement age, and some hung on until past their optimum usefulness. My experience at the Huntington convinced me that trustees ought to retire not later than age seventy-five.

No ideal system of trustee governance of privately endowed libraries has yet been devised. Some institutions suffer from too close surveillance by resident trustees. Others are handicapped by absentee trustees or trustees who have only a glimmer of understanding of the functions of a library. Those Huntington trustees who lived nearby could not resist the temptation to meddle in management. They met too often and gave too much advice. One or two developed crotchets that were genuinely disastrous. James R. Page, for example, professed complete disdain for the research program, saw no reason to pay scholars to do research, scoffed at the notion of buying "a lot of trash" (meaning photostats, reference books, and pamphlet literature). He wanted to use the library's funds to buy more pictures for the art gallery. He himself collected prayer books and antique silver and would have been willing to see the library accumulate old silver. Although he diverted some funds from the acquisition of books, fortunately the other trustees usually managed to restrain him. And yet Jim Page was in many ways a generous and genial man. On a small board of five, however, one crotchety fellow can cause trouble. The Huntington would have been more fortunate if the founder had arranged for a larger and more broadly representative board.

By and large, however, the board of trustees acted with good judgment and carried out the founder's intentions. I found them a pleasant group to work with. My only complaint was that Millikan treated me more like a son than an administrative officer, and it was sometimes tedious to get official sanction for actions that had to be taken within a given time limit. I soon learned that the only satisfactory method of operation was to face the chairman with a fait accompli and listen to a fatherly lecture if he did not approve.

From time to time pressure was exerted to induce the Huntington Library, a tax-exempt institution, to devote more of its energy and income to services for the general public, but it never lost sight of its primary obligation to learning on the highest levels. Although it arranged exhibitions that would be instructive to the laity, these were never allowed to interfere with more serious work.

The art gallery, the grounds, and the botanical gardens attracted throngs of visitors, but they all remained secondary to the main purpose of the institution, which was research and the advancement of learning. Not even the occasional impact of an erratic trustee was sufficient to deflect the library from its charted course. Over the years the Huntington has set an example that other similar foundations have been well advised to emulate.

CHAPTER V

An Uncloistered World

A POPULAR CONCEPT of a scholarly library is the stereotype of a repository of dusty books where academics in green eyeshades retreat from the world of action. The Huntington Library was no such place, and we were all so busy with a multitude of outside activities that we had to ration our time for the more important professional obligations. Soon after my arrival at the library, Farrand warned me that Southern California was littered with organizations all eager for speakers, and to accept only those requests that seemed most desirable. William B. Munro put it more bluntly: "This is the greatest country for *free* speech I have ever known." A few academics, retired from Eastern universities and then living in Southern California, liked to be heard and were eager to talk to women's clubs and miscellaneous organizations; they had set a misleading example, and the scholars at the Huntington were beset with requests to talk, here, there, and yonder—all for free. Only the exercise of the utmost tact would sometimes get us off the hook when some well-known hostess was determined to capture a scholar for her favorite book club. Professional groups were another story, however, and we all accepted our responsibility to participate in local and national organizations.

Farrand had assured me that members of the research staff would be encouraged to carry on their studies elsewhere when necessary, to teach a reasonable amount at neighboring institutions if they wished to do so, and to serve on whatever professional boards seemed desirable. I was soon deeply involved.

Caltech drew upon the Huntington staff to teach some of the courses in the humanities which all graduate students were required to take. Soon after my arrival I was asked to teach a course of my own choosing in history or literature, themes which I alternated term to term. Many Navy V-12 students, potential officers, passed through my classes and were generally interested in historical topics.

The most fascinating class I taught at Caltech consisted of commissioned officers in the Navy and the Army Air Corps who had been sent there to study jet propulsion in the early days of its development. There were one or two Navy captains and Army colonels, the rest lieutenant colonels, commanders, and lieutenant commanders. Not realizing who my students would be on the first night of the semester, I went to the assigned classroom expecting to see half a dozen students physically unfit for military service, for this was at the height of the war. The room had been preempted by men in uniform, and I waited a discreet time before asking if they had not come to the wrong place. "We are waiting for a fellow named Wright," a spokesman replied. Looking at the group, I decided that the routine topic on English poetry already announced would be unsuitable so I changed gears abruptly and offered a course in "The Background of Revolution in the Modern World," beginning with Voltaire and ending with Darwin's *Origin of Species*. I had never taught or heard of such a course but it seemed something that military officers ought to know, and I thought I could keep a few jumps ahead of them. Rarely has a teacher had a livelier class. We began each Tuesday evening at seven o'clock, and it was usually ten or after before they let me go home. "First time I've had a chance to think since I left the Academy," a West Pointer commented. One of the older officers was disappointed when he could not find a complete set of Voltaire's works in any local bookstore. If the military "brass" found the course enlightening, they never knew, I hoped, how fresh the information was to their instructor.

As Farrand had predicted, other opportunities for teaching were not lacking. I enjoyed all my classes, for this was an era when college and university students still had good manners, dressed reasonably well, and were interested in learning rather than in cultivating their own egos and saving the world by straggling through the streets bearing banners. A course at the University of California at Los Angeles on bibliography and research methods, offered in the graduate school of English, allowed me to make many friends among the students, some of whom were later conspicuously successful as university teachers. One of these was Ada Nisbet, who did a term paper in my class on English commentary on America from Dickens to Rudyard Kipling. This paper led to an excellent doctoral dissertation on Dickens and a definitive work on English criticism of America. Miss Nisbet in time became a distinguished graduate professor of English at UCLA, in one of the best departments of English in America.

My course at UCLA gave me great satisfaction, for the students were particularly stimulating and attractive. Not in all the years that I taught there did I encounter any evidence of rudeness or youthful arrogance. Contemplating the attitudes of students in recent years, I am grateful that my academic experience was all achieved in a period when students and instructor worked together with mutual respect—and with enthusiasm. Not every student was brilliant, to be sure, but all displayed a zest for what they were trying to do.

The UCLA class met on Monday afternoons. Frequently I dined afterwards with other members of the faculty: Franklin and Kay Rolfe, Tom and Elizabeth Swedenberg, or some other congenial souls. Conversation was lively, and a gaiety of spirit prevailed. None of us dreamed of the grim problems that would overwhelm universities and academic life in a later period.

As if classes at UCLA on Monday afternoons and at Caltech on Tuesday nights were not enough, I was lured into teaching on Thursday evenings a course at Pomona College on the history of ideas in America. As at UCLA, the students were an extraordinarily attractive and intelligent group, many of whom have remained friends to this day. I have encountered them from time to time in surprising places. Years later, when I was asked to write a scenario on Columbus for a television series called "The Saga of Western Man," one of my former students at Pomona, Patricia Sides, turned up as assistant producer on that series.

Although these three classes constituted what would be considered a full academic load for a professor nowadays, they did not interfere with essential research or administrative duties at the Huntington. Visiting professorships for brief periods permitted teaching at other universities as well: during the summer of 1935, two courses in the English Renaissance—one graduate, one undergraduate—at the University of Michigan; in the spring of 1942, at the University of Washington, the Walker-Ames Lectures which resulted in the publication of a little book entitled *Religion and Empire: The Alliance between Piety and Commerce in English Expansion, 1558–1625* (1943); in the summer of 1946, two graduate courses in history at the University of Minnesota. In brief, any fear that a career in a research library would divorce me from academic experience and the stimulus of students had long since been dispelled.

Godfrey Davies of our staff also taught a graduate course at UCLA, and we sometimes rode over together. He had served as historical consultant for a Hollywood studio on the movie version of *Forever Amber,* an assignment that earned him much ribbing from his colleagues, but it resulted in an acquaintance with a variety of Hollywood types. Occasionally we dined with some of them, an experience that convinced me that no novel about the movie colony could possibly exaggerate the reality.

For several years Paul Green, a Pulitzer Prize-winning dramatist from the University of North Carolina, was frequently in Hollywood, for he had written a script for a movie called *Cabin in the Cotton* that so impressed the moguls of the screen that he quickly became a favored writer and a sage, much to his own surprise and not always to his liking. We played golf every Saturday afternoon, sometimes on the Fox Studio golf course in Los Angeles and sometimes in Pasadena. One afternoon Paul arrived looking perplexed and worried. "What's the trouble?" I asked. "Sam Goldwyn wants me to come back for fifty weeks and offers $100,000," he replied. Compared with Paul's academic salary at Chapel Hill in those years, Goldwyn's temptation looked compelling, but by the following Saturday Paul appeared looking serene and content. "What about Sam Goldwyn's offer?" I asked. "I turned it down," he reported. "Hollywood does something to your soul."

That did not end Paul's work in Hollywood but it illustrated his distrust of long stays in that atmosphere. He telephoned me once from Chapel Hill with a request to inspect a house in Hollywood that he had been offered. It turned out to be the residence of Ann Harding, then a well-known actress. The house was a wondrous thing, a pseudo-Italian creation with a sunken courtyard spanned by a replica of the Bridge of Sighs in Venice, a pirate's cave equipped with a casket of fake jewels, a great hall, across one end of which was a huge smoked-up fireplace and mantel, and other atmospheric touches too numerous to describe. Housing was scarce in Hollywood; Paul had three children and needed space; so the deal was closed for three months' occupancy. On the day the Greens moved in they got a cleaning woman to wash down the smoke-stained mantel. Unfortunately, the rental agent turned up just as she was getting under way with scrub-brush and soap.

"Oh, Professor Green, Professor Green, don't let her do that! That chimney's been genuinely antiqued. Cost fifty dollars to get it smoked up proper."

Much of Hollywood was equally phony. My experiences with its denizens were sometimes official and sometimes informal but they were always astonishing and occasionally appalling.

One morning at the Huntington three "researchers" from a Hollywood studio appeared to investigate the background for a movie version of Hawthorne's *Scarlet Letter*. Clearly not one had ever been in a rare-book library before and they were bewildered. The reading room attendant came to me in distress and asked what we could do for them. The most learned of the trio filled out his reader's application card with proof of academic credentials: he signed himself "D.D.S."—doctor of dental surgery. "Got any more letters like the scarlet letter?" he asked. When we discovered that they really wanted information about crime and punishment in colonial New England, we set them to work reading a handful of books quickly assembled. But they were in a hurry. One was heard to comment: "God, look at that pile of books. A man could read a week in this place."

We did not go out of our way to educate Hollywood, but we did try to provide accurate historical information when we were asked.

An Uncloistered World

During the filming of *The Rothschilds* a frantic call came from the studio about three o'clock one afternoon: "Did the Stock Exchange in London at the time of the Battle of Waterloo mark up quotations on a blackboard?" Somehow we dug up the information, but the correct answer now escapes me.

All members of the research staff felt an obligation to do a certain amount of speaking at professional gatherings in California and elsewhere. Because we were a tax-exempt institution, we could not evade all requests from civic organizations, burdensome as some of these assignments were. Now and then a disgruntled group of California citizens would start a movement to have our tax exemption repealed. During one of these episodes the Jonathan Club in Los Angeles asked me to talk at one of its famous breakfasts. Members included a number of influential businessmen and politicians, and it was expedient for me to go.

The occasion was memorable. A man in white pants and sweater first came out and put the old boys through calisthenics. After these setting-up exercises a lady of uncertain age rendered a set of Russian folk songs. A parson said a lengthy grace, and we were then allowed coffee and eggs. Presently it was my turn to speak. Master of ceremonies was a man named Seltzer. All regular members of the club wore moon-sized medallions with their nicknames inscribed thereon. Mr. Seltzer was inevitably designated "Bromo." "We will be on the air," he informed me, "and we want you to speak just seventeen minutes." The shorter the better, was my silent agreement. Then Bromo launched into his introduction—on the air. The speaker was represented as the greatest orator since Demosthenes, and the Jonathan Club was conferring an immense blessing on the state of California by sharing such a cultural event. Bromo clearly loved the sound of his own voice, and by this time the guest speaker was unrecognizable in his true identity. Finally Bromo wound up his oration like a pitcher getting ready to throw a curve ball: "Ladies and gentlemen of the radio world, it gives me great pleasure to present Mr. L. B. Smith." Never was a speaker more relieved to be pseudonymous.

The three Pasadena institutions that shared a faculty club in the Athenaeum (California Institute of Technology, Mount Wilson

Observatory, and the Huntington Library) established a remarkable rapport that was beneficial to all. Caltech and Mount Wilson, being older than the Huntington, were already recognized on both sides of the Atlantic as leaders in their areas of professional competence, and the Huntington Library from early in its development was determined to equal the other two in contributions to learning. For that reason Farrand brought scholars from abroad and encouraged the research staff to take part in national and international professional organizations. Both director and trustees were convinced that the published results of research at the Huntington would soon establish the library's reputation as a germinal center of learning. That proved to be the case, and the exchange of ideas at the Athenaeum between representatives from the three member institutions, always as between equals, was provocative and stimulating.

For institutions that had international connections of significance, the provinciality of the Eastern establishment vis-à-vis the "Far West" was puzzling. Although nearly all the great universities were represented in Pasadena, some of them acted as if their distinguished alumni had vanished into the vast Pacific. Occasionally this provinciality had unfortunate results for job hunters from some of the Eastern universities. For example, O. J. Campbell, one of our perennial Visiting Scholars from the University of Michigan, reported that George Lyman Kittredge, the doyen of the English department at Harvard, had once tried to palm off a third-rate Harvard Ph.D. on Michigan with the remark: "He's good enough for the Middle West." Michigan, according to Campbell, vowed never to hire another Harvard man for its English department. The belief that nothing much worthwhile could be found west of the Charles River was deeply ingrained, usually in converts who themselves had come from the great open spaces. Hyder Rollins, a Texan, became a professor of English at Harvard and a devout Cantabrigian. At an annual meeting of the Modern Language Association in Boston, Hyder called my hotel and asked: "Are you coming over here this afternoon to meet the celebrities?" Puzzled, I inquired, "What celebrities?" "Why, the Harvard English Department," Hyder replied. "We are giving a tea this afternoon, you know."

This attitude, fortunately, was not the prevailing mood at Harvard, and the history department there was particularly helpful in supporting Robert G. Cleland's program at the Huntington for the study of the history of the Southwest. After a visit to Harvard in 1944, one of my reports stated: "Professor Frederick Merk spoke in the highest terms of Mr. Cleland's own work and expressed enthusiasm for our projects. Several recent Ph.D.'s who did their work under Professor Merk's direction will be available after the war." One of these was Rodman Paul, who came to Caltech, wrote a valuable book on mining in California, and remained an intellectual asset to the region. Dean Paul Buck showed genuine interest in the Huntington's activities and suggested the names of several historians and cultural anthropologists who might be helpful. Howard Mumford Jones, by this time dean of the School of Arts and Sciences at Harvard, also made useful suggestions. The same 1944 report further noted: "With the exception of Harvard, the Eastern universities showed little interest in studies of the West. I could discover no one at Yale, Columbia, or Princeton who might be useful to our projects."

Harvard and the Huntington collaborated in the distribution of a chronological card catalogue of English books printed before 1641. Under my supervision, Miss Lucile Klotz and other research assistants arranged on cards in chronological order all the titles listed alphabetically in Pollard and Redgrave's *Short-Title Catalogue of Books Printed in England . . . 1475–1640*. We then permitted William A. Jackson of the Houghton Library at Harvard to duplicate these cards and sell them to other libraries. This catalogue became known as the "Harvard Chronological Catalogue"—but it was made at the Huntington Library. Professor Charles McIlwain declared it to be one of the most useful historical tools available.

Occasionally Eastern provinciality caused downright annoyance and precipitated action. One man who scoffed at the unenlightened attitudes of the Eastern establishment was William A. Nitze, a brilliant professor of Romance languages who had retired from the University of Chicago and moved to Los Angeles, where he had a home in walking distance of the UCLA campus. Nitze was particularly concerned because the American Council of Learned Societies appeared not to know about anything in the West. To remedy this ignorance, he insisted that Waldo Leland, then president of the ACLS, pay a visit to Southern California, and he called upon me to help impress Leland with the significance of the humanities in the West.

We rounded up some of the most alert scholars in the region, took Leland to see various universities and colleges, pointed out how the ACLS was missing the boat, and so persuaded him of the importance of the West that he agreed to the founding of the Pacific Coast Committee for the Humanities of the ACLS. In 1946 this committee began publishing a magazine, *The Pacific Spectator*, edited by John W. Dodds, head of the humanities division at Stanford, with Miss Edith Mirrielees as managing editor. Nitze himself served as chairman of the committee with Louis B. Wright as vice-chairman; other members were John Dodds, E. Wilson Lyon, president of Pomona College, and Archer Taylor, professor of German at the University of California at Berkeley. Hugh Dick, then a junior member of the English department at UCLA, served as secretary. We also had a large advisory committee representing many Western institutions.

The meetings of our committee, usually at Stanford, were memorable occasions. The Pasadena delegation would arrive by overnight train and would be entertained by Dodds and his hospitable wife at breakfast. For the rest of the day we would plan the intellectual stimulation of the Pacific slope. Nitze was a dynamic personality, with imagination and wisdom. Under his guidance we planned conferences that would bring scholars in the humanities together to discuss professional problems. We made a point of looking for bright young men to fill vacancies in Western colleges and universities. Because professional duties frequently took me to the East, department heads in various institutions asked me to interview candidates and make recommendations. Some of the resulting appointments added to the vitality of Western faculties. Our committee encouraged significant publications, discouraged pedantry when we could, and tried to stir lagging humanists to a realization that they had an obligation to utilize their talents in the promotion of genuine learning—not to settle for mere tweedledum and tweedledee.

My colleagues on the committee induced me, not unwillingly, I must confess, to publish in the first issue of *The Pacific Spectator* (Winter, 1947) a philippic against pedantic obscurantism entitled "The Breakdown of Intellectual Communication." The piece did not win any friends among the avant-garde, and a few critics thought the new magazine was off to a poor start with such an old-fashioned contribution. A few paragraphs will indicate the point of view of our committee as well as that of the author.

> The vogue of obscurantism, shared by the poet with prose writers of the avant-garde, represents a loss to society of intellectual leadership sorely needed in a materialistic world. The self-imposed retirement behind barriers of cultism has removed from the stream of positive leadership minds which might have contributed to the elevation and freedom of the human spirit.
>
> This flight from life by active minds is a negative disaster. Some critics, however, have seen a more sinister and positive evil in the trend toward cultism among the literati. *The Times Literary Supplement,* for example, on March 18, 1944, printed as a leading article, "Cultic Twilight," which drew a gloomy parallel between some of the Nazi hocus-pocus and analogous "myth-discoveries" among fashionable literary coteries. "Mythogenesis is a cult of our day," the *Times* observes. "It has sent a literary movement in this country and America into a frenzied derangement of words—and in Europe it has driven a nation mad and laid Europe in ruins.... The racial myth preached by the Germans turns history into fable; the literary myth turns art into legerdemain. Words before sense is one of the literary mottoes, and if words are too ingrained in meaning to be mishandled, then invent some that can by no possibility be interpreted except by the inventor—who will leave a key to the claque so that future generations may not study in vain...."
>
> Blame for the obscurity into which so much of humane learning has fallen must be shared alike by all of us who ply the trade of scholar, teacher, and interpreter of letters. For too long each in his corner has worried his own particular bone and growled at the approach of an intruder. But everywhere there are signs of an awakened consciousness of the obligation, not only to society, but to learning itself. If learning is not to die, smothered in its own

pedantry, it must acquire an awareness of its public relationships and particularly of its obligations to other members of the fraternity of scholars. In every profession new voices are making this demand with an appeal to common sense and enlightened self-interest. Everywhere there is a realization of the need for better communication.

This movement must not be confused with a degeneration into journalism—always the fear of scholars. Accurate and technical scholarship, learned and difficult criticism, we must continue to encourage. Never was there a greater fallacy than the belief that all learning, scholarship, or criticism must be gay, simple, and alluring to the passing reader. We shall continue to need many an abstruse and tedious study. Someone should say a word for the poor devil who counted the syllables in Chaucer—that perennial illustration never forgotten by the enemies of exact scholarship. Had he not performed that weary labor, we would never have recovered the secret of Chaucer's musical verse, and the world would have been the loser. But we must ask ourselves whether we have done our best to write for the understanding of all who might need our scholarship, our poetry, and our criticism. We must search our souls against pedantry.

One of Will Nitze's hopes was that the Pacific Coast Committee for the Humanities and its journal would indicate to the Eastern establishment and the rest of the world that the West was no longer a frontier of gunmen and cattle rustlers. Perhaps we had some small success but ancient prejudices die hard. For me the activities of the committee meant a personal gain: an enduring friendship with Nitze and my other colleagues and a friendship with Waldo Leland that lasted until his death. In time I was to serve as a member, treasurer, and vice-chairman of the ACLS which Leland headed so long.

The prospect of the end of the war led to a number of intellectual activities in 1944 in which I represented the Huntington Library. A report for February 14, 1944, previously mentioned, lists some of these. One was the creation of the Institute of Early American History and Culture at Williamsburg, Virginia. My own interest in this organization was intense, and for several years I took an active part in it. Its field of activity coincided with research in American colonial culture then under way at the Huntington Library. My report on the Institute's beginning notes:

On December 29 and 30 [1943] a meeting was held in Mr. John D. Rockefeller's offices in New York to consider means for advancing the investigation and interpretation of American civilization in the period up to and including Jefferson's second administration. Mr. Rockefeller and his son John D. Rockefeller III are both greatly interested in this project [creation of the Institute]. Many millions of Rockefeller money have gone into the physical restoration of Williamsburg, Virginia—the best example of a colonial town. Mr. Rockefeller is now interested in something more than a museum, and he proposes to foster research and historical writing in cultural history.

The meeting in New York was attended by Mr. Rockefeller's representatives, officials of the College of William and Mary, and a group of historians interested in this period.

It was decided to create an Institute for Early American History and Culture, to have its headquarters in Williamsburg. The Institute will be conducted jointly by Colonial Williamsburg, Inc. (the Rockefeller organization), and the College of William and Mary. Its policies will be guided by a small Advisory Board. As soon as war conditions clear somewhat, a small permanent research staff will be gathered at Williamsburg and fellows will be appointed. The library facilities at Williamsburg will be greatly expanded by the Rockefeller organization. Scholars of the Institute, however, will work wherever their projects dictate.

Since the Huntington Library is particularly rich in Virginia material and in other colonial fields, opportunities will occur for mutual help. At the meeting of the Board I expressed the view that we would be interested in the activities of the new organization and would cooperate wherever possible.

The editorial policies of the *William and Mary College Quarterly* have been completely revised, and this journal will be the official publication of the Institute for Early American History and Culture.

Another project to promote the study of Anglo-American civilization under the auspices of the Institute for Advanced Study at Princeton, with the active collaboration of the Huntington Library and the John Simon Guggenheim Memorial Foundation, was enthusiastically discussed but, alas, adequate funding by the Institute was not found. This failure was a disappointment to Frank Aydelotte, director of the Institute and chairman of the Advisory Board of the Guggenheim Foundation, and to others involved. My report of 1944 describes the plans.

Plans are being made by the Institute for Advanced Study at Princeton, in cooperation with Princeton University and the Guggenheim Foundation, to set up a section devoted to the study of the European and British backgrounds of American civilization.

A report on what might be done, which I was asked to present, was accepted as a basic plan of operation.

Within the next few years the Institute has fairly definite assurances of receiving large sums of money which can be devoted to this purpose.

The plan is to appoint professors of the Institute and fellows who will carry on their research and writing wherever they can do it best except for two short terms each year when they will be expected to be in residence in Princeton and to participate in seminars at the Institute.

The policies of this organization will be guided by a small and realistic Advisory Board.

Plans and a few appointments may be announced this year, but the program will not be fully developed until the war is over.

In a good many cases, scholars appointed by the Institute will need to work at the Huntington Library. Furthermore, the Institute is desirous of having the cooperation of members of the Huntington Library research staff. For example, from time to time, the Institute would like specialists from our staff to present reports and lead discussions in seminars there. I suggested that a certain amount of correlation of our own seminars with theirs might be possible, and I gave assurance that we would welcome scholars of the Institute to the Huntington Library.

My stay at Princeton during the period of this discussion was made miserable by a case of mononucleosis which I fought out at the Princeton Inn. When I finally was able to leave, Charles McIlwain, retired from Harvard and living at Princeton, offered to help me to the train at Princeton Junction. During the war porters were unavailable, and the kindness of this distinguished historian in helping a younger colleague to carry his bags onto a Pennsylvania train earned my eternal gratitude.

Membership on the Advisory Board of the Institute of Early American History and Culture proved a great satisfaction to me, for this board brought together some of the leading historians of the United States and gave an opportunity for the exchange of ideas and for congenial friendships. The annual two-day spring meetings at Williamsburg were convivial occasions, long to be remembered.

Another member was Alfred Knopf, the New York publisher—witty, sometimes caustic, but always stimulating and entertaining. In that somewhat sedate period of dress, Alfred's brilliant shirts and flamboyant neckties were only exceeded in color by Williamsburg's spring flowers. Alfred had been often at the Huntington Library, and we had already become friends, for he was profoundly interested in the West and was eager to publish Cleland's books and other Western historical works. Unhappily most of my own books at this time fell outside Alfred's immediate interest, and I could boast only one of his imprints, *The Atlantic Frontier*. For many years both Alfred and I served our statutory term of three years on the Institute board, retired for a year, and were reelected.

For a time I served as one of the editorial board of the rejuvenated *William and Mary Quarterly* and was on the editorial board of the *Journal of the History of Ideas* when that periodical was getting under way.

In 1942 the Guggenheim Foundation invited me to become a member of the Advisory Board, and thus began for me an official connection that lasted for twenty-nine years—until 1971. At this time Aydelotte was chairman of the Advisory Board and the Selection Committee, and not the wildest fantasy would have led me to dream that I would succeed him on his retirement in 1950. Being the newest member of the board in 1942 was sufficient honor. Henry Allen Moe, the secretary-general of the Guggenheim Foundation, whom I had known since he interviewed me for a fellowship in 1928, exerted a tremendous influence on American learning, and I was happy to have an opportunity to observe his methods, which were original and wise. But more of that later.

In 1945 the Guggenheim Foundation asked me to become a member of the Committee of Selection for the United States and Canada, a committee that included in these early years Dr. Florence Sabin, a physician and research associate of the Rockefeller Institute; Carl Sauer, professor of geography at the University of California at Berkeley; Wallace Notestein, professor of history at Yale; Linus Pauling, professor of biochemistry at Caltech, later a

109

Nobel laureate; Edwin Bidwell Wilson, professor of statistics in the Harvard School of Public Health. Wilson was one of the most learned—and most fascinating—men I ever knew, and I particularly treasure my long association with him. But more about him and other members of the Advisory Board later.

This chapter has dealt with a few of the extracurricular activities engaged in by some of us on the research staff of the Huntington in the first two decades of its development. It would be tedious to enumerate all the boards and committees on which we served. Let it suffice to say that our goal was to keep the Huntington Library in the main stream of American scholarship. The duties that this involved were sometimes arduous and included what seems in retrospect an incredible amount of speaking to this and that organization. How we prepared all the papers we presented, it is now difficult to comprehend.

Perhaps we were a bit naive in our zeal for learning. If we had stopped to contemplate our tasks, we might have remembered that some of the things we were trying to do had been on the agenda since Aristotle's time. But we were ambitious, enthusiastic, and convinced that significant erudition was worth the battle. Luckily for us, the dismal pall of hypocritical morality that stifles so much activity in Academia today had not descended upon the world. We never felt any pangs of guilt because we were not being our brother's keeper—to the distress of our brother—as so often happens today. We would have been horrified at any suggestion that we ought to squander our research funds "doing good" by the anonymous populace, providing them with entertainment or with programs of uplift. That, we would have argued, is the function of welfare organizations or of churches, but certainly not of a research library. We believed we had a high vocation to stimulate learning in its most advanced forms, and if some prophet of doom had warned us of an impending corruption of learning in the guise of righteousness, we would have been incredulous. Perhaps it is well that one cannot see into the future. If we had possessed that ability, it would have robbed us of incentive—and of a great deal of pleasure.

CHAPTER VI

Agony of Decision

IN FEBRUARY 1947, Charles W. Cole, president of Amherst College, wrote me as follows: "As you probably know the trustees of Amherst [who are also the trustees of the Folger Library] are looking for a new Director for the Folger Library to replace Dr. J. Q. Adams. My friend Professor [William] Haller of Barnard, and a number of other people, have told me that you can probably give us more help, advice, and assistance than anybody else in the country on this problem. I am going to be in Los Angeles March 6–9. I will communicate with you as soon as I get in town to see if I can arrange to come out and see you at the Huntington Library. I hope it will be possible to get together with you because I do feel you can help us greatly in our problem. I am looking forward to the opportunity of meeting you." My reply by telegraph was: "Will look forward to seeing you while in Los Angeles. Please plan to have luncheon with me at the Huntington Library one day while here."

That was the beginning of my association with the Folger Library, but at first it was strictly in an advisory capacity. President Cole came out and spent a day with us at the Huntington and gave us an opportunity to show him something of the working of an active research library. He explained that the trustees of Amherst College now faced a serious problem of trying to transform the Folger from a static collection into an efficient library for advanced scholars. They had received a great deal of criticism from all parts of the country because of the Folger's ineffectiveness as an institution and lack of hospitality to any except a small group of favored friends. What could they do? The trustees were being bombarded with letters suggesting needed improvements at the Folger, and

111

action was imperative. Where could they find an effective director?

Cole's statement came as no surprise, because it was common knowledge that the Folger was an unhappy place to work. It had virtually no reference collection to go with its rare books; the reading room, given over exclusively to eighteenth- and nineteenth-century editions of Shakespeare, was dark, ill-ventilated, and as hot as the Black Hole of Calcutta in summer. A guard with a pistol stood outside the entrance to the offices and reading room, which was barred by a heavy rope. Only a few readers, it was commonly averred, were ever admitted, and they had to have sponsors known to the staff. A letter from Don Cameron Allen, professor of Renaissance literature at Johns Hopkins University, summed up the complaints of many scholars—complaints that had become a major concern of the Amherst trustees: "A reference collection would help but decent and intelligent working conditions would go farther. My impression has always been that nobody ever gave a damn whether you worked there and they were happy to see you leave." So that was the problem with which Charlie Cole was wrestling.

We talked a great deal on that day in March, and he went away with a list of some of the ablest Renaissance scholars in America, any one of whom, in my opinion, would have made an imaginative director of the Folger Library. To a discreet query as to whether I would be interested, I emphatically ruled myself out of consideration. My own situation was too satisfactory in every respect to warrant a change. Furthermore, the problems of the Folger were so complex that only a reckless gambler would want to risk the throw of those dice.

But Charlie Cole impressed me enormously. Here was a historian with vitality, vivacity, imagination, and general good sense. I wished him well and could only envy an institution that had him for its administrative head. On March 22, 1947, he wrote: "I want to thank you again for the grand time you gave me at the Huntington. My only regret is that I did not have much more time to talk to you and see the Library. As it was, I got from you, and the way the Library is run, a great many helpful ideas, and I am sure I will be turning to you again and again for aid, comfort, and advice. I wish that San Marino were not 3,000 miles away."

Later, in the summer, Eustace Seligman, a member of the legal firm of Sullivan and Cromwell in New York and chairman of the Folger Committee of the Amherst trustees, invited me to lunch at Santa Barbara, where he and his wife were spending a vacation. He too had the problems of the Folger on his mind and asked many questions about what could be done to improve its reputation in the academic world.

I gave such information and advice as I could dredge up, and he asked if I would be willing to come to New York in October to tell the full board what the Folger might do to make itself more useful. Although I was trying to finish a book, and my publishing schedule was pressing, anything that one could do to advance learning appeared to be an obligatory public service, and I agreed to make a brief report to the Amherst trustees on the opportunities that lay before the Folger.

Because I had no personal interest in the Folger beyond its utility to scholarship in fields where my interest lay, I could view its problems with complete objectivity and felt no obligation to hedge my comments with tactful ambiguity. Hence the October report was critical—but positive rather than negative. The Folger might have pursued policies that had earned it the ill-will of many scholars, but that could be remedied by positive action to make it a genuine institution of learning, not merely the repository of a recherché collection on Shakespeare. My notes, scribbled on half-sheets during the train trip to New York, are still readable. They emphasized the significance of the acquisitions made during the administration of Joseph Q. Adams, the first director. Adams had been determined to gather as many Renaissance books as possible while they could still be found on the open market at reasonable prices. He had negotiated the purchase of the Harmsworth Collection, which transformed the Folger overnight from a mere Shakespeare collection into a significant Renaissance library. This now imposed upon the Folger an obligation to develop research in every aspect of sixteenth- and seventeenth-century civilization above and beyond its accustomed, and conventional, Shakespearean studies.

The Folger must shift its emphasis from preciosity to utility. That was an obligation to learning that scholars throughout the land were demanding. Any director whom the trustees appointed would have to implement such a program. The Folger should make an effort to gain the support and friendship of scholars everywhere in a broad spectrum of learning—something it had previously neglected.

It was imperative for the Folger to acquire an adequate reference library and to make a useful catalogue, not an elaborate bibliography of rare books that would never be finished (its current endeavor).

The reading room should be humanized with proper lighting, ventilation, and air conditioning. Noiseless rental typewriters should be made available to readers.

In order to encourage scholars to come to the Folger, a series of conferences on pertinent topics might be held; more short-term fellowships might be made available to really competent people; and a reduction in the budget for unnecessary guards might be devoted to some aspect of scholarship.

The Folger had an opportunity to collaborate with other research institutions. For example, it would be desirable to work out a plan for joint fellowships offered by the Huntington and the Folger (something already of interest to me). The two institutions might even think of sponsoring publications of mutual interest. We might work out a scheme for noncompetitive buying of rare books.

The Folger should immediately launch a campaign to procure the basic books required by a scholar to carry on any significant research. It should give priority to such purchases and defer spending its limited book budget on rarities until this need had been satisfied.

The Folger might contemplate raising money for rare-book purchases by selling some of its hoard of duplicate editions, something that a few bibliophiles would regard as heresy. But it would be better to have two really significant books than two copies of the same book with the mere possibility of a variant spelling in one.

Some alterations in the interior of the building might be necessary to improve facilities. Air conditioning should be installed.

The trustees should be aware that *any changes* would be certain to result in criticism from a few members of the staff, from a few cronies who had special privileges at the Folger, and from a few Shakespeare idolaters who regarded any dilution of Shakespeare's works housed in the Folger Library as a profanation.

My remarks based on these notes were listened to intently, and when I had finished the chairman of the full board asked me if I could wait outside the board room in case the trustees had any further inquiries to make. Within a few minutes he reappeared and asked me to come in again.

"If we agreed to all of your suggestions, would you be willing to accept the directorship?" was the question he asked.

My surprise was genuine and complete. It had not occurred to me, after my clear statement to both Cole and Seligman of a lack of interest in such an offer, that the trustees would again ask if I could be available. So I thanked them for the expression of confidence and asked for time to think it over.

Back in my hotel, I again made notes, still preserved on the hotel's stationery, listing this time the assets of my job in California versus the new opportunities in Washington. On paper the assets in California were clearly superior, and a move looked foolish, financially and academically. And yet Cole and Seligman were men whom I instantly liked, and the full board of trustees had impressed me as a remarkable group of men with whom it would be easy to work. I would go home to California, talk it over with my wife, and contemplate the future.

Although the Amherst trustees had offered me an adequate salary in 1947 dollars, my total income in California was greater, and a move East would entail financial loss. The trustees had assured me that the Folger had a commodious director's house on Foxhall Road, one of the most favored streets in Washington, but it was not likely to be as charming as our Spanish house in San Marino, with its olive tree in the patio, its fountain, its kumquat trees and camellias. We had friends throughout California, especially in our immediate region, and why should we leave them for the transient society of political Washington? My research projects could be carried on in San Marino with a minimum of frustration; furthermore the Huntington guaranteed me all the research assistance I could use. One of my assistants was Marion Tinling, a girl of remarkable skill who had collaborated with me in transcribing from the shorthand and editing *The Secret Diary of William Byrd of Westover, 1709–1712*. Already projected was a paperback edition of Shakespeare's works, each play in a separate cover. The publishers had assured me that such an edition would provide a royalty income that would be a welcome supplement to a retirement pension. Why leave all this to take an administrative job in Washington?

But the Amherst trustees had made their offer attractive too. Adequate research assistance of my own choosing would be available. My research projects (including the single-play edition of Shakespeare's works) need not be abandoned. Some years later, when the first play was ready for publication, it was with some regret I agreed to its being called "The Folger Library General Reader's Shakespeare." Lingering hostility to the Folger here and there made me dubious about this title, but something was necessary to indicate to the public that the Folger was not merely a mausoleum where nothing happened. Christian Herter, then a congressman from Massachusetts, had told Charlie Rugg, general counsel for the Amherst trustees: "You have got to let the public know that something worthwhile goes on in that whited sepulchre over there. If you don't, the Folger Library is going to find itself on the tax rolls." Acting on that hint, we put the Folger name on the edition but it remained my property. It was impossible ever to ascertain whether the name hurt or helped the sale of the books.

On one of those October days in 1947, when every influence was arguing against my accepting the Folger offer, our own trustees had a meeting scheduled. As usual it fell to my lot to go over to Millikan's office at 11:00 A.M., brief him on what had to be done at the board meeting, and give him the papers that he, as chairman of the board, needed to sign. We had lunch together at the Athenaeum and parted to meet again in the board room at the library at 2:00 P.M. By that time Millikan had forgotten what I had told him and lost the papers—not unusual in his last years as a trustee. Jim Page at this meeting was beating his favorite tom-tom about the folly of paying scholars to come to the Huntington when we ought to be looking for another Gainsborough portrait for the art gallery. Suddenly I knew I was tired, tired of arguing with old men who reminded me of my grandfather—and who, in their kindly fashion, treated me like a grandson. At that moment I decided to go to Washington.

But other motivations had been operating on my subconscious. Life had become too easy, even with all the frustrations that a board of ancient trustees precipitated. The critical work of developing the Huntington Library had been done. I believed, perhaps naively, that it would run now on its own momentum. If I remained in San Marino, life would continue to be pleasant but the excitement would diminish with the passing years. I was now forty-eight years old. Unless I was willing to settle into the Nirvana that so many Californians appeared to relish, I must seek a new life. The last lines of Tennyson's "Ulysses" haunted me:

> One equal temper of heroic hearts,
> Made weak by time and fate, but strong in will
> To strive, to seek, to find, and not to yield.

Age forty-eight was too early to yield to Nirvana.

When I went to tell Millikan of my decision, he gave me a grandfatherly lecture on the folly of accepting an administrative post: "Some people will praise an administrator for what he does, but it is far less important than a man's research. Anybody can be an administrator; few have the capacity to complete research of great importance." This was the view of a Nobel Prize winner in physics, but he had forgotten that the research worker whom he was addressing had been burdened also with administrative labors at the Huntington, often with responsibility without authority. Furthermore, the administrative post to which I was going provided an opportunity to develop new fields of research. Surely that was worthwhile, for me and for the profession.

My letter of acceptance was sent to President Cole in late October. My tenure at the Folger would begin on July 1, 1948. In the meantime, Charlie Cole and I had much planning to do, and I exercised a sort of remote control of affairs at the Folger.

CHAPTER VII

Problems of the Folger Library

THE PROBLEMS OF THE FOLGER LIBRARY that so perplexed and troubled the trustees of Amherst College in 1947 were of long accumulation and did not reflect on the judgment of Joseph Q. Adams, an honored and distinguished scholar who had served as head of the library, first as acting director and then as director, from 1934 until his death on November 10, 1946. Adams, who had been a brilliant professor of English at Cornell University, was a South Carolinian and a long-time friend of mine. Whenever I visited Washington I called upon him and profited from his wise and witty conversation. Many times he explained that he believed his first obligation at the Folger was to use his energy and the money available to him for the acquisition of Renaissance books that might never come into the market again. Adams was correct in his assessment of the situation. He had remarkable success in adding to the Folger collections books and manuscripts of immense literary and historical value.

In the meantime, if other elements in the Folger's development suffered, it was not Adams's fault. Stanley King, who became president of Amherst College in 1932 and was ex officio liaison officer between the library and the trustees, has described the early days of the Folger in a charming essay, *Recollections of the Folger Shakespeare Library* (1950). Much that King leaves vague can be read between the lines.

Henry Clay Folger, who left his fortune to found the library that bears his name, remains a somewhat shadowy figure because, unlike some other captains of industry, he was a quiet, studious man who avoided the trappings of social splendor and was rarely

119

the subject of newspaper publicity. A graduate of Amherst College in the class of 1879, he went to work for the Standard Oil Company and, when anti-trust action split up the company, became president of the Standard Oil Company of New York. Thrifty and conservative, he accumulated a fortune, not one of the great fortunes but several millions, with which he endowed the library.

Undramatic and sober as was Folger's life, his accomplishments illustrated so clearly the opportunities in the United States for a young man to rise in the world by his own diligence and integrity that I was asked on a number of occasions to describe his career on the "Voice of America." He had demonstrated the value of the work ethic, and, in the end, he had given back to the public all he had earned to create something that he believed would improve our cultural life. The "Voice of America" discovered that listeners in other nations found the quiet life of Henry Clay Folger of greater interest than the doings of more dazzling types.

Folger was born in New York City on June 18, 1857, the son of a wholesale milliner in moderate circumstances.[1] He was a lineal descendant of Benjamin Franklin's maternal grandfather, Peter Folger, one of the pioneer settlers on Martha's Vineyard and Nantucket. Young Henry Clay Folger gained his early education at Adelphi Academy in Brooklyn, where he had as a classmate Charles M. Pratt, son of one of John D. Rockefeller's partners. This friendship was fortunate for Folger because the two boys went together to Amherst, and, when they graduated, young Pratt's father gave them both jobs in the oil business.

Young Folger's letters written to his mother from Amherst give an indication of his developing character.[2] Much time was devoted to Latin, Greek, and mathematics, but he was careful to assure his family that he was not neglecting his health. He took regular exer-

---

[1] In *The Folger Library: A Decade of Growth, 1950–1960* (Washington, D.C.: The Folger Library, 1960), I gave a brief summary of Folger's career. Some material in this chapter is excerpted from that publication.

[2] I am indebted to Mrs. Laetitia Yeandle for transcripts of these letters from the Folger Archives. I have altered the punctuation and capitalization in two or three instances.

cise, sometimes in the gymnasium but often merely taking walks. He had a boy's healthy appetite and was eloquent on the subject whenever any classmate got a box of provisions from home. Henry's letters home assured his parents of his regard for thrift. One of his fellow students had received a dressing gown, "a very handsome one in drab and red," and Folger wrote home that he needed "some sort of garment to put on while studying to save my coat." On one occasion he wrote that "I have some sewing to do this afternoon; my pants are ripped." When he indulged himself by buying a few envelopes with the college seal, he sent his next letter "in a monogram envelope so you can see the monogram. We like it very much, but each envelope cost a cent and a half, so we don't use them often."

Folger and his schoolmates tried various ways of saving money. On January 9, 1876, he wrote his mother: "Frank brought up with him a small flat-iron and last night he washed and ironed.... By this we can make quite a saving." A week later this thrifty scheme of doing their own laundry came to grief. After washing his clothes, he decided to dry them on top of a warm stove and "set out for a skate ... thinking I had saved a quarter of a dollar." When he returned the garments "were reduced to cinders.... I intend to try the experiment again next week and if it fails then will no longer cheat my washerperson.... I will put a line around the stove then." After further scorchings of towels and handkerchiefs, the boys began "to debate whether or not it is a real saving to wash our own clothes" and decided not.

In his senior year Henry wrote his mother that "base-ball fever has again attacked the fellows.... I have neither money nor time to invest in that way [i.e., buy a season ticket] but shall see the College games."

Although Folger could not spare time for all the baseball games, he did find time in his last semester to play Dick Deadeye in a performance of Gilbert and Sullivan's *H.M.S. Pinafore*. Music was one of his delights, and he liked to sing. On May 18, 1879, he wrote his mother: "Today [we heard] a returned missionary, who should have been eaten abroad rather than suffered to be served up to our more fastidious tastes. We had a mighty pleasant sing on the front steps this evening. Music will be something I will miss when I leave College."

In a letter of June 15 to his mother, he made a comment that had great significance in the light of later events. A member of the faculty whom he disliked (and called "the Fossil") had been asked to preach on the last Sunday before Folger's graduation. He wrote: "As this is our last Sunday, we are having the Fossil, a very impolitic movement on the part of the President if he wishes us, in the future when we are rich and able to endow the College, to have pleasant recollections of our last days here." But he was cheered at the praise he had received for his part as Dick Deadeye in *Pinafore:* "They say Deadeye did quite well considering that he was an amateur in acting as well as in singing."

Concerning graduation events, he wrote on June 22: "Friday evening was devoted to the President's reception. Quite a success in its way, but my ideal of a stupid evening—chin [talk], promenading, and a light supper. I was supremely unhappy.... Moody is preaching today. I don't like him. I can stand bad grammar and poor language, but coarseness in the pulpit seems to me disgustingly out of place."

These letters were indicative of a sensitive character, a young man of cultivation and good taste, who early in life would find in William Shakespeare a satisfaction that others might have sought in sports, gallantry, or the "good life."

On his last day at Amherst, he was not yet clear as to his future course: "I'm undecided about next year—about what I ought to do. It is not seldom [*sic:* often?] that a fellow has two courses open to him, and the reasons seem equally strong for either." Unlike St. Paul, when the scales fell from his eyes, he did not go over into Macedonia, but into an oil company—a decision that was lucky for Amherst and the Folger Library.

While working for the oil company, Folger studied law at Columbia University and received the LL.B. degree in 1881. As a result of extra courses in political science at Columbia, Amherst College awarded him an M.A. degree the following year.[3] On Oc-

[3]Some information adapted from *The Folger Library: A Decade of Growth.*

tober 6, 1885, Folger married Emily C. Jordan, a graduate of Vassar College, who was to share his interests and his enthusiasm in book collecting for the next forty-five years.

At Amherst College, Folger had heard Ralph Waldo Emerson deliver one of his last lectures and had been inspired by Emerson's comments on Shakespeare. He had also enjoyed the college classes in English literature and had won a prize for an essay entitled "Dickens as a Preacher." At Vassar, Emily Jordan had written an essay on Shakespeare which may have helped to shape her own later interests. Soon after leaving college, Folger bought a cheap little set of Shakespeare, the Handy Volume Edition, in thirteen volumes, published by Routledge. The Folger Library still has the set. From this beginning grew one of the greatest collections of Shakespeare in the world. In 1886 Folger bought a copy of the Halliwell-Phillipps facsimile of the First Folio of 1623, for which he paid what was to him at that time the stupendous sum of $107.50.

From this time onward Folger was a "collector" with a particular avidity for Shakespeare Folios. By the end of his career he had garnered seventy-nine copies of the First Folio of 1623; fifty-eight copies of the Second Folio of 1632; twenty-four copies of the Third Folio of 1663–64; and thirty-six of the Fourth Folio of 1685. At some point in his collecting of Folios he conceived the idea that the collation of multiple copies would reveal something significant about the text of Shakespeare, but precisely what would be disclosed is not clear. Actually, this collection of multiple copies has proved of greater interest to students of Elizabethan printing than to editors of Shakespeare.

While he was beginning his career as a collector of books, Folger was prospering in business. Although he never became fabulously wealthy, he acquired a fortune that permitted him to indulge his fancy for rare books. After holding the presidency of the Standard Oil Company of New York from 1911 to 1924, he became chairman of the board until his retirement in 1928.

Because he and Mrs. Folger had no children, they devoted their interest—and their fortune—to book collecting and to planning a library that would eventually house their acquisitions. Although Folger's insatiable appetite for Shakespeare Folios gave him the

123

reputation of having a single-track mind interested only in Shakespeare—a reputation that has dogged the Folger Library ever since—actually his interests were much broader than Shakespeare, and he laid the foundation for the great scholar's library of Tudor and Stuart history and literature that the Folger Library has become.

A pathetic irony of Folger's life was that one of the most sensitive, intelligent, and well-read of the great collectors of his period never saw his books spread out before him and did not live to see his library building completed. On June 11, 1930, he died, two weeks after the cornerstone of the building was laid. Two years later the building was finished, and the books he had brought together with so much thought and effort were placed on the shelves. Before this, as each parcel of books had arrived, Mr. and Mrs. Folger had unwrapped them, listed their titles in little black notebooks, and shipped them away for safekeeping because there was not room for them in their house. This procedure earned for Folger an unfavorable reputation as a miser of books, and he was the object of critical comment by scholars on both sides of the Atlantic, who accused him of buying books to store away in vaults where they would never be seen.

Folger confided his plans for a great research library to few people except his wife. Although work on a mysterious building at the corner of Second and East Capitol Streets in Washington actually got under way in the spring of 1930, hardly anyone except his legal counsel, the architect, and the builders knew what it was to be. Curiously, even the president of Amherst College did not know that the trustees of the College had been designated as administrators of Folger's bequest until he read the story in the *New York Times* shortly after the donor's death.

The terms of Folger's will provided that a substantial proportion of the income from his bequest would go to Amherst College in compensation for the services of the trustees of the college in administering the trust.

Mrs. Folger survived her husband by six years and lived to see the Library in operation. When she died on February 21, 1936, she left her residual estate to the trustees of Amherst College for the benefit of the Folger Library.

Although Folger was himself a New Yorker with academic degrees from Amherst College and Columbia University, he chose as the site for his library a block adjacent to the Library of Congress in Washington because he realized that Washington inevitably would be a center for research. Proximity to the Library of Congress, he knew, would be an advantage to scholars working in his own library. The wisdom of his choice has been amply demonstrated.

For the architect of his building, he chose Paul Philippe Cret of Philadelphia, who persuaded him that the Elizabethan structure which he had in mind would not be suitable in a Washington setting. Instead, Cret designed a dignified exterior in white marble, classical in simplicity, with an emphasis upon vertical and horizontal lines, a building modern in interpretation yet belonging to no period. Along the north wall are nine bas-reliefs by John Gregory depicting scenes from Shakespeare's plays. The architect achieved an Elizabethan atmosphere in the paneled main reading room and the exhibition gallery. A replica, much reduced in size, of a characteristic Elizabethan playhouse occupies the east end of the building.

The founder probably never dreamed that his library would attract large numbers of scholars from all over the world. He conceived of the reading room as a place where a few interested people would gather in the genteel atmosphere of a gentleman's library. As a result, the practical facilities needed by a busy research library were lacking, and in later years the Library has undergone a few architectural modifications to make it efficient without destroying its architectural beauty.

The Folger Library opened in 1932 with the books acquired in the founder's lifetime. But a collection of books is not a library, and the transformation of a collector's acquisitions into an efficient research library is a slow and sometimes tedious process requiring expert knowledge and patience.

The first two or three years were consumed in housekeeping details, and the first significant development of the collection as a library began in 1934 with the appointment of Adams as director.

During his twelve years' tenure the library made phenomenal growth.

One of the extraordinary opportunities in the history of twentieth-century libraries came in 1938 when the Folger Library managed to acquire the great private collection that had been brought together by Sir Leicester Harmsworth at Bexhill in Sussex. The story of the negotiations leading to this purchase has been told by Stanley King in his *Recollections*. Rarely in the history of libraries have the scope and purpose of a significant institution been changed overnight by the purchase of a single collection. Yet that is precisely what the acquisition of the Harmsworth Collection did for the Folger. One day it was a tidy little library with a remarkable collection of the Elizabethan period focused upon Shakespeare. The next day it was one of the four most significant libraries in the world for English books on every subject printed before 1641, books listed in Pollard and Redgrave's *Short-Title Catalogue of Books . . . 1475–1640*. Because this catalogue includes all the titles then known to the compilers to have been printed in England or in English within the inclusive dates, it is convenient to refer statistically to the period "before 1641." The original Folger collection concentrated upon belles lettres; the Harmsworth Collection was as broad as the field of human life and thought. Although Harmsworth had himself acquired many fine books of belles lettres, his collection and the original Folger nucleus complemented rather than duplicated each other. The original Folger books listed in Pollard and Redgrave's *Short-Title Catalogue* numbered something over 6,000 titles. In the Harmsworth Collection the Folger acquired approximately 10,500 titles.[4] With the acquisition of this collection the Folger Library shifted its emphasis from a concentration upon literature to a concern for the whole of the civilization of the periods covered by its collections.

During Adams's administration other unusual opportunities

---

[4]The significance of this acquisition is pointed out by Louis B. Wright, "The Harmsworth Collection and the Folger Library," *The Book Collector*, 5 (1957): 123–28, from which a few of the foregoing statements have been taken.

occurred to procure fine books in the period before 1641, and he made the most of them. In a report published in 1942, covering the preceding history of the Library's development, he enumerated many of the most noteworthy acquisitions: a group of approximately 450 titles not included in the first Harmsworth purchase, found by Adams in a stable at Bexhill and later bought from the Harmsworth trustees; a large number of rare copies of Elizabethan plays; many miscellaneous books of great rarity published before 1641; valuable works of music for the early period; a drama collection in manuscript beginning with three rare morality plays of the fifteenth century and including a number of sixteenth- and seventeenth-century English plays; a remarkable collection of manuscripts preserved at Loseley House, Surrey, including a collection of letters of John Donne and documents concerned with the Blackfrairs playhouse; an extraordinary collection of 137 documents, for the most part personal letters, dating from the early seventeenth century (the gift of Arthur A. Houghton, Jr.); and the Dobell Collection of John Dryden and Drydeniana. These are merely a few of the highlights in the assiduous collecting carried on by Adams. The report of his activities up to 1941 required sixty-one pages.

The acquisition of the Dryden collection and other important late-seventeenth-century items was significant, for it rounded out dramatic materials for the Restoration period that Folger himself had begun to collect, and it gave an impetus to the more active collecting of materials from the second half of the seventeenth century that the Library has pursued in later years.

Few libraries have acquired such valuable books in so short a time as the Folger received during Adams's administration. He was a discriminating and persistent hunter of books, and the Folger is under an eternal debt to him for his accomplishments. He gave his energies to book collecting, and it is fortunate that he did. The routine development of a library program could wait; the opportunities to acquire rare books and manuscripts obtained by Dr. Adams will not occur again.

The extensive collections concerned with almost every phase of the civilization of Tudor and Stuart England, brought together during the Folger's first sixteen years, made the organization of the materials into an effective working library imperative.

Adams had recruited a small group of Elizabethan scholars as members of his staff. These included James G. McManaway, Giles E. Dawson, Dorothy E. Mason, and Paul Dunkin. McManaway and Dawson were drama specialists; Miss Mason had worked on the variorum edition of Spenser at Johns Hopkins University; Dunkin was a classicist and an expert cataloguer. All four of these staff members remained with the library for many years and contributed to its development. But they were specialists, more interested in scholarship than in solving administrative problems that the library faced after Adams's death. Their concentration on their particular interests had resulted in a neglect of public relations and a failure to establish a broad base of good will. When my appointment as director was announced, I received a barrage of letters, a vast dossier that I have retained, offering suggestions about what the Folger Library ought to do to serve the interest of learning—and to improve its image in Academia.

The trustees of Amherst had also been receiving many letters of complaint and they took steps to insure that the Folger Library would become more aware of its obligation to the scholarly public. A long letter to the new director signed by Charles W. Cole, President of Amherst College, and Eustace Seligman, chairman of the Folger Committee of the Amherst Trustees, outlined the wishes of the trustees. Because it immediately became the blueprint for the transformation of the Folger into an effective working library, it is reproduced here in its entirety:

> In your thinking and planning for the future of the Folger Library, we thought it might be helpful to you to have a statement of the general position and policy of the Folger Committee and of the Board of Trustees and we, therefore, are sending you this summary in the belief that it will be of use to you, both now and after you take up your duties at the Library.
>
> We have made a study of the relations of the Folger Library to American learning. We have given particular attention to its strength, and its potentialities as an active scholarly institution contributing to the advancement of significant learning in the literary,

intellectual, and social history of the sixteenth and seventeenth centuries. By the acquisition of the Harmsworth Collection the Folger Library assumed an obligation to extend its area of scholarly activity beyond Shakespearean research to include the social and intellectual background of Shakespeare's age and the social forces which grew out of that age.

We, and the other members of the Folger Committee, have consulted a number of scholars in an effort to find out what scholars most want from the Folger Library and how it can best serve the needs of learning. From the advice received it is clear that the time has come to take a further step in the Library's development in order that it may become a more effective research institution and take a more active part in historical study.

The Trustees of Amherst College, therefore, have appointed you director to carry out a policy looking toward the active encouragement of research and would wish you to take such action as may be necessary to give the Library greater practical utility in the advancement of literary and historical learning.

To that end, you should proceed with the development of a reference collection to be easily accessible to scholars using rare books and manuscripts. It will be remembered of course that the proximity of the Library of Congress makes an extensive collection unnecessary, but in the opinion of all working scholars consulted, the efficient use of rare books and manuscripts depends upon the accessibility of standard reference works, critical editions of authors represented in the Folger collections, the most useful biographies and historical treatises, and similar works constantly needed in research.

A simplified catalogue of all reference works should be made as rapidly as the books are acquired, and the catalogue should be made easily accessible to readers.

The reference collection should be placed in the reading room, if possible, where books can be consulted with a minimum of delay and without the need of expensive servicing by the Library staff. This practice, followed by the British Museum and other well-regulated libraries, is urged by scholars who have felt the handicap of the Folger's lack of accessible reference works.

It is desirable that a simplified catalogue or checklist of the Library's holdings of rare books and manuscripts be made easily accessible to readers.

It is desirable that the Library take all practicable measures to increase the ease and efficiency of research, and that it enlist the cooperation and friendly interest of scholars qualified to make the best use of the collections.

You should make a study of the physical arrangements of the entire building with a view to the more efficient use of space, the saving of time in routine operations, and the elimination of unnecessary expense.

It is desirable that the Library continue its policy of acquiring significant source materials in the field of its strength. Concerning the purchase of rare books, we have received a great deal of counsel from scholars deeply interested in the Library's future. The burden of this advice is that the Folger Library should make a careful distinction between rare books which may be merely bibliographical curiosities, or of interest only as collectors' items, and those which are useful tools for research. Many books are valuable to collectors simply because they are rare or represent variants in printing. The Folger's funds are insufficient to permit the buying of collectors' items because of some slight bibliographical or antiquarian interest.

You should study the problem of supplementing rare materials by the judicious purchase of photostats and microfilm of books which cannot be obtained otherwise or which may be too expensive to warrant the purchase of originals.

The Library already possesses many duplicate copies of rare books. The discreet sale or exchange of these duplicates to enable the Library to increase its collection of significant books may be desirable. It may be possible likewise to sell or exchange some of the material, aside from books, in the collections of the Library and to purchase books with the proceeds.

You will, we hope, make a study of the public exhibitions to see whether a shorter open period, say from 1:00 to 4:30 P.M. five days a week, might effect a saving in the time of the staff and possibly an economy in the cost of guards and janitors. A careful investigation should be made of the present methods and the present cost of the service of guards and janitors with a view of economizing on this heavy outlay. You should likewise investigate the need of maintaining the present bindery and the cost thereof.

You should also explore the possibility of cooperation and collaboration between the Folger Library and other research libraries and institutions. Such cooperation might take the form of temporary exchanges of staff members, joint appointments of research fellows, joint publications, non-competitive book buying, exchange of photostats and microfilm, etc.

The efficient operation of a small closely knit institution like the Folger Library depends upon the harmony and cooperation of its staff. You should stand ready to take whatever steps may be necessary to insure efficiency and harmony in the staff by the adjustment of their duties and responsibilities as changing conditions may require. We are conscious of the loyalty and perseverance of the staff of the Folger Library and believe that their cooperation and teamwork in the period of transition will bring results pleasing to both the staff and to scholars who will use the Library.

The implementation of this mandate was not easy. Fortunately I had the full support of the trustees and the loyal cooperation of the staff that I had inherited. McManaway and Dawson took time from academic projects they had under way to help in the reorganization of the Library. Miss Mason was responsible for improving relations with readers. And Dunkin a little later was responsible for making the catalogue into a useful bibliographical tool.

One of our first changes was to take pistols from the guards and remove a barrier blocking entrance to the reading room. The appearance of the place began to look less like a fortress and more like an institution of learning. Because the guards did not put in a full day as guards, they took over most of the custodial duties and thus enabled us to eliminate several janitors. Only one guard, newly hired, complained. After a few days he decided to quit. "My wife won't let me touch a broom," he explained. "That's woman's work." I told him I too had been exposed to brooms but had never felt it demeaning, and thus we parted. Our guards were a remarkable group of men. The captain in charge, Harold Byrd, had been a carpenter during the construction of the building. Another, John Wolff, had also worked on the building and knew the location of every hidden pipe and electric circuit, some of which had been changed after the architects' blueprints were completed. We made him superintendent of the building. One engineer, Charles K. Rogers, eighty-four years old and still vigorous when I came to the Folger, had worked on the Panama Canal and had a wide-ranging curiosity, including a concern for old books. Now and again he would bring in a useful item purchased in a second-hand bookstore and present it to the Folger.

The recruitment of an efficient and loyal staff, both professional and custodial, had priority in my obligations, and the time devoted to this duty over the years was well spent. It seemed to me necessary for the head of the institution to know what was going on in every department and then to delegate responsibility to those best able to carry out their respective duties. To do that an executive must know his people, and I saw to it that my door was always open to anyone with a problem, from an apprentice engineer to the head of a professional department. Although all staff members knew that they could come to my office and talk over their difficulties, no one ever wasted my time. Through the years I was able to regard all the staff as respected—and respectful—friends. It was my observation that one did not have to encourage "hail-fellow-well-met" familiarity to accomplish this but to show genuinely sincere interest in staff members as individuals.

The competence of the Folger staff and their devotion to the well-being of the institution proved the Library's greatest asset during my twenty years as director. Their knowledge, skill, and loyalty were such that I never had a moment's concern when official duties took me overseas for a month at a time or longer.

To serve as assistant to the director, I brought from the Huntington Library Eleanor Pitcher, who was placed in charge of acquisitions. She already had years of successful experience at the Huntington in book purchasing. After the reorganization of the Folger we accelerated our buying program. Miss Pitcher, a remarkable detective in search of rare books, was detailed to spend half of each year in Europe with headquarters in England. She scoured Great Britain and the Continent and found booksellers unknown to most collectors. I also tried to get around to many of them and to establish friendly relations. We discovered one highly effective technique of outwitting competitive buyers: we paid our bills immediately on receipt of the books. Many small booksellers operated on a shoestring without capital, and prompt payment saved them interest charges at their banks. American libraries frequently took months to process bills. We paid promptly and were given first offer of books in our fields of interest.

Antiquarian booksellers often proved to be fascinating personalities, sometimes eccentric, frequently learned, almost invariably men of their word, and usually good company. One of the oddest types that I encountered was an amateur archaeologist and a collector of books for himself. By trade he had been a wigmaker. Yet he had a house in the south of England filled with books: room after room piled with books, sometimes in chaotic heaps in the middle of the floor. Miss Pitcher and I once spent a day there searching through the piles. We sometimes had to turn over rubbish with a hayfork while the erstwhile bookseller dug up Roman pottery in his garden. At the end of the day he came in, looked over our selections, and put prices on them. "But I can't sell you that one," he would sometimes say. "I didn't know I had it and want it for my personal collection. Thank you for finding it." I registered a hope that I would outlive him and buy from his heirs the books he would not sell.

The Folger reading rooms, it was obvious, would be the key to our success in winning the good will of the academic public. Miss Mason was ultimately made reference librarian and proved of invaluable assistance to scholars with difficult problems. She made hundreds of friends for herself and the Folger Library by her skillful assistance.

To administer reading-room services, we appointed Mrs. Elaine W. Fowler as supervisor. She had excellent qualifications as a graduate student of English literature and history combined with a knowledge of business organization acquired in a number of years with International Business Machines Corporation. As the wife of a captain in the United States Navy, she also had considerable experience in public relations and was the soul of tact. Although vigilant to protect the collections, she gave the impression that the reader was always right, and she and her staff invariably made readers feel welcome. The reading room received extravagant praise for its speed and efficiency in producing books and manuscripts required by readers. One English scholar declared that he could accomplish more in the Folger Library in three months than he could in a year in any library in Great Britain.

But this effectiveness was not accomplished in a day or a month. It resulted from several years of hard work. Our first undertaking was the installation of air conditioning throughout the building. The rare-book vaults were already cooled by an antiquated carbon dioxide system, but the rest of the Library lacked even adequate ventilation. For example, the main reading room, a beautiful Gothic interior with dark red oak timbers and stained glass windows, was virtually unendurable in warm weather. The lighting was handsome, ecclesiastically dim, and hot. So we began the installation of modern air conditioning during 1948, my first summer in Washington. I soon understood the apocryphal legend that British diplomats got hardship pay for serving in Washington in the summer. I found myself virtually glued to my office chair. Paper on which I tried to make notes was so damp and flimsy that the ink ran or the pen punched through. And every afternoon at closing time the heavens opened with a deluge, as if the Almighty wished to punish government workers on their way home for indolence during the day. I longed for the dry heat that I had left in California.

Next after air conditioning came the transformation of the reading room into a convenient place to work by putting reference works on the surrounding shelves. For some curious reason which I never comprehended, the reading room contained, not useful works, but eighteenth- and nineteenth-century editions of Shakespeare rarely if ever used. The few reference books possessed by the Folger Library were hidden away somewhere below stairs—and there was no adequate catalogue of them. The early theory behind the lack of a reference library was that a scholar could read a rare book in the Folger and use reference works across the street in the Library of Congress. This arrangement, of course, was utterly impracticable. A time check soon showed that the Folger catalogue staff alone, by frequent trips to the Library of Congress, lost more time—and therefore money—than the needed reference works would cost.

The Huntington Library had gathered an excellent reference collection and I simply got permission to photograph their catalogue cards of reference works in our fields of interest; we then used it as a buying list. In a much shorter time than I believed possible we had a working library that saved time for both Folger cataloguers and readers.

The Folger catalogue, such as it was in 1948, was also a curious anomaly, the creation of Edwin Willoughby, an eccentric who had been made head of the catalogue department sometime before. He invented a system of classification based on the name "William Shakespeare." Fortunately few reference works had been bought and thus classified. We quickly adopted the Library of Congress classification system and tried to forget "William Shakespeare" as a key to the location of books. More serious was a scheme to catalogue or rather to describe the rare books in infinite detail. The result had been an attempt at an elaborate bibliographical description on cards, even to hand-drawn pictures of watermarks in the paper and any other bibliographical curiosity. I calculated that it would take more than two hundred years to complete his task, even if we never bought another rare book. Even worse was the discovery that many bibliographical descriptions were inaccurate.

We had no recourse but to find another slot in the library for Willoughby and to make Paul Dunkin chief of the catalogue department. Dunkin was both competent and wise. He soon had a loyal catalogue staff diligently recataloguing both rare and modern books. Within a few years the Folger had a catalogue that any library might be proud to possess. When Dunkin resigned to become a professor of library science at Rutgers University, he was succeeded by Lilly Stone (now Mrs. John L. Lievsay), who carried on the traditions of accuracy and effectiveness that Dunkin had established.

Until he finally reached retirement age, Willoughby was a problem. If he did a stint at the reading-room desk, he would usually fall asleep. Working in the stacks on some bibliographical problem, he liked to sing—in ghostly tones that sometimes frightened new staff members unfamiliar with this phenomenon. Having written a monograph on the King James version of the Bible, Willoughby fancied that the archbishop of Canterbury might give him an honorary degree of doctor of divinity. To our embarrassment, he wrote the archbishop about the matter—on Folger Library stationery. Sometime later, at a reception at Lambeth Palace, the archbishop asked me quizzically about a "Folger man named Willoughby." I have now forgotten what I answered. Willoughby confessed to a colleague that he hoped to get a D.D. degree because he believed that St. Peter would pass him through the pearly gates if he had such a certificate. Poor Willoughby has long since been gathered to his reward, but he had to go without the archbishop's passport.

Our photographic department attained a reputation for excellence under the direction of Horace Groves, a man remarkable for his quiet efficiency and versatility. He had begun as a bookbinder but learned about photography as a hobby and soon became a professional. Horace was also a humanitarian, ready always to visit the sick, to help in any emergency, and to assist a staff member in distress. Every institution has great need for such a person, and Horace "without portfolio" filled an essential spot.

The Folger was fortunate in finding a bookbinder and restorer of unusual skill and devotion, a German-trained master craftsman named Robert Lunow. No book was so tattered and torn, or worm-eaten, that Lunow could not find a way to repair it, and his artistic bindings took prizes at exhibitions.

Among the unusual personalities I inherited in 1948 was a shy young secretary named Virginia LaMar. One of my first social duties was to present her with a staff wedding gift when she married a man named William Freund. Unhappily, the marriage did not endure, and under her maiden name, she later collaborated with me in editing the whole corpus of William Shakespeare's works. Miss LaMar eventually became my executive secretary and editor of all Folger Library publications. She was a prodigious worker, with one of the keenest minds and best memories I have ever encountered. Although she had gone to a good school, she had never darkened the doors of a college; yet she was one of the best-educated persons on the Folger staff. The work she did as editor of the Folger publications would have deserved a Ph.D. degree several times over. Many a time some learned academic with the usual panoply of advanced degrees turned in a manuscript that Miss LaMar found wanting and corrected—corrected tactfully so that the scholar got full credit for accuracy and learning.

When I arrived at the Folger Library in 1948, I already had plans, as I have mentioned, for an edition of Shakespeare's works, each play in a separate cover. Indeed, I had accepted the post with the understanding that I would have adequate assistance in carrying this task to completion. I considered the arrangement an essential insurance against the woefully inadequate retirement plan then in effect at the Folger. But not for ten years did I have time to begin the task of editing Shakespeare. When I did, I found in Virginia LaMar a skillful collaborator. In the end, we shared such royalties as we earned on a fifty-fifty basis, and she got full acknowledgment on the title pages as joint editor.

This edition was no scissors and paste job. For ten long years we labored at the task—on Saturdays, Sundays, evenings, holidays, and any other time we could salvage. Miss LaMar, meanwhile, was carrying a full load of responsibility as executive secretary and editor of Folger Library publications.

We collated every single word in every play and poem written by Shakespeare with Folio and Quarto versions as well as with the best modern editions, and we wrote notes that we believed would be clear and simple enough for the understanding of ordinary readers. We consciously avoided academic jargon and abracadabra. The plays have served a useful purpose. A photograph published in *The Army Times* in 1969 showed a private in Vietnam going into action with a Folger edition of *The Taming of the Shrew* fastened to the back of his helmet.

Virginia LaMar's death from pneumonia in January 1968 was a great loss to the Folger Library—and to learning. Two days before her death, Eleanor Pitcher also died. Thus the Folger staff was bereft of two of its most effective members.

Luckily we had able understudies at the Folger. Megan Lloyd became executive secretary and editor of Folger publications. Miss Lloyd had been a cataloguer, but she was familiar with all aspects of the Library and was a woman of unusual competence. In college she had majored in history and was interested in publishing. I felt extremely fortunate in having so able a person to succeed Miss LaMar. For several years Elizabeth Niemyer had been Miss Pitcher's understudy and had gone to Europe a number of times to learn all she could about booksellers. She had acquired an unusual knowledge of both booksellers and the Folger's acquisitions policy. Consequently she could carry on the work in which Miss Pitcher had been so successful.

For executive officer the Folger had been fortunate in adding to its staff Philip Knachel, a scholar who had taken his doctorate in medieval history at the Johns Hopkins University under the direction of Dr. Sidney Painter. Knachel had an interest in Tudor and French history. As he had also taken a degree in library science, he was placed in general charge of all technical library services. When I retired in 1968, Knachel, unfortunately for the Folger Library, declined to be considered for the directorship. Knachel had both the technical knowledge and the broad general scholarship ideal for a research library like the Folger. For a year, however, he ran the library with efficiency while the trustees searched for a successor. During that time the staff and the public found in Knachel an acting director who was both popular and effective.

Other members of the staff we gathered were equally competent and showed a remarkable interest in the activities of the Folger Library. Many could have earned more income elsewhere than the salaries that we were able to pay, but they steadfastly declined to be lured away. Our employment policy was to choose the brightest people we could find, give them technical training on the job, and keep them as happy as possible by letting them learn as much as they could about all aspects of the library's departments. Because the Folger is primarily a research library devoted to scholarship in Tudor and Stuart literature and history, we gave at intervals lectures on these subjects to which all staff members were invited to attend on library time.

We also began a publishing program that we hoped would induce staff members to develop intellectual hobbies that would result in publications over their names. In time, the Folger Library brought out a number of pamphlets under the general title of "Folger Booklets on Tudor and Stuart Civilization." The authors of a number of these were junior staff members who had developed an interest in themes like Elizabethan gardening or sports and pastimes from their acquaintance with the literature encountered in their routine duties. These booklets, incidentally, have had an enduring popularity and have been widely used in schools. Each was illustrated with pictures from the Folger collections. Although the series included items by seasoned scholars, one of the primary purposes in the beginning was to encourage the Folger staff to participate in scholarly activities and to feel that they were part of a significant enterprise, not just cogs in a machine. It was my conviction that no institution could be much better than the staff that ran it, and the Folger made every effort to maintain a well-disciplined and happy staff. The quality of our personnel was a marvel to every visitor, professional and otherwise, who came to the Folger Library.

Both staff and visiting scholars made important contributions to the publication program, especially as editors of significant texts in the series "Folger Documents of Tudor and Stuart Civilization." Louise Clubb, a former member of the staff and now a professor at the University of California at Berkeley, compiled a valuable catalogue of Italian plays in the Folger Library. John L. Lievsay, a former Folger Fellow and later professor of comparative literature at Duke University, made an important analysis of the library's other Italian holdings, an indication of the diversity of the Folger's materials.

CHAPTER VIII

"Our Enterprise Is First of All a Library"

On MAY 20, 1929, Henry Clay Folger wrote to Alexander B. Trowbridge, consulting architect, expressing his appreciation of a satisfactory conference about the building in progress. But he added that "it seems best to write" to confirm the results of their conversations. The essential portion of his letter follows.

> 1. We must try to keep in mind that our enterprise is, first of all, a Library, and while there are other features which we hope will be interesting to the public, that of the "Library" is all important. It will therefore be unwise to consider anything in connection with the theatre construction which encroaches on the space set aside for the main library room.
> 2. I have read again all the literature I have about the theatre construction, and am inclined to think any effort to reproduce permanently any one of the theatres known by name will involve too much risk of criticism, based on what is now known about such [a] theatre, or may later be discovered about it. Had we not, therefore, better try to construct a theatre which will suggest the several Elizabethan theatres, in a general way, rather than try to copy simply one of them?—that is, better be indefinite, and design something which will incorporate features from several of the theatres, and can be described simply as a theatre such as was used during the Shakespeare period. I am sorry to reach this conclusion, but of course lack of knowledge may lead us to offer something which may later be found incorrect. Yours very truly, H. C. Folger.

On June 24, 1929, Folger wrote to Paul P. Cret, the principal architect, quoting a note that he had previously sent to Trowbridge about the name of the building: "We have now come to the conclusion that the simplest form will be the best. Let us then put

140

on the building 'FOLGER SHAKESPEARE LIBRARY.' After all, our enterprise is primarily a Library, and all other features are supplemental." On August 10, 1929, he replied to an inquiry from Cret: "Shall the Theatre be fitted for Moving Pictures? No. The Theatre is to show the conditions under which the Elizabethan plays were presented, primarily, and any other use by us will be supplemental."

As it turned out in my time, the little theatre, designed as an exhibit and not as a place for the performance of plays or motion pictures, proved an embarrassment. Thoughtless visitors were constantly remarking: "What a lovely little theatre! Why don't you have Shakespearean plays here?" Folger had never dreamed of encroaching on library time, library energy, or library expense by using the little period room as a living theatre. The room could seat comfortably only about 250 people; the back areas of the stage were too cramped for practicable theatre production. Once in 1949 we permitted the Amherst Masquers (the college's play group) to stage *Julius Caesar;* it took me two weeks to work out of my legal difficulties, for I discovered that we had violated District fire laws, zoning laws, and committed other infractions. Furthermore, we had demonstrated that the Folger stage was unfitted for play production without alterations. And clearly we would violate the founder's wishes if we tinkered with the stage construction. So we confined our use of the theatre to lectures and musicales.

Actually, as anyone knows, the effort to produce plays and run a library within the same small physical structure would mean a devastating encroachment on the library's facilities and the staff's energies and time—not to mention the drain on the budget. We conceived of our vocation as scholarship, not neighborhood entertainment with amateur theatricals. In this decision we had the full support of President Cole of Amherst, himself a historian deeply concerned that the Folger should fulfill the trust that the founder had placed in the college trustees—that they should always remember Folger's injunction: "Our enterprise is first of all a Library."

During my twenty years as director, I was always conscious of the thrifty outlook of my New England trustees who, I knew, would take a dim view of any unnecessary drain on the budget. As a man of Scottish and French Huguenot ancestry myself, I shared the thrifty views of Amherst's treasurer, Paul Weathers. We sometimes disagreed over the precise allocation of funds, but we never failed to agree that we must live within our overall budget. In every year we were able to turn back various amounts to be reserved for contingencies, and we were therefore able to take advantage of many book-buying opportunities that came up unexpectedly in the course of the years.

The Amherst trustees, in whom Folger had vested his trust, were an extraordinarily broadminded and wise group to deal with. In my later years the chairman of the board was John J. McCloy, lawyer, financier, diplomat, and man of learning. Dealing with him was always a pleasure because of his knowledge, good will, and wisdom. The chairman of the Folger Committee was Eustace Seligman, a learned and brilliant lawyer and a man of many diverse interests. I greatly enjoyed my association with him and always left a meeting with him stimulated and elated. The principal liaison between the Amherst trustees and the Folger administration was President Cole. No institution could have been more fortunate. As a historian who had done a great deal of research in French economic history of the seventeenth century, he knew at first hand what a research library ought to do, and he supported our program with enthusiasm. No administrator could hope for more intelligent or wiser collaborators than Eustace Seligman and Charlie Cole. My lot was made easy because of their vision, and the Folger Library would have been kept from squandering its funds and energies in extraneous endeavors—even had its administration been so ill-advised as to try.

Through most of my years at the Folger, I was fortunate, as Amherst College was fortunate, in having trustees who were intelligent, informed, and wise—men willing to determine policy on the basis of their own knowledge and assurance, not from something they learned at second hand. I attribute the Folger's success to this factor more than to any other one influence. Institutions can be ruined by ill-informed trustees who get bees in their bonnets about what they would like to see the institution do. Sometimes such trustees are influenced by doctrinaire friends, by promoters of fanciful schemes, or simply by self-conceit. They convince themselves that they know best, and then vanity prevents any change of mind. If the truth were known, appalling numbers of institutions in America have suffered calamities, occasionally of major proportions, from the ignorance or vanity of headstrong trustees.

Conscious of Henry Clay Folger's expressed wishes and supported by the unanimous votes of the Amherst trustees, the Folger Library refused to be diverted from its set purpose of becoming an effective library for the study of Tudor and Stuart history and literature—the best possible for both its source material and its staff assistance.

We sought to establish an international reputation for the encouragement of learning in these fields. To that end, we invited some of the most distinguished scholars in Europe, Africa, the Far East, and the Western Hemisphere to lecture, give seminars, or spend periods of study at the Folger. Our roster of visiting scholars read like a *Who's Who* in the fields of Tudor and Stuart civilization and eighteenth-century drama. They proved extremely helpful, not only in giving us—readers and staff alike—the benefit of their knowledge and experience, but also in reporting from time to time the availability of books and manuscripts for purchase and, occasionally, in using their influence to help us to get them.

Among the outstanding scholars we brought to the Folger were the late Sir John Neale, the great historian of Queen Elizabeth I and her parliaments; the Earl of Crawford and Balcarres, then chairman of the trustees of the British Museum and also of the National Gallery of Art in London; Professor Conyers Read, biographer of Lord Burghley and Sir Thomas Walsingham; F. P. Wilson, professor at Merton College, Oxford, authority on Elizabethan drama and many other subjects; Frederick Hard, president of Scripps College, a Spenser specialist and student of the influence of art on literature; Dougald MacMillan, professor at the University of North Carolina and a Restoration and eighteenth-century drama authority; Arthur Humphreys, professor at the University of Leicester, an inspired Shakespeare editor and one of Great Britain's distinguished scholars in many fields; H. S. Bennett, professor at Emmanuel College, Cambridge, interested in the Elizabethan reading public; Garrett Mattingly, chairman of the history department of Columbia University, specialist in Renaissance diplomacy and author of the best of all books on the Spanish Armada. A booklet he wrote on this subject for the Folger series, adding new details to the story, was his last publication before an untimely death.

Another distinguished scholar, working on a book later published under the title *Othello's Countrymen*, was Eldred D. Jones of Fourah Bay College, Freetown, Sierra Leone. A graduate of Corpus Christi College, Oxford, Jones won many friends in this country, and made an extremely favorable impression during a visit to academic institutions in the South.

William Haller, professor emeritus of Barnard College, the authority on Puritanism and an old friend from British Museum and Huntington days, was our resident "Nestor," an important influence at the Folger as he had been at the Huntington. A. G. Dickens, professor at the University of London and soon to be director of the Institute of Historical Research there, came to work at the library, as did Craig Thompson, professor and librarian at Haverford College (later of the University of Pennsylvania), translator and editor of Erasmus, who wrote a number of the Folger booklets.

Levi Fox, director of the Shakespeare Birthplace Trust at Stratford-upon-Avon, spent a summer comparing Folger Shakespeareana with the holdings of the Trust archives at Stratford. Sir Frank Francis, director of the British Museum; David Quinn, professor at the University of Liverpool and author of significant books on sixteenth- and seventeenth-century exploration—these and scores of other scholars of great distinction were a source of stimulation and assistance to the administration and to their fellow readers.

These scholars came by invitation of the Folger Library. We also established a fellowship program for less experienced scholars who might apply for short-term grants. But because we wanted to exercise the same care in the selection of Fellows as we did in the choice of senior visiting scholars, we retained within the administration control of the selection process rather than farming it out to a committee whose members might not be aware of our objectives or be as familiar with academic personnel as were the Folger authorities themselves. This procedure enabled us to develop a remarkable "alumni" group, a list of Fellows of which any institution might be proud.

A pleasant and useful ritual was afternoon tea, served each day at 3:00 P.M., to which all readers and staff members in rotation were invited. We discouraged a coffee break in the forenoon as a waste of precious time in a short day. But the set tea period brought scholars and staff together with an informal opportunity for the exchange of ideas. Sir John Neale once asserted that the brief afternoon teas at the Folger were one of our most valuable assets, a time for communication among men and women of diverse ages, interests, and talents.

Between 1948 and 1968, the Folger Library added to its collections more than 70,000 books, not to mention manuscripts. More than half this number could be classified as rare or scarce items in the Tudor and Stuart period, or—to give inclusive dates—from about 1476 (when printing was introduced into England) until the death of Queen Anne in 1714. A survey of our resources in 1948–49 showed that we were then already the second library in the world in the number of English books published before 1641, exceeded only by the library of the British Museum (now known as the British Library). We also had the largest collection in the world of significant works by and about Shakespeare.

To build to this strength, we established a policy of buying only source material that would be useful to scholars, never items that were merely curious or possessed of some typographical variant of interest only to collectors. Our touchstone was always that a book or manuscript must have continuing utility to learning. When another Shakespeare Folio was offered to us, we said, "No thank you." We gave the same answer to offers of literary manuscripts already edited time after time, of no conceivable use to any scholar. One bookseller eagerly reported to us a very rare item that "a Shakespeare library simply could not refuse." It was an edition of *Hamlet* printed on cork sheets. Barring some scholar pursuing evidence of printing on cork—an unlikely topic—we could foresee no use for this expensive rarity and turned it down.

145

But we diligently explored bookshops from Edinburgh to Vienna in the effort to collect items that would illuminate the life and times of Tudor and Stuart England: works on economics, religion, literature, learning, science, technology, law, travel, exploration, music, the arts, drama—in short, everything that would help a scholar reconstruct any aspect of those momentous years.

Our search was always interesting and sometimes dramatic in the memories of past ages that it evoked. I recall a particularly poignant moment for a student of humanism when the proprietor of Erasmus House in Basel, standing in the very room in which Erasmus died, pulled from the shelf a book of selections from Plutarch, *Ex Plutarcho versa per Des. Erasmum Roterodamum.* It had been printed in Basel by Johannes Froben in 1520 and was edited by Erasmus, illustrated by Hans Holbein, and dedicated to Henry VIII. We bought it—at a reasonable price.

We discovered many rare and historically valuable items but never the kind of things that make headlines in the newspapers— no unknown manuscript of Shakespeare, Milton, or anything so sensational. But we brought to light thousands of valuable books and manuscripts that scholars find invaluable.

We once bought a whole parish church library, from the little church of Shipdham near Norwich in East Anglia. The church had decided that it had no need for the books, which had been on shelves in the church since early in the seventeenth century and had never been disturbed. The spines of the bound books had rotted away from exposure to sunlight but the pages inside were as clean and crisp as on the day they were printed. The catalogue announcing the church's decision to sell its library stated: "It may be added that the sum realized will be used to meeting the heavy expense of repairs to the roof and additional cost of £175 for new heating apparatus, both of which are of great urgency at the present time; to form a library of modern books for the use and edification of the parishioners; and to be used towards the reduction of the dilapidations assessment on the rectory and premises." The books, dealing with Tudor and Stuart economics, science, politics, and religion, are now safe in the Folger Library, and the parishioners of Shipdham Church, we hope, are dry, warm, and edified.

On another occasion we discovered at Arbury Hall, in Warwickshire, a notable collection of manuscript newsletters written from London by professional news writers to members of the Newdigate family between 1674 and 1715. The collection, numbering approximately four thousand separate issues, is one of the most important groups of newsletters in existence for this period. The letters supply news of interest to a man of affairs resident in the country. They report the movements and activities of the royal family; give information about domestic politics, foreign and military affairs, the wars abroad and deployment of ships; and relay news from the New World. They also supply gossip that throws light on social history.

A collection with a peculiar pertinence in Washington is the Bagot Papers, obtained in 1954: more than a thousand documents illustrating Elizabethan political log-rolling. The Bagot family controlled political patronage in Staffordshire during the reign of Elizabeth I and were energetic in their efforts to get ever more special concessions from the central government in London. Numerous letters to Lord Burghley, the Earl of Essex, or other officials in power urge favors for Stafford or some Stafford man. The Bagots, like any congressman in Washington, regarded their immediate constituents as their first obligation, a situation that only students of politics-in-the-abstract expect to change.

Although we were eager to find significant books and manuscripts in our period, we had an informal agreement with the British Museum that we would not bid against British research libraries for anything that might be construed as a "national treasure," documents that should rightfully remain in Great Britain. The agreement proved beneficial to us because we received cooperation that we could not otherwise have expected.

Valuable collections of manuscripts privately owned we microfilmed. Through the courtesy of the Marquess of Salisbury, we were permitted to microfilm the Cecil Papers at Hatfield House, the most valuable single archive outside the Public Record Office for sixteenth- and seventeenth-century history. The Marquess of Salisbury retains the right to give permission for the publication in toto of any document, but he granted the Folger Library permission to allow scholars to use the papers and to quote from them for their purposes. The Folger gave a microfilm copy to the Marquess, and he in turn presented it to the British Museum where scholars in London can now study the papers conveniently.

The goal of the Folger Library was not to be merely a repository of books and manuscripts waiting for scholars to use them. It sought to become a research institution that would make a positive contribution to learning. To do that, it made its resources available to any mature scholar. Because its facilities were limited and its treasures fragile, it was, like the Huntington, obliged to exclude undergraduates and casual readers interested primarily in satisfying a normal human curiosity. But nothing in the Folger Library was reserved for special use, not even by members of the library's own staff. The library did not undertake to protect anyone's claim upon any book or document that he or she contemplated editing and publishing. All accredited scholars had free access to Folger documents, subject only to the normal precautions necessary to protect rare and fragile materials from damage. So important was this principle of unrestricted use that the trustees of Amherst College, at their meeting on January 30, 1954, passed the following resolution.

> In the interest of learning, the Folger Library believes in the free dissemination of information in its historical source materials and in the multiplication of copies of rare documents which may serve to advance learning. As a token of its belief in the wide distribution of rare materials, it has microfilmed its unique sixteenth- and seventeenth-century books and permitted other libraries to acquire film copies.
>
> The Folger Library has traditionally followed a liberal policy in granting permission to any qualified scholar to use the rare materials in its possession. It does not try to impound material for the special use of its own staff. The Library takes the position that learning is best served if qualified persons have free access to all documents. It does not undertake to insure anybody's special claims to a particular document in its possession. In short, no one, not even a member of the Library's own staff, is permitted to stake an indefinite and exclusive claim to the right to use or reproduce any document in the Folger Library. The Folger Library will make an effort to inform scholars about previous requests for permis-

sion to edit or reproduce documents, but it will assume no responsibility for protecting any scholar's "right" to reproduce a Folger document, or to publish materials based on it.

The Folger Library believes that it has an obligation to protect its documents against physical damage or any sort of misuse, and it also reserves the right to withhold materials from persons not qualified to use them in the interest of learning. The main concern of a research library should be the advancement of learning, which can be served best by freedom of investigation and freedom to publish the results of research. To this end, the Folger Library wishes scholars to have access to its documents with the least possible restraints on their use. Because the Trustees of Amherst College, who administer the Folger Library, believe that it is desirable to affirm this traditional policy as a matter of record, they have approved this statement.

Gathering rare books and manuscripts and making them available to scholars did not prove an exercise in solemnity at the Folger Library. The staff came from a varied background but everyone had a sense of humor, seemed to enjoy life, and got on with more harmony than can usually be found in small institutions. Miss Pitcher, assistant to the director, was by nature a disciplinarian and sometimes scared the daylights out of maintenance workers who she thought might be shirking a task. But she had a saving sense of the ridiculous, and the staff learned that her bark was worse than her bite. She also had a sense of history and was a moving spirit in preparation for a celebrated Elizabethan dinner that we gave for the staff as a trial run for a larger festival in 1964 to celebrate the four hundredth anniversary of Shakespeare's birth.

We knew that one of the favorite Elizabethan potations was mead, a drink famous in England since Saxon times but not available in Washington, D.C. She enlisted the help of a junior colleague, Jean Miller, procured some stoneware crocks, bought some honey (the necessary ingredient for fermentation), and sought the yeast to make it work. Alas, the particular kind of yeast favored by mead makers of old could not be found. But Dr. Henry Allen Moe, president of the Guggenheim Foundation, a friend and a man learned in the lore of drink, heard of our problem and offered to help. He thought he could procure the yeast in Great Britain, which he did. We set the honey, yeast, and water to fermenting in the north basement. During the process, Philip Knachel arrived as a newcomer to take up his duties as Assistant Director of the Library. Miss Pitcher undertook to give him a tour of the building. He noticed the crocks and sniffed.

"What is in the jars?" Knachel inquired.

"Oh," replied Miss Pitcher with elaborate unconcern. "Just mead."

"Mead! What is it doing here?" Knachel wanted to know.

"This is where we *always* make our mead," Miss Pitcher responded sweetly—as if the making of mead was a normal part of library routine.

The dinner, cooked entirely by the staff, was a great success and encouraged us to arrange for a similar affair in the summer of 1964 when approximately 150 guests from all over the world visited the Folger Library as part of the American celebration of the Shakespeare anniversary. This time, of course, we had to employ caterers, who received careful instructions about the preparation of Elizabethan dishes, including whole roast suckling pig. Our mead manufactory, moreover, was inadequate for so large a number, and we had to settle for more prosaic ale and wine.

Miss Pitcher was never one to bear fools gladly, and her antipathy for both fools and frauds was ill concealed. A professor from a German university once turned up at the library and by his unreasonable demands and bad manners made himself disliked by everybody. Encountering Miss Pitcher by the readers' mailbox after closing time one afternoon, he berated her and the United States Post Office for niggardliness in having only one postal delivery a day. "In Germany," he gloated, "we have three." Miss Pitcher turned upon him a cold eye and replied: "If we did not have to spend our tax money restoring your country, we could afford a good mail service again, too."

Eccentric readers sometimes contributed to staff gaiety. One of the oddest—and best liked—was a hulking English bachelor named John Crow, until his death a lecturer at the University of London. After he had spent a period as guest lecturer at the University of California at Los Angeles, a friend drove him east across the continent. The desert sun faded Crow's tan suit, on the south side only, to a soft gray, but Crow did not seem to mind being parti-colored like a character out of the commedia dell' arte. Apparently he had only one suit. On the way to the library on a memorable morning, his braces, not surprisingly, gave way. He arrived clutching a generous gathering of pants and asked at once to be conducted to the bookbinder. Robert Lunow, undaunted, took a piece of book leather and patched him up. Thereafter Crow enjoyed boasting to everyone that he could now claim to be a rarity "bound by Lunow."

The discovery of nylon shirts was a great event in Crow's life, for it saved him the necessity of patronizing a neighborhood Chinese laundry. The proud owner of two nylon shirts, he brought the soiled one periodically to the Folger, washed it, and hung it out to dry in a section of the stacks that was open to readers. Though we endeavored to provide our readers with every reasonable convenience, that was a little too much. Thereafter I appointed Giles Dawson "Crow-keeper," with instructions to see that this shirt-washing scholar did his laundry elsewhere.

Every library and museum attracts strange personalities. Though some of our readers were eccentrics, they were screened according to their scholarly attainments and needs. But the exhibition galleries were of course open to everybody. One familiar visitor was an earnest middle-aged man whose daily ritual it was to march back to a large clock that had not run since the late seventeenth century, solemnly set his watch by it, and march out. Eventually I had the clock repaired rather than have him keeping the wrong time, but apparently he did not care for twentieth-century time and quit coming.

Visitors often made interesting observations prompted by objects on exhibition. I have treasured a comment made by Miss Meta Glass, then recently retired president of Sweet Briar College. We were inspecting a rather poor bust of Shakespeare in the main reading room. Miss Glass remarked that good busts were rare, expecially those being made nowadays. "In an unguarded moment I let a sculptor do a bust of me," she observed. "And I have it in my little house in Charlottesville. Every night when I go home, I look at the thing and say, 'One of us has got to move.'"

151

It was not generally known that the ashes of Mr. and Mrs. Folger are preserved behind a bronze plaque at one end of the Jacobean reading room. But all the guards were aware of this, and they gleefully informed recruits to the guard force that ghosts sometimes walked the oak-paneled premises of a night. The audible creaking of wood, contracting with evening temperature changes, served to confirm their warning. Three days after an especially promising-looking guard had gone to work, he came to my office and announced that he had to quit. He was a retired army sergeant and I hated to lose him. When I asked why he had to leave, he explained: "You see, sir, every night when I walk through that reading room I seem to feel something behind me, and it's all I can do not to break and run."

Readers multiplied, books and manuscripts accumulated, and we found that we had to have more space. Already we had floored and finished the lowest basement room as a book stack but that too was insufficient. So in 1959 we let a contract for the construction of a new wing to the building, utilizing a parking lot in the rear and sacrificing a lawn for a new parking area for the staff. The architects were Harbeson, Hough, Livingston, and Larson of Philadelphia, successors to Paul Cret, the original architect. The building contractors were William Lipscomb Company, successors to the contractors who had erected the original structure. In both firms men who had worked on the earlier building were still active and directed the new construction. When it was concluded, the design was so close to the original, and the material so similar, that it was all but impossible to tell that the new wing was a later addition. One useful byproduct was a roof garden over the new wing—discreetly hidden behind a parapet—where we could have tea, staff luncheons, and even parties in good weather.

We did everything we could to make the institution attractive, convenient, and effective as a research library. It was obvious that privately endowed research libraries would be required to bear an increasing burden in supplying the needs of the learned world. In recent years, more and more, the specialized research libraries have had to increase their services to the humanities in the same way that advanced laboratories in physics, chemistry, or biology enable the top echelon of specialists to carry on research in pure science as distinguished from the application of science to industry.

Without investigations in pure science, engineers would run out of new developments. In the same way, a few scholars working quietly in research libraries are adding fresh knowledge in the world of literature, history, and the arts, and equipping themselves to take the leadership of the graduate schools. Research libraries are helping to provide the scholars essential to educational leadership. Without such men of learning at the top, college and university education in America would lapse into mediocrity. The influence of the specialized research library in maintaining the quality of educational leadership cannot be measured accurately in quantitative terms. It is not related to the great *number* of readers. It does relate to the influence of a relatively small body of learned scholars whose works transmit to others the truths of history and the insights of literature which eventually reach the common stream of popular education.

Because of the burden of teaching in the universities, the increased demand upon university libraries, and the general distraction of academic life, the specialized libraries now serve university faculties as places of refuge where they can work free of interruption. As never before, the special library is needed by the scholar who can find neither time for research nor the source materials on his own campus.

The privately endowed library as an independent research institution devoting part of its income to subsidizing scholarly investigations is peculiar to the United States and is a development of the past half-century. The responsibilities of these endowed libraries are constantly increasing, and the next quarter of a century inevitably will see them occupying a still more important place in higher learning.

One of the gravest problems facing American society today and, indeed, the societies of other countries as well, is the maintenance of a sense of quality in education, with the preservation in our civilization of the classical tradition and of those elements of distinction in the arts that once went with aristocratic background and training. The tendency in American education in our time has been to level down to the lowest common denominator and to forget that somewhere, somehow, we must preserve the beauty and wisdom, and the standards of excellence, that will never be found in mediocrity.

Coincidental with the zeal for leveling down in education has come an attack on learning itself. It has been fashionable to abuse the scholar engaged in research as an ivory-towered academic, innocent of practical affairs and even incapable of teaching. In some circles theorists have made a distinction between scholars and teachers, as if they were mutually exclusive. Such talk and such ideas are both naive and unrealistic, but they have done much harm to learning and to education.

The best teacher almost invariably is a good scholar, and the worst teacher is frequently a glib and empty performer who scorns research. Because universities and colleges are now so crowded with students, many faculty members have difficulty finding the time to be learned men and women, and the emphasis is often upon making them efficient transmitters rather than scholars. Unhappily, what they have to transmit will become stereotyped if they have no opportunity to refresh their stock of knowledge by study in their fields of specialization.

A few privately endowed research libraries, the Folger among them, will have an increasing obligation in the future to serve the interest of scholarship and higher learning without bowing to the fashion for mediocrity. Inevitably they will be accused of elitism, as if that were a state of iniquity. But as Thomas Jefferson, the great apostle of democracy, realized, a society without an intellectual elite capable of supplying leadership is a society headed for degradation and eventual decay.

Research libraries have an obligation to create oases where academic leaders can find refreshment and inspiration. During the Dark Ages a few monasteries kept alive the desire for learning. In a similar way today institutions like the Folger must join with the universities in combating forces of darkness almost as overwhelming as those that nearly wiped out classical culture in the eighth century.

The main responsibility of these research libraries is to the few, to the leaders who can best use them. They must never relax their efforts to improve their facilities and to increase their holdings in those materials needed by scholars who can make distinguished and enduring contributions to the advancement of learning.

CHAPTER IX

Extracurricular Activities: Near and Far

WHEN A PRESIDENTIAL NOMINEE for the librarianship of Congress was being questioned by a senatorial committee in the summer of 1975, two or three senators seemed unduly concerned lest he spend government time writing a book. The nominee, a Pulitzer Prize-winning historian, was viewed with grave suspicion: if he salvaged a few moments from routine administration to read a book, they were convinced that such a deed would be malfeasance in office. If he did nothing, or dozed in a corner somewhere after a few cocktails at luncheon, a custom honored in the Senate, that would merely prove him a clubbable and ordinary fellow to be respected and approved by the inquisitive committee. But to read a book—and write one—heaven forbid! The Treasury should be warned of a wastrel.

This attitude struck me as a reversion to a kind of Neanderthalism that afflicts government, especially when faced with a nominee of intellectual attainments. A nonentity of immaculate dreariness would never be held in doubtful suspense. My own experience with boards of trustees had been so different from the attitude of the august Senate that I could scarcely believe that continued intellectual activity would be considered a liability. My trustees, both at the Huntington Library and the Folger, had encouraged me to participate to the limit of my capacity in activities that they believed would redound to the credit of their institutions. That any conscientious administrator would neglect his appointed duties for such activities was of course unthinkable. Administration does not mean becoming a helot slaving away at trivia. An alert administrator has to see beyond his own bailiwick, take part in what is going on elsewhere, and continue to keep his mind alive—even by reading and, if heaven is kind, writing a book.

Earlier in this narrative I have mentioned the encouragement that wise trustees gave to administrative and other officers of their institutions to participate in outside activities. The far-sightedness of this attitude ought to be obvious. The recluse administrator may learn about every cranny and crevice in his own shop, but he is not likely to receive the stimulation that will enable him to give his own institution the significance it should have.

My own experience at the Huntington and later at the Folger Library convinced me that officers of academic institutions, particularly libraries, need to maintain contacts with a world beyond their own specializations—even to do a bit of trout fishing when the opportunity offers. A day above the timberline on a clear mountain stream can purge the mind of much nonsense. Good conversation with alert friends around a campfire is also an antidote for pedantry, a malady that academics ought to fear like the Black Death.

A happy fate has provided me with good companions, in and out of Academia. They have always been stimulating, sometimes exciting, often merry and entertaining, occasionally critical—but always helpful in widening one's outlook and stretching one's imagination. I have already mentioned my fishing companions of the high altitudes and my delight in conversation with Howard Mumford Jones at Chapel Hill, the Huntington Library, and the University of Michigan when he was professor there. Talk with Howard on any occasion was invariably provocative and entertaining. He could fire off volleys of fresh ideas about how to save the railroads from their own stupidity and presently be talking about the quality of German poetry of the nineteenth century. A stodgy professor once commented, "Howard Jones is too brilliant." Brilliant he is but never superficial. His fecund mind has served as a whetstone for all those around him, and his capacity for human understanding has made him an enduring friend.

Among friends made during my brief period as a lecturer at the University of Washington in Seattle was an altogether different type. Angelo Pellegrini, a second-generation Italian, was a teacher of speech and an authority on food and drink. Angelo finally put his gastronomic ideas into a book entitled *The Unprejudiced Palate* (1948), a charming essay with an utter misnomer for title because every page illustrates Angelo's splendid prejudices about food. From him I learned much about the influence of the kitchen upon man's mind as well as his body. Thomas Carlyle once commented sourly that "all the ills of the world come from the frying pan." Angelo was equally convinced that the way to salvation led through the kitchen.

To librarians, however, salvation lies in books, and their greatest frustration is a lack of time to sample the tempting wares that pass through their hands in the order of business. Contrary to popular misconception, librarians do not spend their days reading books. Much of their bookish education must come from communication with their fellows and with others concerned with their trade. A significant part of my own bookish education has come from booksellers and collectors who have directed me to things I ought to know about—and books that are essential in any man's education.

The long years spent as a member of the Selection Committee of the Guggenheim Foundation, referred to earlier, were an experience of continuing education. The Committee, never more than seven men, read all of the hundreds of digests, even in areas in which we had no special knowledge. We had referees and special committees to advise in such fields as the fine arts and music, but we served as the final court and made the ultimate decisions. We all benefited from the broad acquaintance that the late Henry Moe, president of the Foundation, possessed, and the immense learning of E. Bidwell Wilson, a senior member of the Committee. Wilson, professor of statistics in the Harvard School of Public Health, was a brilliant mathematician, an economist, and a physicist, and he knew more than most of us in other fields besides. A man of urbane knowledge of the world, he was also a connoisseur of wine.

Our Committee learned a great deal about scholars other than the applicants for fellowships. For example, we soon learned to discount the inveterate liars among graduate school instructors who make all their geese into swans. We also had to be aware of the few who are too severe.

The elimination of the very poor candidates was easy; the selection of the very best was also obvious; but to discriminate among the middle group—the majority—required the judgment of Solomon, which none of us presumed to have. Nevertheless we worked over the applications conscientiously and came up with the wisest selections in our capacity. Of course we made mistakes, both of commission and omission, but by and large our record proved good. The great body of former Guggenheim Foundation Fellows is a very distinguished group.

The meetings of the Committee of Selection were always occasions for the exchange of ideas. Each of us learned a great deal from our colleagues. In my last year, the other members of the committee were Marc Kac, mathematician; W. F. Libby, Nobel Prize-winning chemist; Robert K. Merton, economist and sociologist who succeeded me as chairman; Charles Muscatine, professor of English literature; Marcus Rhoades, biochemist and botanist; and Samuel E. Thorne, professor of the history of law. Henry Moe had established a tradition of ending each working day with a memorable dinner at the Century Association, a tradition maintained by Gordon Ray when he succeeded Moe as president of the Foundation. If we worked hard, we also enjoyed good fellowship and conviviality.

On my retirement in 1971, my colleagues composed a resolution that would admirably serve as an obituary. When inscribed in Gothic script on a great sheet and framed, it weighed forty pounds. Modesty forbids me to quote it, but the members of the Committee reported that, as chairman, I had "directed their activities without haste but without rest." I then learned for the first time that my selection as a Fellow in 1928 was what the English call "a near thing." The resolution noted: "After a battle of the titans behind the scenes to determine whether at the age of 29 he was 'as yet of Fellowship size,' his sponsor, Edwin Greenlaw of Johns Hopkins, prevailed at last over Kittredge of Harvard and Tucker Brooke of Yale." No wonder Greenlaw had admonished me so earnestly not to let him down! My appreciation was profound. The scroll hangs in my study and is reprinted in the reports of the president for the preceding years of 1969 and 1970.

In 1951 the History Book Club asked me to become one of three editors entrusted with the selection of historical works for adoption by the club. The other two editors were Dumas Malone and the late Walter Millis. Malone and I have remained on the editorial board ever since. This association has been intellectually profitable, for it has forced me to read many books that otherwise might not have come to my attention. It has also given me a sense of disillusionment at the poor judgment and lack of wisdom of many publishers. Much trivia, passing as history, pours from the presses to sink into deserved oblivion. What goes on in the minds of publishers and their advisors continues to baffle me, for much that they bring out has neither value as history nor the promise of profit for the publisher. Yet year after year, worthless rubbish continues to find its way into print.

An organization that has made an enduring impression on the development and activities of modern libraries is the Council on Library Resources. The Council had its origin in two meetings held at the Folger Library on January 15 and March 31, 1955. The Ford Foundation at that time was being bombarded by requests from libraries for grants. It seemed desirable to have some agency that could receive such requests, determine their worth, and fund them if possible. Fred C. Cole, who at the time was on leave from Tulane University as consultant for the Ford Foundation, came to me with the problem. The Ford Foundation would make a small grant to the Folger if we would convene a body of scholars, scientists, and librarians to discuss ways and means of solving some of the problems faced by research libraries and would then make a report to the Foundation.

The first meeting consisted of about fifty individuals representing every aspect of learning concerned with research libraries. Discussion was cogent and lively. We heard reports of the alarm of university administrators over the expense of maintaining libraries and the need for ever-expanding space to house books and periodicals resulting from the explosion of knowledge. Hard-pressed librarians complained at the unsympathetic attitude of finance officers; one librarian ruefully commented that it would take acres of buildings just to house the catalogues if books continued to multiply at the current rate until the year 2000. Reduction of printed works by microphotography, someone suggested, might solve the problem. This prediction prompted one book-lover to an impassioned outburst on the tragedy of losing the smell of old leather and the "feel" of a finely bound book. A cynical scientist retorted that we could spray computer cards with the synthetic perfume of old leather and thus ease the agony of the book-lover.

The discussions at this preliminary conference produced a body of facts and opinions that had to be refined at a second meeting of a much smaller group. At both meetings, Leonard Carmichael, then Secretary of the Smithsonian Institution, took an active part and made many useful suggestions. The members of the conferences agreed that we should propose to the Ford Foundation the creation of an organization that would devote its efforts to finding solutions of the problems of libraries with particular emphasis on the larger research institutions.

Members of the conferences had turned in a great quantity of written suggestions. Someone had now to digest the material and shape it into a practical proposal that would be acceptable to the Ford Foundation. On a hot July day, Fred Cole met me on the top deck of the liner *United States* as I was about to sail for Europe. For two hours, until sailing time, we discussed every angle of the report. In the end I agreed to submit a draft proposal which I wrote crossing the Atlantic and sent back by airmail to my secretary for retyping. This version, worked over by Fred Cole, W. McNeil Lowry of the Ford Foundation, and myself, became the charter of the Council on Library Resources which the Ford Foundation agreed to sponsor with an initial grant of $5,000,000.

A board of directors consisting of scholars, scientists, and librarians, with diverse skills and qualifications, was selected. The Ford Foundation appointed Gilbert W. Chapman, president of Yale and Towne Manufacturing Company, chairman of the board. I became vice-chairman. The board elected Verner Clapp, associate librarian of Congress, president of the Council. He at once organized a staff, set up shop in Washington, and began submitting proposals for studies and laboratory experiments to attack the most urgent of library problems.

The Ford Foundation had envisioned a board of directors, all specialists of one sort and another, who would contribute their special knowledge at regular board meetings. Chapman, accustomed to boards of directors who left everything to management, saw no reason for the directors to do more than approve once a year the actions of management so long as these officers performed satisfactorily. After some persuasion, he agreed to greater participation of the board in decisions. He resigned as chairman in 1965.

The new chairman, Whitney North Seymour, Sr., a distinguished New York lawyer, proved remarkably sympathetic with the objectives of the board and has been of immense help. When Verner Clapp reached retirement age in 1967, Fred Cole, who had long since left the Ford Foundation and Tulane University to become president of Washington and Lee University, was persuaded to take the presidency of the Council that he had done so much to create. For a number of years, the Council has had the advice of Sir Frank Francis, retired director of the British Museum, who has served as consultant.

Since its creation, the Council has become a potent force in the library world, with programs abroad as well as in the United States. After a meeting of the International Federation of Library Associations (IFLA) in Moscow, which I attended as observer, we decided to appropriate funds to help defray expenses of an efficient secretariat. The Council has also taken the lead in fostering computer applications to libraries where practicable, in encouraging and helping to fund the development of new and useful types of equipment, in bringing about far-reaching cooperation between libraries both at home and abroad, and in studying methods designed to restore and preserve books printed on deteriorating pulp papers. A method of manufacturing a permanent type of wood pulp paper, developed at the Barrow Laboratory in Richmond, Virginia, with a grant from the Council on Library Resources, would alone have justified its existence. Renewed grants from the Ford Foundation have enabled the Council to expand its activities and to provide funds for fellowships and internships designed to improve the quality of library leadership.

In the autumn of 1964, the American Historical Association

found itself without an executive secretary. Boyd Shafer, who had ably served in that capacity for several years, had resigned to accept a professorship in a Middle Western college. Julian Boyd, president of the American Historical Association in 1964, persuaded me to serve as an interim executive secretary while we looked for a replacement. Because my own office was only two blocks from AHA headquarters, I agreed to supervise activities until the end of the year. My labors in this capacity were not very strenuous—nor very effective, I fear—for they did not interfere with my regular duties as director of the Folger Library. At least, however, we kept the ship afloat until we obtained the services of Paul L. Ward, who had recently resigned as president of Sarah Lawrence College.

One memorable event of that year was a dinner party that Julian and I arranged for Alfred Knopf, Sr., publisher of many historical works. It was a dinner with many tributes to Alfred, who for many years had himself given delightful dinners for his friends among the historians. Lest we fail to come up to the standards of his own hospitality, we enlisted the best culinary talent of the Sheraton-Park Hotel, and I searched the town over for Alfred's favorite vintage wine, to discover only two precious bottles. The other guests had to be content with less favored vintage years, but they never knew that their bottles differed from those on Alfred's table.

Julian Boyd's presidential address that year was entitled "A Modest Proposal to Meet an Urgent Need." It stressed the importance of a residential center for scholars in Washington, a sort of international house, where research workers in all the historical sciences could find temporary quarters, meet one another, and exchange ideas. "Graduate students and seasoned veterans alike who come here from this and many other countries have no place to live and associate with others of like purpose, no staff of experts to advise them how to take advantage of the incomparable library and archival materials, no guidance or assistance," Julian asserted. "... The need to remedy this glaring defect on the cultural landscape of a great capital is overwhelming, is long overdue, and is increasing in dimension with every passing year." In my own newsletters from the Folger Library, I had long been pleading for the creation of an international house for scholars. For a time it looked as if the Federal government would sponsor such a house during its rehabilitation of Pennsylvania Avenue, and President Johnson even sent a quartet of architects to the Folger to discuss the matter with me.

But our efforts were wasted and the plan came to naught. Secretary Dillon Ripley of the Smithsonian Institution persuaded the Woodrow Wilson Foundation to establish a small, exclusive organization under the aegis of the Smithsonian—the Woodrow Wilson International Center for Scholars—which each year invites a few individuals to come as Fellows and dine together at intervals. Washington still lacks any adequate center for most scholars, who must live about in such boarding houses as they can find if they plan to carry on research in the libraries and archives of this city.

One of the most fascinating institutions with which I have been officially connected is the Henry Francis du Pont Winterthur Museum at Wilmington, Delaware. In 1955 Mr. du Pont invited me to become a trustee, and I have served in various capacities on that board ever since. My years as a member of the executive committee have been an education in the operation of a complex museum.

Of all the people I have known, Henry F. du Pont was one of the most remarkable personalities. Utterly without pretense or pomposity, he was passionately interested in a variety of activities: the collection of early American artifacts of the decorative arts, the development of magnificent horticultural exhibits and an azalea garden without parallel, the operation of a farm with a famous dairy herd, the stimulating of studies in American decorative arts, a devotion to the Episcopal Church, and the cherishing of a host of friends on both sides of the Atlantic.

The hospitality of Harry du Pont, as he was known to his intimates, was unbounded. He took pleasure in serving on his table the finest products of his farms and dairy as well as exotic delicacies, and he seemingly never forgot the preferences of his guests. Once at dinner I exclaimed over the excellence of some *marrons glacés*. Thereafter, Harry never failed to have *marrons glacés* for me each time that I returned.

Walking through the azalea garden with him one spring afternoon, I asked where he found a head gardener. "I am head gardener," he answered. Carrying a small notebook, he entered the name and number of any azalea that was not blooming at its appointed time. The next day it would be moved to take its place among the "late bloomers," and a more alert plant would take its place. He prescribed the precise furnishings and arrangements of all the period rooms in the museum and was probably the nation's most expert authority on Early American furniture. It was an extraordinary privilege to know him and to have a part in an enterprise of such value to our cultural history.

Harry du Pont's generosity was unlimited when it came to providing for the museum and all its surroundings. At his death, some retrenchment was necessary. For example, the dairy herd had to be sold and farming curtailed by planting most of the land in grass. Someone estimated that butter from the dairy herd had cost four or five dollars a pound to produce. The fields and woods remain, however, as an example of the general appearance of a Delaware farm. "The time will come when young people in this region may want to see what a real farm looked like," Harry once told me. So he wanted to keep the estate intact. He would have preferred to see crops being grown and the dairy still in operation.

Another personality of unusual fascination for me was President Harry S. Truman. It was my fortune to have a hand in the founding of his library and his research institute at Independence, Missouri. On June 3, 1955, Cyrus Eaton, the railroad magnate and industrialist, arranged a huge dinner at the Hotel Cleveland in Cleveland, Ohio, to raise money for the Harry S. Truman Library Fund. He asked me to make the principal speech, probably because he was aware that I knew about Mr. Truman's interest in history and could be depended upon to stress that aspect. Mr. Truman told me on one occasion that he had learned to read history as a child and had been an avid consumer of historical works ever since. "See these glasses," he said, pointing to his spectacles. "When I was a little boy I had to wear glasses and could not play ball for fear of breaking them and damaging my eyes. I read all the history books I could lay my hands on in the Independence library. My teacher then got more books on history and biography for me from Kansas

City, and I read them. More interesting than novels." His detailed knowledge of history sometimes proved an embarrassment to his speech writers, for if they made a blunder he would spot it. As a birthday gift one year, the White House staff gave him a set of the *Dictionary of American Biography*. "That was the biggest mistake we ever made," declared David Lloyd, one of his staffers. "The Old Man knows more history than any of the rest of us now; with the *DAB* handy, he can always catch us in a mistake."

Aware of this background, I entitled my talk, "A Defender of Learning," for Mr. Truman had often expressed a desire to promote historical scholarship in America. When Julian Boyd presented the President with the first volume of his monumental edition of the writings of Thomas Jefferson, Mr. Truman responded with a proposal to create a commission to support the editing and publication of the works of other great historical figures in America. He actively encouraged the work of the National Historical Publications Commission, which by now has promoted editions of the writings of many American statesmen.

After the formalities of the dinner were over, Mr. Truman invited Julian Boyd, Lyman Butterfield, editor of the Adams Papers, and me to come over to his suite in the hotel; he talked until long after midnight about historical matters. When the Harry S. Truman Institute for National and International Affairs was created, we three were among the trustees appointed, and we have remained on that board ever since. We looked forward to the annual meetings, for Mr. Truman was usually present and took an active interest in the Institute's scholarly endeavors. Always a good raconteur, he told many stories of events and personalities that had been a part of his own experience. My regret is that I did not keep a notebook, for some of the anecdotes and narratives I have not yet seen in print. Perhaps he did not want them published, though not once did he ever say that any were "off the record."

One anecdote that he told with gusto concerned Daniel Webster and Henry Clay. On a certain drizzly evening these two nineteenth-century statesmen, both far gone in drink, were stumbling down from the Capitol to their boarding house on Pennsylvania Avenue. The streets were wet and, in those days, slippery with mud. Webster slid into a ditch, and Clay undertook to help him up. He pulled and hauled, but liquor and the footing betrayed him. He, too, fell in. "Dan'l," he said, "I can't get you up but I can lie down beside you." "That," said Mr. Truman, "is what is known in politics as moral support."

The year 1964 was a busy one for me. The Shakespeare Birthplace Trust at Stratford-upon-Avon decided as an international gesture to add two American life trustees to its board, and Eugene Black, then president of the World Bank, and I were elected. In the meantime, the National Geographic Society had asked me to write a story for its magazine on "Shakespeare's England," and had followed up with an invitation to become a trustee.

My association with the National Geographic Society has been stimulating and has given me an enormous respect for the organization. On my retirement from the directorship of the Folger Library in 1968, the Geographic offered me an office and asked me to serve as historical consultant and to write a number of historical chapters in some of its publications. My associates have been congenial and the work exciting, so that at times I have wished I had retired from the Folger sooner. Activities for the Geographic have resulted in much travel. One expedition sent me exploring all the places associated with Queen Elizabeth I for an article in the magazine and a chapter in *This England,* one of the Society's distinguished books. An exploration of out-of-the-way places in Italy resulted in chapters in another Geographic book, *The Renaissance.* Inspection visits by the Research Committee of archeological and other projects funded by the Geographic have given me a chance to see more of Europe, much of Turkey, and some of South America, even to the remote Galapagos Islands. Thanks to the Geographic, "retirement" has proved a busy and rewarding period.

Life in Washington, itself, provides unusual opportunities for the observation of world events and participation in affairs of continuing interest. For an individual with a taste for history and for writing, few cities can equal the nation's capital, though the city has its obvious shortcomings. Nearly every important world figure sooner or later comes here, and Fate frequently throws into one's path personalities who otherwise would remain mere names and abstractions. It was our luck to know many members of the fluctuating diplomatic set and to make friends soon scattered to the ends of the earth. When these friends are sent off to far places, about the only consolation for their loss is the thought that it would always be possible to cash a check in Kabul, Samarkand, or Cairo.

When Russell Wiggins was editor of the *Washington Post* and Alfred Friendly its managing editor, they emphasized urbanity and good manners that have all but vanished from journalism in the 1970s. They also had a keen sense of history and a recognition of the value of American traditions. The *Post* in their time published many valuable articles on American history, for Russell Wiggins himself was vitally interested in the period of Jefferson. He contrived to get Julian Boyd and other historians to contribute essays that were informative and often amusing. From 1962 to 1964, I contributed several editorials a week to the *Post,* editorials on unimportant subjects, to be sure, for my line was that of the short familiar essay, sometimes on a subject of historical interest, often merely facetious. But it was fun to do. It is said that a man never gets printer's ink off his fingers, and the opportunity to write editorials took me back to my unregenerate youth.

Whether the numerous boards on which I have served received much benefit from me, they have contributed both to my education and to my pleasure. During ten years' service on the editorial board of the John Harvard Library, from 1958 to 1968, I learned about a vast collection of books long out of print that someone believed should once more be made available. We authorized the republication of many of these through the Harvard University Press. Its then director, the late Thomas J. Wilson, believed in the program and enthusiastically supported it.

An organization always certain to supply both stimulation and pleasure has been the Board of Visitors of Tulane University—the creation of an imaginative physicist, Joseph C. Morris, who until the day of his death was the source of a constant stream of brilliant ideas. He was convinced that Tulane, traditionally controlled by a small local Board of Administrators, needed to be stimulated by industrialists, scientists, and humanistic scholars chosen from many areas of the nation. The meetings are always lively and provocative.

I have been a member since 1965, and from 1972 through 1974, I served as chairman. But discussion is not the only enticement of these meetings. The cuisine of New Orleans is famous throughout the land, the oysters unexcelled by even the most succulent from Chesapeake Bay, and we dine each night in Lucullan disregard of cholesterol and other hazards.

The American Philosophical Society Held at Philadelphia for Promoting Useful Knowledge is an institution that has given me much satisfaction. A member since 1948, I always suspected that my election was a case of mistaken identity, for most of my colleagues at that time were older and more distinguished men. But after years of seasoning, I have lately served on the executive council and as vice president, first under the presidency of Leonard Carmichael and more recently under President Julian Boyd. No learned society in America can boast a wider variety of interests than this, the oldest, founded by Benjamin Franklin and later presided over by Thomas Jefferson. One always has the feeling that Franklin is somewhere in the wings ready to promote some project or invention useful to the nation.

All in all, life for me has been a sequence of stimulating experiences, sometimes laborious, sometimes exciting, never boring. Until old age overtook me, I cannot remember being aware of fatigue. Some new interest has always beckoned, to crowd out thoughts of weariness. It is difficult for me to comprehend the current fashionable condemnation of the "work ethic" and the adulation of a "life-style" (that deplorable cliché) of indolence and self-indulgence. That way lies boredom and unhappiness. I am grateful to my ancestors for providing a persistent instinct for curiosity about the great world and a respect for diligence that permanently inoculated me against boredom.

Long ago, Rabelais warned against "peeping out at life through a little hole" and exhorted his readers to maintain "a gaiety of spirit in contempt of fortune." This is not always an easy injunction to follow, but it ought to be Everyman's goal.

169

Index

Adams, Joseph Q., 111, 113; distinguished record at Folger, 119 ff.; purchase of Harmsworth Collection, 113, 126, 129
Allen, Don Cameron, 112
American Council of Learned Societies (ACLS), 104–6
American Historical Association (AHA), 162–63
American Philosophical Society, 169
Amherst College, trustees of: open book policy at Folger set by, 148–49; responsibility of, for Folger Library, 111, 124, 128, 141–43
Arabella Huntington Memorial, 60
Arbury Hall collection (Warwickshire, England), 147
Arliss, George, 88
Army Times, 137
Arundel-Lumley collection, 31
Athenaeum, 90, 91, 101 ff.
Atlantic Frontier, The (Wright), 109
Aydelotte, Frank, 21, 107, 109
Ayres, Harry M., 76

Bacon, Roger, xix
Bagot Papers, 147
Baker, C. H. Collins, 56, 59
Balderston, Katharine, 81
Barefoot in Arcadia, ix

Barrett, C. Waller, xvi
Barrow Laboratory, 162
Baskervill, C. R., 77
Battle Abbey Papers, 71
Becker, Carl, 76, 88–89
Bell, James Ford, xvi
Bennett, H. S., 143–44
Bentley, Gerald E., 26, 77
Beutner, Sister Mary Louise, 80
Biblioteca Laurenziana, 46
Bibliothèque Nationale, 44
Billington, R. A., 52–53
Black, Frances. *See* Mrs. Louis B. Wright
Bliss, Leslie E., 59, 72
Block, Maurice, 59
Bodleian Library, 34 ff.
Bodley, Sir Thomas, 36 ff.
Book collectors: American, xii, xx, 32; English, 32 ff.; sentimental values of, 62
Booksellers, 132–33
Boyd, Julian, 163–64, 166, 169
"Breakdown of Intellectual Communication, The" (Wright), 105–6
Bridgewater Library, 64
British Museum, 25 ff., 76; collections in, 30 ff.
Bromley, Mrs. John. *See* Jean Robertson

171

Brooke, C. F. Tucker, 159
Brown, John Carter, xiv
Bryant, Dr. Ernest A., 66
Buck, Paul, 103
Buell, A. W., 72
Butterfield, Lyman, 166
Bynum, Lindley, 72
Byrd, Harold, 131

California Institute of Technology (Caltech), 90, 91, 96 ff.
Campbell, Lily Bess, 74–75
Campbell, Oscar J., 55, 75, 102
Carmichael, Leonard, 161, 169
Catalogues: chronological, made at Huntington, 103; reference, at Folger, 134–35
Cattle on a Thousand Hills (Cleland), 71–72
Cecil Papers, 146–47
Chambers, R. W., 26, 78–79
Chapel Hill. See University of North Carolina at Chapel Hill
Chapman, Gilbert W., 161–62
Chase, Harry Woodburn, 12, 16
Church, E. Dwight, 65
Clapp, Verner, 161–62
Clark Library. See William Andrews Clark Memorial Library
Cleland, Robert G., 70–72, 103
Clements Library. See William L. Clements Library
Clubb, Louise, 139
Cole, Charles W., president of Amherst College, 111; on goal of Folger Library, 141; instructions for new director, 128–31; and liaison between trustees and Folger, 142; seeks advice on Folger, 111–12
Cole, Fred C., 160–62
Cole, George Watson, 65
Council on Library Resources, 160–62

Cracherode, Clayton Mordaunt, 33
Craig, Hardin, 80
Craven, Avery, 55, 75
Crawford and Balcarres, Earl of. See Lindsay, David
Cret, Paul Philippe, 125, 140–41, 152
Crissey, Merrill H., 55
Crow, John, 150–51
Curti, Merle, 76

Dakin, Susannah Bryant, 66
Davies, Godfrey, 55–57, 99
Dawson, Giles E., 128, 131, 151
Dehler, Frank, 26
Dehler, Katherine, 26
Dick, Hugh, 104
Dickens, A. G., 144
Dodds, John W., 104
Donne, John, 127
Dowling, Noel, 26
Dryden, John, xvi, 127
Drury Lane Calendar (MacMillan, comp.), 81
Dunkin, Paul, 128, 131, 135
Dunn, William E., 53
du Pont, Henry F., 164–65
du Pont family, xv
Duveen, Sir Joseph, 59, 60, 66

Eaton, Cyrus, 165
Egerton, Sir Thomas, 64
Egerton Papers, 59
Eleutherian Mills Historical Library, xv
Elizabethan dinner at Folger, 149–50
Elizabethan theatre at Folger, 140–41
Ellis, Arthur, 30
Emerson, Ralph Waldo, 123
Emory University, 47
Enchanted Glass, The (Craig), 80

Erasmus, 146
Evans, Allan, 70–71
Evans, Sir Ifor, 27
Ex Plutarcho versa per Des. Erasmum Roterodamum, 146

Farrand, Max, 47–48, 50 ff., 87, 92–93, 96
Farrand, Mrs. Max (Beatrix Cadwalader Jones), 87–89
Foerster, Norman, 9
Folger, Henry Clay, 119 ff.; and the Folger Library, 140–41
Folger, Mrs. Henry C. (Emily C. Jordan), 123–25
"Folger Booklets on Tudor and Stuart Civilization," 138–39
"Folger Documents of Tudor and Stuart Civilization," 139
Folger Library: Two Decades of Growth, The (Wright), ix, 120 n
"Folger Library General Reader's Shakespeare, The," 116, 136–37
Folger Shakespeare Library, The, ix, xi, 6, 63, 125 ff.; acquisitions, 126–28, 129–30, 132–34, 145–49; and Council on Library Resources, 160; criticism of, 111, 119, 128–31; international reputation of, 143–44; new wing built, 152; open policy on use of materials, 148–49; publishing program, 136–37, 138–39; Shakespearean theatre, 141; staff, 128, 130 ff.
Ford Foundation, The, 160–62
"Founder and His Library, The" (Thorpe), 59–60
Fowler, Mrs. Elaine W., ix, 133
Fox, Levi, 144
Francis, Sir Frank, 144, 162
Franklin, Benjamin, xii–xiii, 169
Frederick Jackson Turner (Billington), 54–55

Freund, Mrs. William. *See* LaMar, Virginia A.
Friendly, Alfred, Sr., 168
Froben, Johannes, 146
Frost, Robert, 69

Gay, Edwin F., 70–71
"Genesis of the Research Institution, The" (Billington), 52–53
Glass, Meta, 151
Gogarty, St. John, 69–70
Graves, Thornton Shirley, 9, 18–19
Gray, Frances (Mrs. Lewis Patton), 14
Green, Paul, 10, 23–24, 99–100
Greenlaw, Edwin A., 9, 10, 18–22, 85, 159
Greenwood Index-Journal, 7
Gregory, John, 125
Groves, Horace, 136
Guggenheim Foundation, The John Simon, xviii, 107, 109 ff., 158; Advisory Board, 109; resolution on Wright's retirement, 159; Selection Committee, 109–10, 158

Hale, George Ellery, 52 ff., 84, 92–93
"Hale Plan," 54
Haller, William, 26, 32, 76–77, 111, 144
Hamilton, J. G. de Roulhac, 17
Hammack, Dan, 72
Harbeson, Hough, Livingston, and Larson, 152
Hard, Frederick, 10, 16, 21, 72, 77, 143
Harmsworth Collection, 113–14, 126–27
Harry S. Truman Institute for National and International Affairs, 166
Harvard University, xv, 102–3
Harvard University Press, 168

173

Haselden, R. B., 59
Hatfield House, 147
Heber, Richard, 33-34
Heffner, Hubert, 10, 81
Heffner, Ray, 10, 80-81
Henderson, Archibald, 12
Henry VIII, 146
Henry E. Huntington Library and Art Gallery. *See* Huntington Library
Henry E. Huntington Library and Art Gallery from Its Beginning to 1969, The (Pomfret), 52
Henry Francis du Pont Winterthur Museum, 164-65
Herter, Christian, 116
Hertrich, William, 58, 60
History Book Club, 160
Holbein, Hans, the Younger, 146
Hollywood, 99-101
Hoover, Herbert, 25, 92
Houghton, Arthur A., Jr., xv, 127
Houghton Library, xv, 103
Howard, Leon, 21, 78
Howell, Almonte C., 10
Hubble, Edwin, 93
Hudson, Hoyt, 76
Humphreys, Arthur, 143
Hunt, Myron, 64
Huntington, Archer M., 53, 92
Huntington, Collis P., 53
Huntington, Henry E., 6, 52 ff.; agents used, 65-66; personal interest in books, 64-65
Huntington, Howard, 53
Huntington Botanical Gardens, 58
Huntington Botanical Gardens, The (Hertrich), 58
Huntington Library, ix, xi, xviii, 47-48, 50 ff., 61 ff.; art collections, 59-60; book collections, 63 ff.; botanical gardens, 60; collection policy, 66-68; community of scholars, 69 ff.; conferences, 82-86; governance, 92-95; hospitality, 87-90; as pioneer research institution, 57 ff., 94-95; publications program, 82; public relations, 73 ff., 90-91; staff, 57 ff., 91-92
Huntington Library Bulletin, 64, 82
Huntington Library Quarterly, 52, 59, 64, 82, 84-86

Indiana University, xvi
Institute for Advanced Study (Princeton), 107
Institute of Early American History and Culture (Williamsburg), 106-9
International Federation of Library Associations (IFLA), 162

Jackson, William A., 103
James I, 41
James, Thomas, 38-41
Jefferson, Thomas, xiii, 154, 166, 169
John Carter Brown Library, xiii, xiv
John Harvard Library, 168
Johns Hopkins University, 20
Johnson, Francis R., 77
Johnson, President Lyndon B., 164
Jones, Beatrix Cadwalader. *See* Farrand, Mrs. Max
Jones, Eldred D., 144
Jones, Howard Mumford, 9, 56, 77, 103, 157
Jordan, Emily C. *See* Folger, Mrs. Henry C.
Journal of the History of Ideas, 109

Kac, Marc, 159
King, Stanley, 119
Kittredge, George Lyman, 8, 102, 159
Klotz, Lucile, 103
Klutz, "Doctor" and Mrs., 15-16

174

Index

Knachel, Philip A., 138, 150
Knopf, Alfred, Sr., 109, 163
Kocher, Frederick, 77
Koller, Kathrine, 21, 78

LaMar, Virginia A., 136–37
Lander College, 7
Larkey, Sanford, 77
Larpent, John, 66
Lawton, Robert O., 7
Lee, Sir Sidney, 6
Leland, Waldo, 104–6
Lenox, James, xiv
Lenox Library, xiii, xiv
Lewis, Wilmarth, xv–xvi
Libby, W. F., 159
Libraries: intellectual obligation of research libraries, 154–55; privately endowed, xii, xvii; in traditional view, xii; unique quality of private research libraries, 152–54. *See also* Folger Shakespeare Library, The; Huntington Library
Library of Congress, xiii, xv
Lievsay, John L., 139
Lievsay, Mrs. John L. *See* Stone, Lilly C.
Lilly, Josiah K., xvi
Lindsay, David, 28th Earl of Crawford and 11th Earl of Balcarres, 143
Lipscomb Company. *See* William Lipscomb Company
Lloyd, David, 166
Lloyd, Megan, 137
Logan, James, xiii
London, 23, 29
Lunow, Robert, 136, 151
Lyon, E. Wilson, 104

McCloy, John J., 142
McGregor, Tracy W., xvi
McIlwain, Charles, 103, 108
McKerrow, Ronald B., 46
McManaway, James G., 128, 131
MacMillan, William Dougald, 10, 81, 143
Malone, Dumas, 160
Malone, Kemp, 24
Manly, John Matthews, 77
Mason, Dorothy E., 128, 131, 133
Mather, Cotton, xiii
Mattingly, Garrett, 144
Merk, Frederick, 103
Merton, Robert K., 159
Middle-Class Culture in Elizabethan England (Wright), 29, 55
Miller, Jean, 149
Millikan, Robert A., 4, 54, 92–94, 116–17
Millis, Walter, 160
Milton, John, xi
Mirrielees, Edith, 104
Mirror for Magistrates, The (Campbell, ed.), 74
"Modest Proposal to Meet an Urgent Need, A" (Boyd), 163
Moe, Henry Allen, 21, 109, 149, 158
Moore-Smith, G. C., 28
Morehead, John Motley, 16–17
Morris, Joseph C., 168
Munro, William B., 92–93, 96
Muscatine, Charles, 159

National Geographic Society, 167
National Historical Publications Commission, 166
Neale, Sir John, 143, 145
Newberry Library, xvii
Newsletters, Newdigate family (Arbury Hall), 147
Niemyer, Elizabeth, 137
Nisbet, Ada, 75, 98
Nitze, William A., 103
Noble, Marcus Cicero Stevens, 12
Notestein, Wallace, 109

175

Odum, Howard, 9
Othello's Countrymen (Jones), 144

Pacific Coast Committee for the Humanities, 104
Pacific Spectator, The, 104–6
Padelford, Frederick Morgan, 80–81
Page, James R., 93–94, 117
Painter, Sidney, 138
Parks, George, 79
Pasadena social life, 89–91
Patton, George S., 53–54
Patton, Mrs. Lewis. *See* Gray, Frances
Paul, Rodman, 103
Pauling, Linus, 109–10
Pellegrini, Angelo, 157–58
Penn, Maybelle, 15
Pierpont Morgan Library, xvii
Pitcher, Eleanor, 132–33, 137, 149–50
Plutarch, 146
Pomfret, John E., 52
Pomona College, 98 ff.
Potter, Russell, 10, 14
Powell, Lawrence Clark, 62
Powicke, Sir Maurice, 76
Pratt, Charles M., 120–21
Pritchett, Henry S., 92
Prohibition, 12–13
Provinciality, Eastern, 102–7

Quinn, David B., 144

Rabelais, François, 169
Rawlinson, Thomas, 33
Ray, Gordon, xviii, 159
Read, Conyers, 59, 76, 143
Recollections of the Folger Shakespeare Library (King), 119, 126
Reed, A. W., 78–79
Religion and Empire (Wright), 99

Rhoades, Marcus, 159
Ringler, William, 76
Ripley, Dillon, 164
Robertson, Jean (Mrs. John Bromley), 80
Robinson, Henry M., 54, 92
Rockefeller, John D., Jr., 107
Rockefeller, John D., III, 107
Rogers, Charles K., 131
Rogers, Will, 5, 91
Rolfe, Franklin, 75, 98
Rolfe, Kay, 75, 98
Rollins, Hyder, 102
Root, R. K., 76
Rosenbach, A. S. W., 6, 65–66
Rosenwald, Lessing J., xv
Royster, James Finch, 9
Rugg, Charles, 116
Rush, Frank, 72

Sabin, Dr. Florence, 109
St. Gallen library, 46
Salisbury, 5th Marquess of, 147–48
San Marino, 51 ff.
Sauer, Carl, 109
Schad, Robert O., 59
Secret Diary of William Byrd of Westover, The (Wright, ed.), 116
Seligman, Eustace, 113, 128–31, 142
Seymour, Whitney North, Sr., 162
Shafer, Boyd, 163
Shakespeare anniversary (1964), 150
Shakespeare Birthplace Trust (Stratford-upon-Avon), 167
Shepard, Odell, 91
Sherburn, George E., 63–64
Shipdham Church library (Norfolk, England), 146
Short-Title Catalogue of Books Printed in England . . . 1475–1640 (Pollard and Redgrave, comps.), 29–30, 103

Sides, Patricia, 98
Smith, David Nichol, 79-80
Smith, George D., 65
Smithsonian Institution, xiii, 161, 164
Spartanburg Herald, 6
Spiller, Robert, 26
Stevens, Henry, xiii
Stone, Lilly C. (Mrs. John L. Lievsay), 135
Stoudemire, Sterling, 10
Strathmann, Ernest, 78
Swedenberg, Elizabeth, 75, 98
Swedenberg, Tom, 75, 98

Taming of the Shrew, The, 137
Taylor, Archer, 104
Thomason, George, 31-32
Thomason Tracts, 31-32, 76
Thompson, Craig, 144
Thorne, Samuel E., 159
Thorpe, James, 59
Tinling, Marion, 116
Trowbridge, Alexander B., 140
Truman, President Harry S., 165-67; as "a defender of learning," 166
Trustees: encouragement of extracurricular activities, 156-57; obligations of, 73-74
Tulane University, 162, 168-69
Turner, Frederick Jackson, 54-55

United States, 1830-1850, The (Turner), 55
University of California at Los Angeles (UCLA), 98-99
University of North Carolina at Chapel Hill, 8 ff.
Unprejudiced Palate, The (Pellegrini), 157-58

Vatican Library, 46

Walpole, Sir Hugh, 69
Walpole collection, xvi
Ward, Paul L., 163
Watson, Harry L., 7
Weathers, Paul, 142
Webb, Stanford, 21
Wecter, Dixon, 70
Wharton, Edith, 87, 89
White, Helen, 26, 78, 86
Wiggins, Russell, 168
William and Mary Quarterly, 109. *See also* Institute of Early American History and Culture (Williamsburg)
William Andrews Clark Memorial Library, xvi
William L. Clements Library, xvi
William Lipscomb Company, 152
Willoughby, Edwin E., 134-36
Wilson, Edwin Bidwell, 110, 158
Wilson, F. P., 78-79, 143
Wilson, Louis Round, 16-17
Wilson, Thomas J., 168
Winterthur Museum. *See* Henry Francis du Pont Winterthur Museum
Wofford College, 6
Wolff, John, 131
Woodrow Wilson International Center for Scholars, 164
Wright, Louis B.: reporter, 3, 6-7; graduate student, University of North Carolina, 8 ff.; book buying, 17, 145; graduate teaching, 19-20; Johnson Research Scholar (Johns Hopkins), 20; Guggenheim Fellow, 21-22, 159; life in London, 24 ff.; vacation in Europe, 44-46; visiting professor at Emory University, 47; invited to Huntington Library, 48; motor trip across continent (1931), 49-51; at Huntington Library, 50 ff.; invited to join

177

Wright, Louis B. (*continued*)
Huntington research staff, 56; home in San Marino, 90; teaching at Caltech, UCLA, and Pomona, 96 ff.; visiting professor, Universities of Michigan, Washington, Minnesota, 99; talk at Jonathan Club, 101; on Pacific Coast Committee for Humanities, 104; organizational activities, 104 ff.; recommendations for Institute for Advanced Study, 107–8; service on editorial boards, 109; joins Guggenheim Advisory Board and Guggenheim Committee of Selection, 109–10, 158–59; advises Amherst trustees, 113–15; accepts Folger directorship, 115–18; extracurricular activities, 156 ff.; becomes an editor of History Book Club, 160; helps to form Council on Library Resources, 160–61; at meeting of International Federation of Library Associations in Moscow (1970), 162; executive secretary of American Historical Association, 163; advocates international house for scholars in Washington, 163–64; invited to become trustee of Winterthur Museum, 164; at founding of Harry S. Truman Library, 165–66; trustee of Harry S. Truman Institute for National and International Affairs, 166; elected life trustee of Shakespeare Birthplace Trust, 167; serves as trustee and historical consultant for National Geographic Society, 167; writes editorials for *Washington Post*, 168; serves on editorial board of John Harvard Library, 168; serves on Board of Visitors, Tulane University, 168; serves on executive council and as vice president, American Philosophical Society, 169
Wright, Mrs. Louis B. (Frances Black), ix, 20

Yeandle, Laetitia, 120 n

179

Of Books and Men

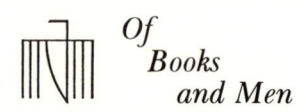

Composition by The Composing Room of Michigan, Inc., Grand Rapids Michigan.

Printed offset lithography by Thomson-Shore, Inc. of Ann Arbor, Michigan.

The paper on which the book is printed bears the watermark of the S. D. Warren Company and was developed for an effective life of at least three hundred years.

Designed by Larry Hirst